To Western Woods

To Western Woods

The Breckinridge Family Moves to Kentucky in 1793

Hazel Dicken-Garcia

Rutherford ● Madison ● Teaneck
Fairleigh Dickinson University Press
London and Toronto: Associated University Presses

Associated University Presses
440 Forsgate Drive
Cranbury, NJ 08512

Associated University Presses
25 Sicilian Avenue
London WC1A 2QH, England

Associated University Presses
P.O. Box 39, Clarkson Pstl. Stn.
Mississauga, Ontario,
L5J 3X9 Canada

The paper used in this publication meets the requirements
of the American National Standard for Permanence of Paper
for Printed Library Materials Z39.48-1984.

Library of Congress Cataloging-in-Publication Data

Dicken Garcia, Hazel.
    To western woods : the Breckinridge family moves to Kentucky in
1793 / Hazel Dicken-Garcia.
        p. cm.
    Includes bibliographical references and index.
    ISBN 0-8386-3342-0 (alk. paper)
    1. Kentucky—History—To 1792—Biography.   2. Kentucky—
History—1792–1865—Biography.   3. Breckinridge family.
4. Breckinridge, John, 1760–1806.   I. Title.
F454.D53   1991
976.9'03'0922—dc20
[B]   89-46408
                                                                               CIP

PRINTED IN THE UNITED STATES OF AMERICA

For the Descendants of Those Who Migrated

Contents

Illustrations

Acknowledgments

This book about communication in the early westward migration focuses on one family's move, and thus it is to the Breckinridge family that I owe the greatest debt. Family members who preserved letters and documents during the American Revolution, the founding of the new nation, and the westward migration knew the importance of events in which they participated, and they kept careful records. We are all the richer because they did. Particular appreciation also goes to the Smithsonian Institution, Washington, D.C., for the research fellowship that enabled me to spend a year studying the westward migration and to discover the Breckinridge family papers.

All research and writing are collaborative efforts that could never get done without the assistance of individuals always too numerous to name. Among a few that I am especially indebted to are James C. Klotter, of the Kentucky Historical Society, for encouragement, for countless suggestions regarding sources, and for reviewing and commenting on an early draft of the manuscript; Marilyn Grant, for editing, proofreading, and ever-valuable suggestions and comments; Kevin Duchschere, for assistance in researching the James Breckinridge Collections at the University of Virginia; and Sandya Rao, for assistance in locating materials. Of course, the completed project is the sole responsibility of the author; those who assisted are by no means accountable for its shortcomings.

Those who generously granted permission for use of materials were especially important to the development of this book: Particularly, I am grateful to Mrs. Helen Congleton Breckinridge for permission to use her unpublished work on the Breckinridge family; to Dr. J. Anthony Caruso, for permission to use maps published in his work on the Appalachian frontier; to Dr. Lowell H. Harrison, for permission to use John Breckinridge's 18 March 1792 letter to his brother James; to Michael O. Shannon, for permission to quote the Shannon Family Letters; and to the many manuscript librarians for tireless assistance with requests about copyright ownership of materials. I also wish to acknowledge *Adena: A Journal of the History and Culture of the Ohio Valley*, vol. 3 (Spring 1978) where portions of chapter 1 appeared.

The library staffs, who gave gracious assistance with many ques-

11

tions at various stages of the research, are too numerous to mention, but some merit special thanks: James J. Holmberg, curator of manuscripts, The Filson Club, Louisville, Kentucky; Claire McCann, manuscript librarian, University of Kentucky Libraries, Lexington, Kentucky; Mary Margaraet Bell, manuscripts curator, the Kentucky Historical Society, Frankfort, Kentucky; Patricia Hodges, manuscripts & archives supervisor, Department of Library Special Collections, Western Kentucky University, Bowling Green, Kentucky; and staffs of the University of Chicago Library, State Historical Society of Wisconsin, the manuscripts and periodicals divisions of the Library of Congress, Washington, D.C., and the Geography and Map Division and United States Copyright Office, Alexandria, Virginia.

Finally, *To Western Woods* comes from an untitled poem in which the author Philip Freneau captured much of the spirit of the westward migration to Kentucky. The poem appeared in *The Kentucke Gazette* on 19 July 1788 and in other newspapers and magazines in the late 1780s.

To Western Woods

Introduction: The Westward Migration as Communication History

A few months after Lord Dunmore's War ended with cession of western land by the Indians, news of Kentucky's first settlement in the spring of 1775 spread through Virginia before the settlers reached their new homeland. Presbyterian minister John Brown of Augusta County, Virginia, wrote to William Preston of the excitement, "What a Buzzel is this amongst People about Kentuck?" Complaining that half his congregation had gone, he pondered following, "but Ministers will have their congregations, but why need I fear that? Ministers are moveable goods as well as others."[1] As he wrote, an express rider brought him news of the battles of Lexington and Concord; hence Brown's letter referred to two history-changing events, the American Revolution and the westward migration across the Appalachian Mountains.

Preston, Brown's brother-in-law, lived on the western-most edge of the frontier in Fincastle County, Virginia, when he received Brown's letter in May 1775 (see figure). The next year, part of Fincastle County, which then encompassed what is now the state of Kentucky, became Kentucky County, and sixteen years later, on 1 June 1792, land encompassed by Kentucky County became the fifteenth state of the new nation.[2] During those seventeen years from the first settlement in 1775 to statehood in 1792, nearly seventy thousand people—including Brown and other ministers and their congregations—crossed the Appalachian Mountain range and settled in the area.[3]

This book focuses on one Virginia family's migration during those years. What such a move meant at the time may be unfathomable in an age when one can traverse the globe in mere hours, learn of events as they happen in far-flung corners of the world, carry on dialogues with people separated by oceans and continents, and even travel into space. To those who crossed the mountains in the late eighteenth century, communication facilities of the late twentieth century would have been even less comprehensible. Nor is there much knowledge about how the structures of people's lives and expectations have been shaped by communication developments during those two centuries.

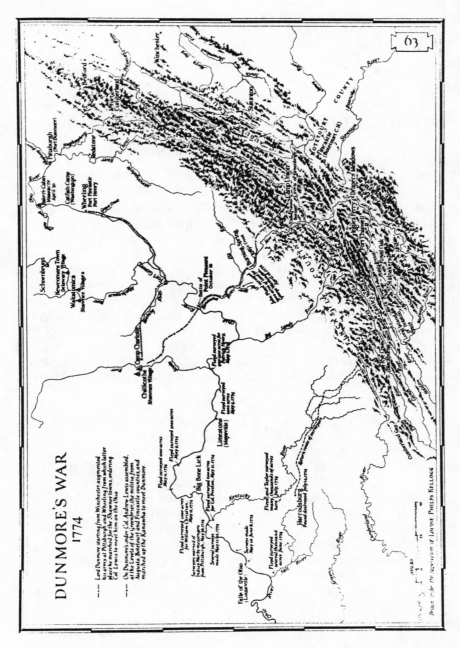

Dunmore's War. Reprinted with permission of Charles Scribner's Sons, an imprint of Macmillan Publishing Company, from *Atlas of American History* by James Truslow Adams and R. V. Coleman. Copyright 1943 by Charles Scribner's Sons, renewed 1977.

Scholars have examined elements, such as transportation, postal facilities, and the various information media, but attention has yet to focus on the communication infrastructure as it has affected lives through history. More than the sum of its parts, communication encompasses not only information, but the means by which information and people can travel from point to point, the means by which people interact, and the means for individual affirmation and identity. Communication is an infrastructure within which individuals live, structuring lives at the same time it links them and knits societies together, conducting them from past to present to future.

That infrastructure's interlocking components, including interpersonal and mediated communication, consist of differing functions and differing levels of function—all of which change in response to developments in communication. At the most basic level are the intimate interpersonal relationships, consisting of family and closest friends, which function to give identity, security, and emotional comfort (dysfunctions are not being considered). At another interpersonal level are the colleagueships, consisting of those with whom one has frequent contact through work, civic, educational, and religious associations, which function as reference groups representing norms and values within which one grows and against which one judges and adjusts one's attitudes and behaviors. Functions of these parts of the communication infrastructure may have changed the least through history.

A quite different, but interlocking, component of the communication infrastructure consists of the physical means by which information is transported; changes in this component over time influence functions of interpersonal communication. Before the invention of the telegraph, information could not be conducted through space apart from human travel. Persons wishing to send messages sought reliable people to carry them, preferably people they knew; hence interpersonal relationships were linked to sending messages. In the late eighteenth century, travel required significant advanced planning for even the most commonplace tasks of today. Unless one lived in a village or town, as few of the southern population did then,[4] buying items not produced at home (certain foodstuffs, supplies, furniture, clothing) or fetching a doctor entailed a trip of a day or more. A family member or servant usually went on such errands; or orders were sent with a neighbor who might be planning a trip. And almost invariably, one wrote letters to be carried by individuals going on whatever errands, for one rarely knew when someone might be traveling that way again. Throughout this book, letters dated a day or two before the happenchance carrier departed indicate the advance planning.

Another component of the communication infrastructure is mediated communication, that which is published in newspapers, magazines, and books to inform, enlighten, educate, and generally circulate ideas. In recent years, literature has increasingly explored how images portrayed through these vehicles (and the more contemporary electronic media) structure lives and influence culture. For example, the way media portray women, it is argued, tends to structure expectations of both men and women from childhood about their roles in society.[5] In this book, newspapers are the most used form of mediated communication, and during the late eighteenth century, women were relatively invisible in them—one indication of change in this element of mediated communication.[6] However, while the thesis here encompasses the prevailing view of this literature, it projects a broader argument: the interlocking components create a communication infrastructure that in itself has a history, and as that history has changed over time, the manner in which it has structured lives has also changed. This infrastructure's history has been shaped by development of its differing components and is therefore integrated with every aspect of cultural change.

Because communication structures the environment in which people live, developments in communication alter experiences over time that influence behavior and attitudes. The integral role of communication in daily lives has perhaps been the greatest barrier to study of this history because it is too nearly inseparable from existence to be examined objectively. In the information age, when communication facilities and their capabilities are taken for granted, the fact that a communication infrastructure has a history is easily overlooked—and yet in no other age, perhaps, has need for study of that history been greater, if knowledge of an essential component of civilization is not to be forever obscured. Throughout this book the thesis is implicit in the sources quoted, for they bespeak the nature of communication and its effects on lives. The sources reveal largely a *freeze-frame* stage in the development of communication, for, by present-day standards, communication forms and facilities changed little during the decades under study.

The westward migration in America, entirely dependent on communication facilities at whatever their stage of development as it progressed, allows for examining communication behavior and role in a particular segment of American history. For both the movement and the communication forms conducting it are written large in the nation's history and are therefore unusually identifiable. The one is inseparable from the other.

Many historians have written of the rapid and massive migration over the mountains, a part of the movement called the Great Upland Migration, because it represents the first shift of population from the coastal area upward to the Piedmont, the mountain ranges, and beyond. Except for travel histories and diary accounts of historical figures and events, no research has focused on what individuals wrote about moving across the Appalachian Mountains. In the 1940s, historian Leland Baldwin lamented "the misfortune . . . that no contemporary with the genius to do it justice saw the epic possibilities of this transit of civilization" and recorded it for "future generations."[7]

Although no contemporary wrote *that* story, many westward migrants wrote letters and diaries, which, with complete files of many newspapers, remain extant, thanks in large measure to the efforts of such visionaries as Lyman C. Draper and Rueben T. Durrett, whose collections are housed at the State Historical Society of Wisconsin and University of Chicago libraries, respectively. Among these sources can be found parts of that story that may be pieced together to reveal communication behavior and the role of communication in the migration. This was the purpose in examining the letters of one family through the preparation and move over the mountains. Although I studied hundreds of letters, diaries, tracts, newspapers, and memoirs from the era, the focus on one family seemed a convenient way to provide a coherent story of what migrating meant to individuals. The family preserved a wealth of papers during the era, and these make possible some reconstruction of its activities. Further, the family is worthy of study for its own sake; a leading southern family before and after the move, it was the origin of one of Kentucky's most prominent families to the present day.

Although the bulk of the book deals with one family's letters, other letters, newspapers, and diaries relating to the migration in this period aided in the reconstruction of one family's migration. To focus on communication, several questions were asked of these sources: Assuming that information influences behavior, what prompted people to move to an untamed wilderness? Communication facilities of the time made social visits across the mountains impractical, and this structured migrants' expectations about future interaction with relatives and friends. How were people affected, knowing the limited possibilities for communicating with friends and relatives left behind? What did migrants express about leaving relatives and friends they might not see again? Considering the communications facilities of the time, what did the move require of any given family in material and emotional terms? What role did communication play in meeting general needs for information and linkage from isolated to settled communities, where friends and relatives remained? What role did communication play in conducting the culture-transforming event that was the westward migration?

The first two chapters, relying on many sources about travel to the Kentucky country during the period, help answer questions about communication facilities during migration. These chapters set the stage for the story of one family's relocation detailed in remaining chapters. These late-eighteenth-century migrants, however, must be viewed in the context of the larger westward migration.

Exactly when the westward migration began might be defined as the date the first family settled west of the Tidewater in Virginia, for, as one student of the frontier has written, in the eighteenth century "the most forward advance of the westward movement was in southwest Virginia and western North Carolina."[8] Most discussions, however, after noting Virginia Governor Spotswood's 1716 exploratory trip to the Blue Ridge Mountain summit, begin with the 1720s. By 1727, the press of settlement led to the decision to survey and extend westward the line between Virginia and North Carolina, and in 1726 or 1727 the first Pennsylvanian's move overland to the Shenandoah Valley of Virginia heralded a flood tide of migration along that corridor[9] (see figure). The westward push of settlement required extending the Virginia line again in just two decades, shortly before Dr. Thomas Walker, of the Loyal Land Company, traveled into the Kentucky country in 1750 in search of 800,000 acres of land for settlement.[10] Walker and explorers who followed over the next several years carried home information about this "place of fields"[11] that spurred others to contemplate moving there.

Migration was slowed, however, first by the French and Indian War and then by the American Revolution. Indians had often found settlers' behavior bewildering during the century and a half of white settlement in America. Despite intervals of comradery, settlers broke promises to Indians and behaved in other ways that belied any real friendship. By the 1750s, in the face of expanding westward settlement, Indians had grown desperate about keeping their land. For most of the rest of the century, they were decidedly on the defensive and took advantage of first the British-French conflict and then the British-American conflict to try to halt westward settlement.

The French and Indian War erupted at midcentury as the English became increasingly impatient with French efforts to establish a line of forts along the Ohio River to deter British access to the interior. By virtue of its 1609 charter, Virginia claimed the western territory, including the Ohio River. In 1749 French emissary Celoron de Blainville planted leaden plates at the mouths of the Allegheny and Ohio rivers to signify France's ownership of the area,[12] and three years

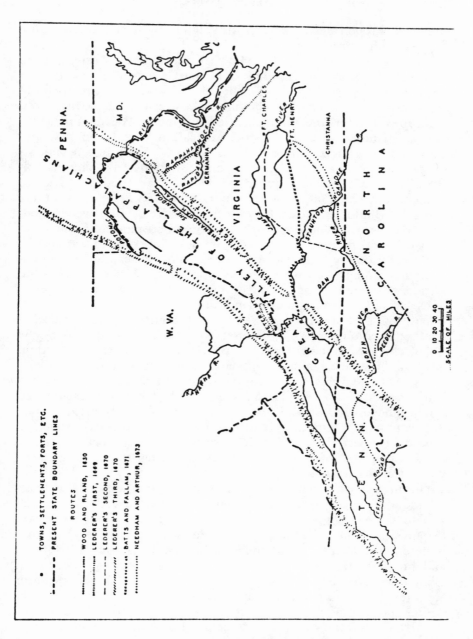

Great Valley of the Appalachians. Reprinted with the permission of the author, John Anthony Caruso, from *The Appalachian Frontier,* copyright 1959, Bobbs-Merrill, p. 12.

later, the French destroyed a British trading post at Piqua, halting English trade north of the Ohio River.[13]

In 1753 the Virginia governor dispatched George Washington to request the French to withdraw from the Ohio Valley. The French refused, and Virginians, on behalf of the Crown, began to build defenses at the forks of the Ohio in 1754. After French troops forced them to surrender, the Virginians, led by George Washington, withdrew a distance, erected a stockade called Fort Necessity, and launched an attack.[14] The French defeated Washington and his troops, however, and British regiments, supported by Virginia soldiers under Maj. Gen. Edward Braddock, then tried to drive the French from Fort Duquesne (Pittsburgh) in 1755. They were sorely defeated. Braddock and half the fifteen hundred troups were killed. The Indians, who had previously vacillated between the French and British, allied themselves with the French and went to war against settlements on the Virginia and Pennsylvania frontiers. Settlers retaliated, and atrocities on both sides instilled anger in both Indians and settlers that seethed below the surface of their subsequent interactions and fed the struggle over land for decades.[15]

With the end of the French and Indian War, King George III, by the Proclamation of 1763, attempted to establish a boundary along the Appalachian Mountains, west of which settlement was forbidden. Settlers, however, ignored boundaries intended to protect Indians' lands, and five years later, the Treaty of Fort Stanwix with the Six Nations and the Treaty of Hard Labor with the Cherokees established a new line extending the territory available for settlement.[16] The following spring, thousands of settlers began crossing the Appalachian Mountains toward Pittsburgh; five thousand had settled in the area by the summer of 1769, and thirty thousand settled there within three years after the treaties.[17]

During the same years, surveyors "on the Ohio" marked off plats awarded to veterans of the French and Indian War while several Indian tribes, who never accepted the Treaty of Fort Stanwix (Miamis, Shawnee, Delawares, Wyandotts, and Mingoes), prepared to defend their land. In 1770 the Shawnee and Delaware joined forces and brought other tribes together in 1771 to form the Northwest Confederacy, headed by Shawnee Chief Cornstalk. As surveying of Kentucky lands continued, isolated raids, pillage, and murders by whites and Indians against each other escalated, leading to Dunmore's War by the summer of 1774. After the battle of Point Pleasant in October 1774, Cornstalk called for an end to the war, and the Treaty of Camp Charlotte opened the Ohio territory for settlement.[18]

Some have said that the first families' attempts to settle in Kentucky provoked Dunmore's War. Evidence suggests that no one lived in Kentucky between the 1750s and early 1775, although explorers visited and sojourned there sporadically. Northern and southern Indian tribes had long guarded the area as a mutual hunting ground and allowed no one to live there. In 1754 hostile Indians destroyed the only known eighteenth-century Kentucky Indian village, Eskippakithiki, which existed near present Winchester from circa 1720.[19]

Explorer Daniel Boone stayed in the Kentucky country longer than any known white person before 1775. He and six others set out to hunt in the area in the spring of 1769. Indians warned them to leave, then captured them when they did not. After the hunters escaped, Indians pursued them and killed one. The hunters then abandoned the trip and returned home—except Boone, who remained in Kentucky two years, hunting and exploring alone except for a short visit from his brother Squire.[20]

After returning to his Yadkin River, North Carolina, home in 1771, Boone began preparing to move his family to the Kentucky country. By the fall of 1773, he had assembled five families to accompany his, and the group set out on the wilderness route on 25 September. Indians saw the women and children in the caravan moving west as signifying permanent settlement, which they sought to prevent by attacking part of the group, brutally killing five, including Boone's oldest son, James, sixteen. Boone wanted to continue the journey, but, after burying the dead, others persuaded him to retreat to Clinch River, Virginia.[21]

While Boone temporarily resided on Clinch River, Indians continued to raid frontier settlements, and Virginia Governor Dunmore asked William Preston to select two couriers to go to the Kentucky country and warn surveyors of the hostilities. Boone, one of two selected,[22] discovered on this trip that James Harrod and a group of men had begun building a fort near the site Boone later settled. After hearing news of the impending Indian war, however, Harrod and the men abandoned those efforts to join the battle of Point Pleasant (present Wheeling, West Virginia) in October 1774.[23]

Boone probably knew the treaty ending Dunmore's War resulted in the Indians relinquishing Kentucky lands, but he apparently concluded that establishing permanent settlements required more resources and settlers than he commanded. He knew North Carolinian Richard Henderson was interested in Kentucky land. Henderson, a judge from whom Boone had a few years earlier sought assistance on a court matter, was retired by 1774 and had decided to buy western land from the Indians, finance the clearing of a road into the Kentucky country, and promote the land and road to entice settlers.[24] He

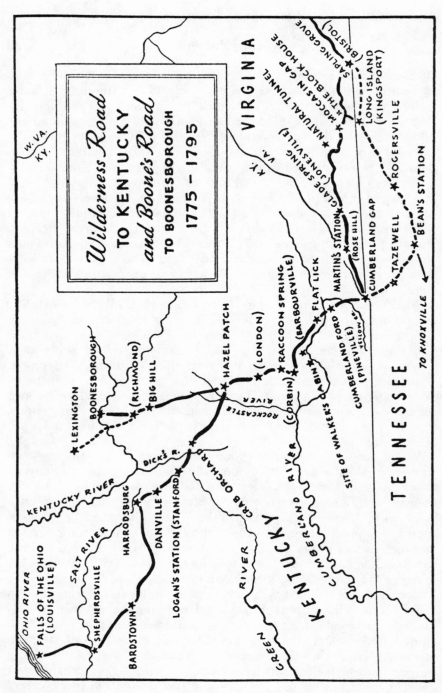

Wilderness Road to Kentucky. Reprinted from Robert L. Kincaid, *The Wilderness Road* (Indianapolis: The Bobbs-Merrill Company, 1947), p. 77.

called on Boone to help. In violation of government policy, Henderson—accompanied by Boone—met tribe leaders at Sycamore Shoals on the Watauga River in March 1775 and bought land south of the Kentucky River. Boone then led the road-cutting crew into Kentucky and began building Fort Boonesborough in the spring of 1775 (see figure) as the first American Revolution battles were fought. He returned that summer to bring his wife and children from North Carolina—and he boasted for the rest of his life that his was the first white family to settle in Kentucky. Other families soon followed.[25]

Peace following Dunmore's War was short-lived, and Indian raids continued into the American Revolution years, when an Indian-British alliance nearly wiped out the new settlements. Confined to small, crowded forts and surrounded by unsanitary conditions, the settlers suffered near starvation and assorted illnesses.[26] By January of 1780, fewer than three hundred people lived in Kentucky.[27] But after the revolutionary war ended in 1781, migration mushroomed. Although Indian hostilities, which abated somewhat after 1782, continued into the mid-1790s, Kentucky settlers began by 1780 to establish towns, schools, churches, businesses, and professional offices.[28] And in late 1784, they met in a convention, the first of ten during the ensuing seven years, to petition for statehood.[29]

The end of British rule in America released a great surge in westward migration. By the 1783 treaty ending the revolution, word of luxuriant land over the mountains had been spreading throughout the eastern population for at least three decades. But, exactly what did people know about the area to which they moved in such numbers after the war?

On the assumption that people base decisions—especially such a momentous decision as migrating—on information, I studied sources for evidence of what people could have known about the area beyond the mountains. I studied them also for evidence of events, plans, and procedures associated with such a move. Newspapers published in the decades after 1769 yielded little information about the tramontane region. Further, the news published about the West was overwhelmingly negative: items told of Indians harassing and murdering settlers and destroying entire frontier communities. Such news seemed unlikely to inspire many people to transplant entire lives hundreds of miles from familiar surroundings. On the assumption that more positive information about the region passed via letters and word of mouth, I studied letters, and a particular set of them became the basis of this book.

The book follows the John and Mary Cabell Breckinridge family letters as they relate to interest in the area that became the state of

Kentucky. Beginning in 1769 and building toward and including the family's move from Albemarle County, Virginia, to Lexington, Kentucky, in 1793, letter excerpts pertaining to Kentucky are here interspersed with newspaper accounts. The book is not, it is important to stress, about details of daily lives in eighteenth-century America; rather, as one means of exploring communication behavior and the role of communication during this early period of westward migration, the book concentrates on what a few individuals recorded about their lives while their activities pertained to the West and to migrating.

Many diaries, spanning the entire westward movement, have been published, most appearing as historical documents in and of themselves, or as part of the history of a particular area's development, or as evidence of what people observed during travel, or as histories of events of which the writers were a part. Although any diary necessarily represents the writer's point of view, little study has focused on that viewpoint. The dominant perspective has been from the diary outward to what it might tell of the writer's times, and not inward to how the times structured the writer's life and expectations. A notable exception is Lillian Schlissel's study of the diaries of women who moved westward during the last half of the nineteenth century.[30] Joanna Stratton's examination of pioneer Kansas women's reminiscences also focuses on individuals' viewpoints and experiences, but her work is not based on diaries and extends to far more than the migration itself.[31] Nicholas Perkins Hardeman relies on family letters and documents to develop an extraordinary history of the Hardeman family through generations across the entire westward migration.[32]

Works emphasizing personal and family records as sources generally tend to focus on one of two distinct waves of the westward migration—the last decades of the eighteenth century or midnineteenth century. Although nearly three-fourths of a century and enormous changes in America separate the two great tides of migration, notable similarities between the writings in the two eras are apparent. For example, people in both periods kept diaries as if with a conviction of the historical importance of the journeys they made. But there also are differences.

Schlissel, who focused only on women's diaries of the later westward migration, referred to hundreds of them. In contrast, women's diaries and letters are conspicuously scarce among those extant from the late-eighteenth-century migration. Since the number of women must have been close to thirty-five thousand of the nearly seventy thousand who migrated to Kentucky (and an equal number that moved into Tennessee) in the last twenty-five years of the century,[33] one is led to speculate about their silence. Although more than twice the number moved across the plains in the midnineteenth century and left more diaries and letters, numbers will not explain the differences.[34]

Other factors, no doubt, include fewer educated women among the earlier migrants, more scarce and expensive paper and writing supplies, less favorable conditions for writing during a cruder means of travel, greater likelihood that diaries and letters in a more primitive era of communication and storage facilities have not survived, and that, during what seems to have been the most prolific diary-writing period for eighteenth-century migrants, *men* were the travelers. Men on exploring trips and first visits to Kentucky were not accompanied by women, and these men wrote many of the extant diaries of this era.

Another difference is the length of the accounts. In contrast to the sparse comment and terse descriptions in the late-eighteenth-century diaries, the later writers often belabored details and descriptions of incidents. Possibly, the later migrants had read diaries and letters from the earlier migration, realized their importance, and deliberately tried to both provide fuller accounts and assure they were saved. Later writers probably had more materials and better conditions for writing. Transportation modes had improved, and, although these provided limited comfort and privacy, they afforded more than earlier migrants had. Steamboats speeded up waterway travel, and both the boats and prairie wagons of the later migration provided places to retire at night, to sit and write perhaps relatively undisturbed. Eighteenth-century migrants slept more often under the stars, or in cabins or "ordinaries," where numerous travelers, crowded into one large room, slept on the floor.[35]

Schlissel notes that the later migrants had to invest extraordinary effort in preparations over a lengthy period of time, and most had moved before or had parents who had.[36] The same was true of earlier migrants, but the two groups differed in the amount of information available about the area they were moving to. Although the mid-nineteenth-century overland passengers' knowledge of the far western United States was limited, guidebooks—albeit flawed with misinformation—were accessible.[37] No such sources were available in the eighteenth century, and early Kentucky migrants knew little about what lay beyond the Appalachian Mountains.

Colonists had lived on the Atlantic coastal plain for more than a century before any ascended the Blue Ridge Mountain summit.[38] And another half century passed before anyone resided on the other side of that summit. Maps available to migrants by the 1770s reveal people's limited knowledge about the tramontane region. A 1744 map

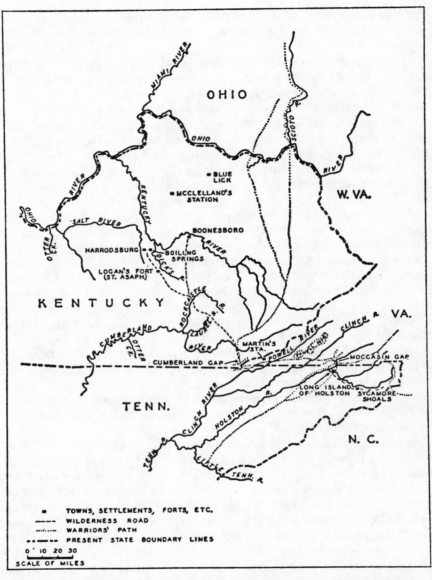

Early Kentucky Settlements. Reprinted with the permission of the author, John Anthony Caruso, from *The Appalachian Frontier,* copyright 1959, Bobbs-Merrill Co., p. 160.

shows the Tennessee and Ohio rivers emptying into the Wabash, the Cumberland River emptying into the Tennessee, and the Potomac and Wabash uniting to form a lake south of present Lake Erie. A 1752 map labels the Alleghany Mountains "Mississippi or Allegheny Ridge"; New River appears as a branch of the Mississippi, and the tramontaine region is labeled, "A mountainous tract of land west of the Blue Ridge, Augusta County, parts unknown. . . ."[39] Of fifty-three maps in Lloyd A. Brown's *Early Maps of the Ohio Valley*, twenty-eight appeared between 1750 and 1778. Of those, six showed the tramontane region but provided limited detail. Two important eighteenth-century Virginia maps, the 1751 Fry-Jefferson and the 1770 John Henry map, show Ohio Valley rivers but lack other details. On the Fry-Jefferson map, "The Allagany Ridge" appears as the western edge of detail. John Mitchill's 1755 map, which Brown calls "the most important and famous map in American history" because of its use to settle boundary disputes through 1783, shows virtually no detail of the Kentucky country.[40]

At most, colonists in the early 1770s had a concept of a French line at or near the Mississippi River because of the chain of forts north to south in that region. Indeed, no one conceived of a distinct place called Kentucky before 1776. Generally, colonists referred to the area as "the western frontiers," "the Virginia frontier," "over the mountains," "on the Ohio," and "on the western waters." The first newspaper mention of the word "Kentucky" appeared in a 3 May 1753 *Pennsylvania Journal*. The item reported that Ottawa Indians had captured some traders "at a place called Kentucky" in January. The first Virginia newspaper use of the word appeared on 8 September 1774.[41] Both references, however, seemed to mean only the river and a very limited adjacent area.

Before 1750, colonists' knowledge of the Kentucky country came from traders.[42] Then, beginning in 1750, explorers and hunters crisscrossed the area.[43] Finally, in 1770 surveyors began marking Kentucky lands granted to soldiers of the French and Indian War.[44] Four Virginia counties successively included the Kentucky country. In the 1750s, the Virginia Burgesses claimed that Augusta County, established in 1738, included the Ohio River; in 1769, Botetourt County was carved from Augusta and included Kentucky;[45] in 1772 Fincastle County was carved from Botetourt and included Kentucky.[46] In 1776 Fincastle County was divided into three counties, none of which was called Fincastle. One of the new counties was named Kentucky and followed the approximate boundaries of the present state. But Kentucky County existed only until 1780, when it was divided into Jefferson, Lincoln, and Fayette counties. By 1792, when Kentucky became a state, those counties had been further divided to give the new state nine counties.[47]

Common to writers among the migrants of both the late-eighteenth and mid-nineteenth century was restraint in recording emotions and personal matters. Stratton and Schlissel portray pioneer women as stoic, although Schlissel notes that diaries occasionally contained bursts of emotion.[48] A reader finds, nevertheless, even less emotion in diaries of the earlier writers, who wrote cryptically. Still, the later writers, despite more verbiage, add little to our knowledge about personal details of lives in transit. One may conclude that taboos prevented mention of bodily comforts, personal hygiene, and sex. Stratton notes that such subjects were treated either euphemistically or not at all.[49]

The general lack of emotion in the writing seems remarkable when one considers that migrants in both eras faced the most emotional of life's experiences: deaths of family members, relatives, and co-travelers by violence, disease, exposure, or accident; burials in the wilderness; conception and pregnancies; births of babies under the most primitive circumstances; illnesses and injuries, especially of young children, while traveling under the most stressful conditions and without access to medical facilities; life-threatening confrontations with Indians and denizens of the wild. One might expect being in transit to heighten the emotional impact of such experiences, causing more effusive comment because travelers lacked familiar support systems.

The absence of emotion in the writing leads a reader to speculate that those courageous people were indeed stoic, that the pain was too great for words, that they functioned within a value structure that militated against expressions of emotion, that they were simply single-minded about the purpose of their writings—which was to provide basic information—or that an understood code governed what one committed to paper. Evidence suggests that early Americans believed only ennobling words should be committed to print, and perhaps the same belief governed even the most personal writing. Certainly, the writers intended diaries to be passed on and read, at least among family members and descendants; and they knew that the means for communicating by letter denied privacy. Perhaps it was by design that nothing hinting of character weakness should be transmitted to contemporaries or to future generations.

Because of the matter-of-fact treatment of emotion-rending events, the dominant characteristic of letters and diaries cited in this book is understatement. While writers discussed effects of moving, the sources betray no clue that people viewed their lives rent by seemingly life-rending events. People wrote of tragedies often in very brief sentences, without elaboration and little hint of the grief they surely suffered.

A diary of what was perhaps the most torturous journey by migrants during this era is illustrative. John Donelson recorded the trip of a group that left Fort Patrick Henry on Holston River in Virginia on 22 December 1779 and took four months on waterways to reach what is now Nashville, Tennessee. During the trip, Indians attacked on five occasions, killing thirty, one of whom they burned after taking him and Donelson's son as prisoners to their village. (Donelson's son was spared when a visiting trader in the village ransomed him.) In addition, one man drowned, one died of exposure, and a baby born on the trip drowned during an Indian attack the next day; five men were wounded; one man got lost; one family, left behind as lost after being beset by Indians when its boat ran upon rocks, managed to escape and catch up with the others before having to abandon the badly damaged boat. Cargo was lost when one boat was damaged and a second boat and a canoe sank on different occasions, and the group ran out of food.

Matter-of-factly recording these events, Donelson wrote that as the company "lay by" at an evacuated Chickamauga town, "the wife of Ephraim Peyton was here delivered of a child." Peyton, traveling overland with another company, would not learn of the baby's birth and death until his company met the Donelson group at their destination. Donelson elaborated somewhat on one of the trip's tragedies. The leader of twenty-eight traveling with smallpox had agreed to keep his boat "at some distance in the rear, for fear of the infection spreading." Indians, "observing his helpless situation, singled off from the rest of the fleet, intercepted him and killed and took prisoners the whole crew, to the great grief of the whole company, uncertain how soon they might share the same fate; their cries were distinctly heard by those boats in the rear."[50]

Mrs. Peyton had no time for grief when her newborn baby was drowned during efforts to escape an Indian attack. Donelson, concerned about her health, wrote that she assisted in getting the boat underway, "being frequently exposed to wet and cold then and afterwards. . . . Her health appears to be good . . . and I think and hope she will do well." Some emotion also shows through his final entry, where he recorded arriving at his destination and finding "Capt. Robertson and his company," who had journeyed overland. "It is a source of satisfaction to us to be enabled to restore to him and others their families and friends, who were entrusted to our care, and who, sometime since, perhaps, despaired of ever meeting again," Donelson wrote, with no reference to the thirty-three who did not survive the trip or that Ephraim Peyton, although reunited with his wife, would never see his firstborn.[51]

Daniel Boone, in his autobiography, matter-of-factly notes the murder of his sixteen-year-old son James while en route to Kentucky in 1773. The one surviving witness related the brutality of the murder. After James and seventeen-year-old Henry Russell were shot through the hips and could not move, James, recognizing one of the Shawnee attackers as a frequent visitor to the Boone farm, pleaded for their lives. But the Indians tortured their victims, stabbing both boys repeatedly and tearing out their fingernails and toenails before finally killing them.[52] Boone's autobiography said of the event, "The rear of our company was attacked by a number of Indians, who killed six, and wounded one man. Of these my eldest son was one that fell." Similarly, he noted the death of his next oldest son Israel, who was twenty-two when killed in an Indian battle nine years later, "The brave and much lamented Colonels Todd and Trigg, Major Harland and my second son, were among the dead."[53]

Although unemotional in recording these deaths, Boone's grief is revealed in a stark statement about discovering in early 1774 that wolves had disturbed James's wilderness grave. Caught in a fierce storm while re-covering the grave, he said he then felt more depressed than at any time in his life.[54] Such emotional statements were rare, however, and an example from William Brown's diary is more typical. Brown kept a diary of his 1782 trip to Kentucky to see a brother whom he had not seen for some time. The two visited briefly on 19 July. William's next diary entry tells of the Battle of Blue Licks (Kentucky) and lists the officers killed; his next paragraph states only, "In this action James fell."[55]

Expressions of emotion appear more often in letters and diaries of women, of men while ill, and of very young men on a first trip away from home. However, it is clear that the young men who wrote of fear believed such feelings were to be suppressed and overcome.[56] The writing of seasoned male travelers occasionally reveals homesickness after prolonged absences from home, but even that is expressed guardedly.

The image of prairie migrants' family life as patriarchal, noted by Schlissel,[57] also appears in diaries and letters of the earlier migrants. Men, deciding to move westward, were eager, determined, fearless, taciturn about leaving behind friends and relatives, and generally unyielding to the pleas of wives and mothers who opposed the move. Women, on the other hand, objected to the move and lamented the separation from familiar surroundings, friends, and relatives. They worried about the trip, what it might involve, whether they were prepared, and how they would fare.

Men anticipated women's resistance in deciding to move but took the posture that "weathering that storm" of protest was but a minor nuisance. Such stances tend to strengthen the notion that men viewed women as weaker, almost childlike in venting emotions. Yet men seemed to expect superhuman emotional strength from women. Men on lengthy sojourns expected wives to handle all their affairs, manage farms or businesses, keep the home, care for their children, and remain faithful while patiently waiting without news as to whether their husbands might be dead or alive. Sweeping generalizations based on the writing of very few are unsafe, of course, and there is reason to think that John Breckinridge waited years for his wife's assent before finally moving despite her protest.[58] Further, when he wanted to move again after arriving in Kentucky, he abided by her wishes.[59] It also appears that James Breckinridge, despite vowing his bones would be buried in Kentucky, never moved there out of deference to his wife.[60] Daniel Boone also abided by his wife's wishes not to move to Florida during the 1760s.[61] And Harriette Simpson Arnow, in what she calls a very rare kind of expression in the diaries and letters, reports that James Smith wrote of cutting short a hunting trip in the 1760s because "as I had already been longer from home than what I expected, I thought my wife would be much distressed, and think I was killed by Indians."[62]

The first of this book's eight chapters, which relies heavily on diaries for background about moving over the mountains in the late eighteenth century, reveals migrants' stoic determination. Chapter two briefly describes the nature of eighteenth-century communication via letters and the postal service. The remaining six chapters divide according to a common pattern in the migration process revealed in the diaries and letters. For example, among the several stages, the first was marked by tales of the new land told by returning explorers, hunters, surveyors, and travelers. The second stage occurred when individuals, whose curiosities were aroused, went to see if the land measured up to what they had heard. (Often, one family member went to reconnoiter and, upon returning, told friends and relatives of the good land, thus setting the second stage in motion all over again.) The third stage encompassed family discussion of such a move: How many family members, or units of an extended family, would move? How would separation from elderly parents and relatives affect them? What was needed for the move, and how might it be procured? What land was available, at what price, location, and quality?

After resolving such questions, the fourth stage—moving preparations—began in earnest and often took two years. Land in the new country was secured or staked; slaves and an overseer often were sent ahead to take livestock and make "improvements" (build a cabin, put in fences and plant crops).[63] Meantime, migrants concluded affairs at home, which included disposing of property, settling business with debtors, creditors, clients, and partners, and engaging someone to handle unsettled accounts. Families then decided on the travel route, secured provisions and transportation facilities, set the moving date, and found or assembled a company to travel with.

The fifth stage was the actual move—the departure and long journey to the new home. Those left behind waited anxiously to hear of safe arrivals. The sixth stage—arrival of migrants at their destination—involved getting settled, but not before writing a letter home about the trip, arrival, activities, and prospects in the new land. An important part of those letters home often included directions about how and when to move, what kind of problems to anticipate, and how to avoid others. And, again, the process was set in motion.

John Breckinridge, one of early Kentucky's most prominent statesmen and a U.S. attorney general, served in the Virginia legislature and practiced law before moving to Kentucky in 1793.[64] Mary Cabell Breckinridge nurtured and influenced descendants and kin for seven decades after she became a mother at age seventeen. To her must go much of the credit for the strength of character, independence, and freedom of thought that permeated generations of a family respected for individual convictions. Throughout her life, Breckinridge kin and siblings prominently espoused opposing political and religious positions, but familial bonds remained steady.

Breckinridges lived on the frontier almost from their arrival in America,[65] and the letters show increasing interest in the West as years passed. In 1769, the year of the first letter quoted here, John was only nine years old, and Mary Cabell was an infant. The first preparations by Breckinridge family members to migrate came in the early 1780s, when John was in his early twenties. John did not declare his own intentions to move until 1788, and other members of the extended family preceded his move in the spring of 1793. That the family took so long preparing for the move and had reliable assistance from relatives already there may be atypical of the usual migration pattern. Further, the family probably was better educated and more financially secure than most. However, regarding communication facilities and their role in people's lives, the Breckinridges' migration may be sufficiently representative to provide insights about the transition others experienced in the move across the Appalachian Mountains two centuries ago.

Although the family papers contain hundreds of letters, only portions of those relevant to the West and the family's move were studied carefully. Some are quoted here at length because they give insights into the state of communication, expanding frontier, and political, social, and economic conditions. Commentary interspersed with newspaper excerpts provide some historical context during the migration years.

Newspaper accounts sketch a running story of events during the years studied. They also give some evidence of what people then might have read about the tramontane region. Some letters referred to specific news articles, but references to newspapers per se are innumerable and evidence abounds that their contents were widely known. Throughout this book, however, I exercise caution by noting that individuals *may* have read given stories where it is highly probable they had. The newspapers cited are primarily those published in Pittsburgh, Pennsylvania, Virginia, and Kentucky—areas central to the early westward migration.

Newspapers were published weekly and consisted of four pages dominated by foreign news. By 1776 only thirty-five newspapers were published throughout the colonies.[66] No Virginia newspaper was published continuously during the years studied, although at least twenty-seven were established during the period. During 1775, Williamsburg, then the Virginia capital, had at least three *Virginia Gazettes*. But no newspaper was published there after Richmond became the capital in 1780. In 1786 Richmond had three newspapers, but for most of the years studied, only one newspaper was published there. Alexandria, Fredericksburg, Norfolk, Petersburg, and Winchester were the only other Virginia towns supporting newspapers that lasted more than a year or so during the period. Except for Norfolk, no newspaper was published in these towns until the mid- and late 1780s. Kentucky's first newspaper began in 1787. Until then, the western-most newspaper in America was in Pittsburgh, Pennsylvania, and it began only a year earlier, in 1786.[67]

Newspapers had circulations of three hundred to one thousand, but the few issues were passed among neighbors, relatives, friends, mere acquaintances, and even to strangers. Unusual efforts were made to circulate newspapers and magazines among western settlements, where people avidly sought news of the East. James Brown advised his brother to send eastern newspapers as expressions of gratitude to westerners who supported his reelection to Congress in 1790.[68] Eastern merchants sending goods to western settlers always mentioned newspapers and magazines being sent—or took pains to explain why none was among the cargo when they could not send them. Soon after *The Pittsburgh Gazette* began publishing, John Blair announced in the 2 September 1786 issue that his boat would deliver newspapers weekly up and down the Monogahela River. John McDonald announced in the same issue that he would deliver the *Pittsburgh Gazette* weekly between Pittsburgh and the Monongahela landing nearest Washington.[69] Although literacy rates were low, the educated few read newspapers thoroughly and talked to others about what they read.[70]

The newspapers, letters, and diaries cited span the twenty-four years during which Kentucky emerged from wilderness to statehood. Important issues for those settling the area included conflicts with Indians, statehood, rights to the Mississippi River, and ownership of Kentucky land. These issues have been examined by many scholars, and it is not my purpose to explore them here. However, because letters, newspapers, and diaries frequently refer to them, each merits sufficient comment to make them identifiable to the reader.

The overriding issue during most of these years involved conflicts between settlers and Indians over western land, the background of which has been sketched above. References to Indians consistently characterized them as the enemy, as "savages." If sources were available to show how Indians referred to whites, the language would, no doubt, be similar. In any event, no letter, diary, or newspaper content treated Indians favorably, and almost none treated them even neutrally.[71]

Statehood was an equally important issue. After the first statehood convention in 1784, factions developed, and achieving separation from Virginia was a long, drawn-out process. The state of communication facilities gave rise to and continually aggravated the issue: The distance of settlements from the state capital meant laws were enacted in Richmond long before Kentuckians could know of, or enforce, them. Further, no legal framework existed—especially in the earliest years of settlement—within which the settlers could deal with emergencies.[72]

Still another issue, which ultimately became bound up with statehood and Indian conflicts, was Kentuckians' rights to use the Mississippi River. When Congress did not act on statehood as quickly as Kentuckians wished, some threatened to secede and join Spain, using the need of navigation rights and ineffective federal measures against Indians as bargaining points.[73]

Finally, a latent issue, which erupted in full force near the turn of the century, concerned legal problems of who owned what Kentucky land. Land was the great magnet drawing settlers to Kentucky. First, many sought prosperity as surveyors of land granted to veterans of the French and Indian War and American Revolution and as agents of others seeking land. Second, farmers seeking better land and futures for their families poured into Kentucky, especially in the 1780s. But many surveyors were careless in specifying locations, and nearly everyone was careless about assuring that plats were duly registered and free of prior claims. Daniel Boone's problems are illustrative. This explorer, builder of the first road into Kentucky, leader of its first settlement, and its defender during its starkest days, wanted, above all, to leave his surviving children financially secure. Although he surveyed and claimed thousands of Kentucky acres under preemption rights, he ultimately lost all of them to later claimants.[74] As disputes over ownership escalated, lawyers followed surveyors and farmers to Kentucky, seeking prosperity in the proliferating work of settling claims. Diverse claimants, trying to prove prior surveys to authenticate claims, led to complicated lawsuits well into the next century.[75]

In summary, while these issues were in the background and are recognizable in letter references, the focus here is the narrative the letters provide of one family's move across the Appalachian Mountains in the late eighteenth century. Ultimately, the letters reflect much about several families, Breckinridge friends and relatives who considered moving—or who did move—to Kentucky. Although commentary and newspaper excerpts provide some context, the letters generally speak most eloquently for themselves. Understatement, referred to above, becomes the letters' strongest message, imparting volumes of quiet courage, strength, and determination, bespeaking a rich heritage of character and elegant simplicity in the myriad personalities who set pen to paper. At the same time, the letters provide at least glimpses into another kind of heritage—that "transit of civilization" that began in eighteenth-century America and settled a continent within one hundred years. Finally, in addition to portraying communication behavior during the era, the letters reveal communication facilities and patterns and their roles in peoples lives' during the early stages of the westward migration.

1
Traveling over the Mountains

Communication facilities in the late eighteenth century dictated a pattern of life for those moving across the mountains that was set in motion long before the move and lasted long after. Including preparations of a year or more, travel of several weeks, and an extended period of getting established in the new home, the pattern was marked by unpredictability. Communication facilities limited migrants' choices, structured their activities and expectations. Choice of routes for the move, which was very limited, determined the kind of transportation required, the season of travel, and migrants' expectations regarding the trip's ease or difficulty and length. Because communication facilities militated against social trips across the mountains, migrants had to alter expectations about the place in their lives given to their most important social ties. They would not see again some friends and family members left behind. They could send letters, but, again, they could not expect to exchange letters on any predictable schedule. What was the substance and effect of such experiences for migrants? This chapter explores what moving over the mountains meant during the last decades of the eighteenth century—a period in which John and Mary Cabell Breckinridge prepared for moving and migrated to Kentucky. Using diaries, letters, and newspaper excerpts in which people recorded their thoughts and experiences, my research focused on what prompted people to move, how they viewed relocation and the trip itself, what preparations it entailed, how migrants fared en route, and what they revealed about experiences related to moving.

Above all, people who moved across the Appalachian Mountains into the Kentucky country in the eighteenth century hoped for a better life. William Hickman's statements typify the hopes: "In the beginning of the year 1776, I heard of a new country called Kentucky[.] [M]y circumstances being low in this world, and having a young and growing family . . . I concluded . . . to go and see for myself." His trip in the late winter of 1776 was difficult, but after returning home he continued to think of the "new country Kentucky" as he increasingly despaired of adequately supporting his family in Virginia. He wrote that in the summer of 1783, "as I was walking among my little corn, on a poor spot, having nine children, I made up my mind to move to that country, as I had an idea of it for years."[1]

Although hope for better lives prompted migrants to move, numerous anxieties about it crowded their minds. The decision represented a greater life-changing experience than at any time since and required long-term attention to details that have long since disappeared from the American culture. The costs were great, especially for migrants who were not well-off financially; they intended, by moving, to increase their prospects. In addition to selling homes and settling affairs, preparation meant acquiring the necessities for a long trip and planning for sustenance in the new home until crops could be produced or other sources of income secured. A letter fragment from someone in Kentucky in 1785 to a friend in the East reveals the former's compassion for the efforts the latter faced in moving. Noting the friend's "determination to see me this fall," the writer sympathized:

> Believe me, my knowledge of the difficulties which attend, & the delays which fall in to obstruct, a man who is about to break up his household & remove from one Country to another, fil[d] me with doubts on the latter Subject, notwithstanding your arrangements here. —My anxiety too on the occasion, might help to increase my apprehensions, for you are sensible from much experience I am persuaded, that we are very proud to doubt the success of any measure, which we warmly desire.[2]

Hickman wrote that he took one year to prepare for the move:

> I then fixed on the day to start, which was the 16th day of August, twelve months. I wound up all my affairs, and started on the 16th of August, 1784. I sold my little place—it was small and poor, but there was a good framed house and orchard on it. The purchaser paid me the money down for it, or I should not have been able to have moved.[3]

Some migrants were wealthier than Hickman, and the memoir of David Meade, published by Bayrd Still, indicates the financial drain even for those. Certainly, the numbers migrating by 1796, the year Meade moved from the James River in Virginia to Lexington, had inflated costs, which Meade could afford more than most; but he complained of prices rising after he crossed the mountains, of rent in Lexington of fifty-five pounds per year for two second-story rooms in a brick building while waiting for his home to be built, and of dwindling funds over the next year. In seven months from the time his family set out, he had spent a thousand pounds. He wrote to his nephews that if they chose to migrate, they should have five hundred pounds beyond travel expenses and a thousand additional pounds for expenses over the first year after moving.[4] In the summer of 1785, a man overseeing the building of a home and growing of a crop in Kentucky for another planning to move there warned: "As we shall be obliged to purchase provisions of every kind, the expence will over-run your calculation."[5]

For every migrant, rich or poor, once the pattern was set in motion, there was virtually no turning back. The planning and commitment to the expenses, the arduous work of protracted, time-consuming preparations, demanded persistent, deliberate care. Such resolute effort, despite ever-present awareness of hazards en route and anxiety about what might await in an unknown land, attests to migrants' belief that they were investing in a better future and that the long-term goal was worth any short-term risks. Implicit in all the recorded messages is a certainty that the development of a vast area lay ahead and that participation in that process offered a momentous opportunity. In a travel account published by George P. Harrison, Moses Austin, commenting on migrants he met on a trip through Kentucky in 1796, noted their resoluteness despite naiveté about what lay ahead for most:

> Ask these Pilgrims what they expect when they git to Kentuckey the Answer is Land. have you any. No, but I expect I can git it. have you any thing to pay for land, No. did you Ever see the Country. No but Every Body says its good land . . . here is hundreds Travelling hundreds of Miles, they Know not for what Nor Whither, except its to Kentucky, passing land almost as good and easy obtain.d, the Proprietors of which would gladly give on any terms, but it will not do its not Kentuckey its not the Promis.d land its not the good inheratence the Land of Milk and Honey. and when arriv.d at this Heaven in Idea what do they find? a goodly land I will allow but to them forbidden Land. exausted and worn down with distress and disappointment they are at last Oblig.d to become hewers of wood and Drawers of water.[6]

Eighteenth-century migrants could choose one of only two routes from the East to Kentucky, both of which required weeks of dangerous, tedious, costly travel.[7] The overland route, via Cumberland Gap, on what is today the Kentucky-Tennessee border, was shorter, but it could take much longer than the river route via Pittsburgh, Pennsylvania. Choosing the river route meant days of travel over treacherous terrain to Pittsburgh, where one usually had to wait for boats to be built and for the Ohio River to rise sufficiently to support passage. But, with the river high enough to support smooth boat passage, travelers could go from Pittsburgh to Limestone (present Maysville, Kentucky) in as few as four days, or all the way to the Falls of the Ohio (present Louisville, Kentucky)—682 miles—in less than two weeks.[8] The wilderness route, on the other hand, took four to five weeks from Williamsburg, Virginia, to present central Kentucky (Harrodsburg), a distance of 713 miles[9] (see figure).

Choosing the route of travel affected the mode of transportation and equipment to be acquired, the time and location for departure, and the company one traveled with. The most favored times for migrating were the spring months, so that travelers might arrive at destinations in time to put in crops for fall harvest. Equally important, spring trips via waterways were usually faster because spring thaws and rains raised water levels, making boat passage swifter. Making the tedious journey as quickly as possible was important because migrants wanted to minimize the length of discomfort and exposure to possible encounters with Indians. The latter could mean the loss of belongings, including provisions, at the least; at the worst, it could mean serious injuries, captivity, or loss of lives.

Of all the concerns recorded in diaries and letters of the earliest migrants over the Appalachian Mountains, that regarding Indians receives most expression. Friends and relatives warned those planning to move about the danger, and migrants often referred to best times to make the trip as the seasons when Indians were less "troublesome." Until serious threat from Indians virtually disappeared by the mid-1790s, travelers reporting on trips almost invariably mentioned them—either "signs" of them or lack thereof—and seemed to equate the ease or difficulty of their passage with whether or not they saw them. Meade, traveling in 1796, repeatedly referred to Indians, noting that "little more than eighteen months ago there was danger in landing upon either shore" between Pittsburgh and Limestone. When his boat met "three large keel Boats rowed by naked Copper colored men—of very savage appearance and working with prodigious exertion," he wrote, "my fears were all awakened and I will confess that I did not feel altogether easy until they were out of sight."[10]

During the earliest years of migrating into the Kentucky country, the wilderness route was safer than the river, where boats became easy targets for Indian snipers on river banks. People traveled in large groups (called companies) and, if attacked, could find immediate shelter in surrounding woods and terrain. After *The Kentucky Gazette*

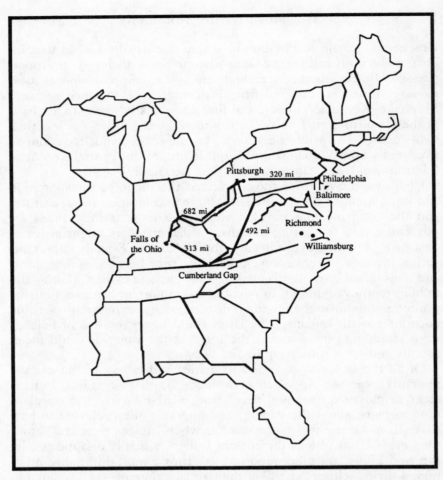

Migration Routes to the Kentucky Country in the Late Eighteenth Century.

began publishing in Lexington in 1787 (spelled *Kentucke* until 14 March 1789) advertisements such as the following, seeking company for a trip to the older settlements, appeared often:

NOTICE: A very large company will meet at the Crab-orchard on the ninth of next month in order to set out the day after on their way through the Wilderness. —It is hoped that each man will be armed with a good gun and not depend upon others to defend him.[11]

Whatever the route, those planning a move always emphasized the company and frequently expressed concern about the kind of people they might have to travel with. No one traveled alone, except when compelled by the most dire circumstances.[12]

Migrants' transportation included packhorses, wagons, canoes, and boats, most common of which, during the latter part of the eighteenth century, was the flatboat. No one means of transportation could carry migrants all the way to their destination. Wagons were common during the first leg. Canoes, often hauled overland on wagons, could be used on tributaries, and boats traversed the large rivers. No mode of transportation was easy, as letters and diaries repeatedly document, and, except for the river portion of the northern route, most migrants probably walked most of the way to Kentucky.

Setting out from homes, movers loaded wagons with all the possessions they would hold, saving space for family members to ride. Daniel Drake wrote of his family, whose "mode of travelling was in two horse wagons" from Philadelphia in the spring of 1788: "Behold, then the departure! These five persons, three of whom were adults [his mother, father, aunt, himself and his young sister], with all their earthly goods crowded into one 'Jersey Wagon,' to be hauled over the steep & rugged Allegheny mountains, and throughout an overland journey of nearly 400 miles by two horses."[13] Migrants moving livestock herded them ahead of or behind the wagons, which averaged about five miles per hour.[14]

Wagons often provided respite for weary walkers, shelter from inclement weather, and comfort for ailing travelers. But they were not always reliable; they often had to be pushed, became mired in mud, or broke, and often were abandoned en route. James Nourse wrote in his diary of a trip to Kentucky from Berkeley County, Virginia, in April 1775, "Sett off with the wagon . . . a very disagreeable day I had of it, walked all the way, and what was worse, Johnston's horses not drawing well was obliged at every bad place which was very often to put my shoulder to the wheel. . . ." After transferring to canoes a few days later, Nourse wrote that canoes afforded no better transportation: "Embarked on board our Canoes . . . the river so low and shallow at places, that a dozen times a day all hands were obliged to jump overboard and lead the Canoes . . . once our Canoe Struck upon a Rock in the Midst of the River, & Edward Taylor was in much danger."[15]

After reaching Pittsburgh, migrants transferred baggage from wagons to flatboats and loaded livestock for the trip down the river. Wagons might also be put on board flatboats because they could be used overland from Limestone or the Falls of the Ohio to the interior. But wagons often were sold or stored to be retrieved later, and travelers were met by friends and relatives with horses and wagons for the final overland passage.

Although wagons were used on land and canoes on tributaries, packhorses moved most eighteenth-century migrants' cargoes to Kentucky.[16] In the diary of a trip via Pittsburgh in 1788, published by John L. Blair, Maria Dewees wrote, "You would be suprized to see the number of pack horses which travel these roads[,] ten or twelve in a drove."[17] People, of course, rode horses where possible, but, except for very young children, packhorses rarely carried people; they were needed for carrying provisions. As Arrow emphasized, "provisions of any kind were scarce in Kentucky,"[18] and travelers tried to transport enough supplies to sustain themselves through the long trip and at destinations until provisions could be replenished through hunting, farming, gardening, and other means. Many spring travelers did not arrive in time to plant crops for fall harvest and had to assure other means to sustain themselves until the following year. One migrant told of hunger among a company of eight families who arrived with only a hundred pounds of bacon and had to subsist the first year on "wild meat."[19]

Food for livestock also had to be transported, especially during winter, when animals could not graze or forage en route. Diaries and letters frequently refer to purchasing corn, hay, and fodder along inhabited portions of the route and to stopping for livestock to graze along uninhabited parts. Nourse, in his diary of another trip in 1779, via the wilderness route, noting "scarce any picking in the woods" for horses, wrote on 30 December of reaching "Roberts mill where we got corn for our horses but could get no kind of fodder." The next day, his company reached another farm, "where we got plenty of fodder at a dollar a bundle." Horses fed on cane, which, in the earliest migration years, grew abundantly along parts of the wilderness route. Nourse wrote that after passing "the last cabin in the settlement" the group "for the first time turned our horses to cane," and after camping by a "good canebrake," the horses "looked as well as when I paid ten dollars for fodder." Cane was so significant that Nourse mentioned it seventeen times in his short diary of the trip from 27 December 1779 until late February 1780, usually noting simply "good canebrake" after the date and camp location. (Such information seems to have been recorded purely for others who would later travel the same route.) Arriving at Boonesborough after nearly seven weeks of travel from Colonel Shelby's in Berkeley County, Virginia, Nourse wrote that he paid "as high as sixty dollars a bushel" for two bushels of corn.[19a]

Cargo was secured on horses with pack saddles, which had to be made or procured for the trip. Writing of trip preparations, Nourse noted on 28 December that he "Set to making pack saddles, getting bells, etc., and Wednesday set off with our pack horses."[20] According to Arnow, the "forked limb of a white oak of a certain shape and bigness made the best of pack saddles." After a tree with the right kind of fork was located and cut down, Arnow explains:

> The forked limb or crotch had only to be cut the right length, the prong chipped out with hatchet and knife to fit the animal's back. A board was then fastened to each fork with wooden pins, and holes bored to receive the iron rings for carrying straps and girths. The main thing was that everything hold, for often the pack-saddle carried children, one slung on either side in a willow or split white oak hamper, or in cold weather swaddled in the feather beds and bed clothing, and all these had to say put on trails so steep the animal sometimes pitched forward or fell on his haunches.[21]

Horses laden with two hundred pounds[22] not only climbed the steepest of mountains, they also trudged through mire, snow, or ice, and swam swift currents, depending on the season; often they lost loads along the way. Dewees, a young wife and mother, wrote of "roads so very steep that the horses seem ready to fall backwards."[23] William Calk wrote of a trip from Prince William County, Virginia, via the wilderness route in 1775, "We start early and travel . . . along a verey Bad hilley way cross one creek whear the horses almost got mired[;] some fell in and all wet their loads." Later, he wrote that in crossing "indian Creek, Abrams saddel turned and the load all fell in." And a few days later, he wrote that the company had to "toat" packs across a stream on a log while horses swam. "One hors ran in with his pack and lost it in the river, and they got it again."[24] Often, travelers had to unload and discard baggage so the horses could travel faster.

People often wrote of fatigue, especially from walking. In 1788,

Dewees wrote: "Sett off for the north Mountain, which we find so bad we are Obliged to foot it up. . . . Find this the most fatiguing days journey we have had." A few days later, she wrote, "Set out for Chestnut ridge. Horrid roads and the Stony's land in the world. I believe every few hundred yards, rocks big enough to build a small house upon."[25] On 14 April 1775 William Calk wrote of coming "to a turable mountain that tired us all almost to death to git over it. . . ."[26]

Travel on the river route meant long layovers at Pittsburgh while people waited for rain and for boats to be built. One migrant told of waiting six weeks in the fall of 1793 for rain, and the Dewees family, who left Philadelphia for Kentucky on 27 September 1788, waited near Pittsburgh for rain from 20 October until 18 November.[27]

Flatboats carried most late-eighteenth-century migrants on large waterways. These preceded keelboats, but the great variety of boats in this era has led to confusion in distinguishing different kinds. Flatboats were also called "arks," "broad horns," "Kentucky boats," "New Orleans boats," "sneak boxes," and "rafts." Rafts, however, preceded the flatboat, and the different names probably referred to shapes or specific features. For example, Kentucky boats were covered only partially, while New Orleans boats were fully covered.[28] W. Wallace Carson says the first ark was built in 1793, but that was, no doubt, a variation of the flatboat, which was used on the Ohio River by 1780 and probably earlier, according to Baldwin.[29]

Flatboats averaged five miles per hour and were large enough for relatively normal living activities aboard. Boats, up to one hundred feet long and capable of carrying fifteen to seventy tons, included space for baggage and furniture, supplies, and living quarters.[30] Some also included space for livestock, but some migrants had more than one boat, including at least one to carry animals and often one to carry furniture and other baggage. David Campbell's company, moving from Maryland to the Falls of the Ohio in 1780, included six families and four boats, one of which carried the livestock.[31] Baldwin reports a receipt from 1800 that provides a description of the boats: "One Kentucky boat forty five feet long, fitted up with three rooms, two chimneys, two windows (of six lights each) a Necessary, a tarred cloth over the cover of two rooms, being old tents, together with Oars, Pump, and Cable 20 lb., also one Batteau and one Tent."[32]

Flatboats cost approximately $1.00 to $1.50 per foot, with fully covered ones being more expensive than those partially covered. Cable, pump, and fireplace cost an additional $10. Some had brick fireplaces and chimneys, while sand-filled boxes or kettles served as fireplaces on others. The average flatboat was fourteen by forty or fifty feet long.[33] In addition to usual daily activities of preparing food, dining, and sleeping on board, classes were conducted for children, farm animals and fowls were attended, and babies were born. Boaters stopped at intervals to put livestock ashore for grazing, take hunting excursions, and secure food or other provisions;[34] and children were sometimes taken ashore for games to break the monotony of travel for them.[35]

The Dewees family's boat was built at McKee's Ferry, twelve miles up the Monongahela River from Pittsburgh. But the Deweeses grew anxious about the water level before reaching that point, and Mr. Dewees and his brother-in-law rode the thirteen miles to McKee's Ferry to assess whether the water would be high enough for travel. Next day, the entire group moved on to McKee's Ferry, and on 18 October Mrs. Dewees wrote of learning that the boat was completed and described it as "resembling Noahs Ark not a little." The next day, she wrote that "our boat is 40 foot long, our room 16 by 12 with a Comfortable fireplace. Our Bed room partitioned off with blankets, and far preferable to the Cabbins we met with after we crossed the Mountains" (she expressed relief at the absence of fleas, which had "almost devoured" them "on shore").[36]

Usually, more than one family shared a boat, and many boats traveled together. Drake had no idea "how many families were crowded onto one boat," or how many boats were in the "flotilla" with which his family traveled to Limestone.[37] Eighteen-year-old William Sudduth, who went to Kentucky in the fall of 1783, wrote that the boat he traveled on "had on board four families and twenty horses." The low water forced Sudduth's company to lighten the boat, and the group decided after a week "to put out fifteen horses and five men to take the horses by land." Low water often forced migrants to lighten a boat's load by removing cargo to paid storage where possible, or hiding it ashore for later retrieval. Even this did not help if water levels were too low. Much cargo left behind simply was lost, and the trip overland often was too much for livestock. By the time Sudduth and his companions arrived at Lexington, he wrote, "nine of the fifteen horses . . . had given out on our journey, my own for one."[38]

The Dewees family worried about low water and grew impatient for rain while waiting to move down the Monongahela River to Pittsburgh. The river would not support the boat laden with all their belongings when they moved on, so they left the horses and baggage to be sent by wagon from McKee's Ferry. After a difficult passage over low water for eleven miles, they stopped a mile from Pittsburgh on 20 October and waited for rain.[39] No travelers wanted to risk boat trouble or interrupted passage between Pittsburgh and Limestone because, as Drake later wrote, the "danger of being attacked by the Indians was too great to justify a landing" during that part of the trip.[40]

Baldwin published a letter from a flatboat captain to his wife that summarizes the work of boat piloting and some routine hazards of river travel:

> I think Jonas will have a second time to go down this river Before he learns not to scratch the Shore fifteen or twenty miles before he can get the boat Stopped and then to run night and day in the most eminent danger and the weather most excessive Cold—when the Boats will run above 100 miles in 24 hours and the nights so dark that the Shores Cannot be known from the water any other way than by throwing Stone or Coal out from the sides and hearing where they light—when his rest cannot exceed 4 hours out of 24, and all the rest be watching and fatigue—when running on an Island how to Carry his boat in the river again—when thrown on land by the ice his Oars run in the earth almost to the handle how to get her afloat again and how to run into a harbour for Safety and live in the boat when it is cold enough to freeze a dog to death—such with but few exceptions has been our Case since we embarked.[41] [Reprinted from *The Keelboat Age on Western Waters*, by Leland D. Baldwin, by permission of the University of Pittsburgh Press, © 1941 by University of Pittsburgh Press, © 1969 by Leland D. Baldwin.]

One constant worry of migrants was dwindling provisions. Some travelers ran out of food, and supplies in the towns along the routes grew scarce as migrants in greater numbers passed through. In the spring of 1789, Joel Watkins complained of insufficient food while he waited at Pittsburgh. On 8 May he wrote in his diary: "Continued at our encampment and made shift to purchase half Bushel of Corn which we parched and pounded to meal, which we thickened water with and sweetened with sugar and drank for diet[,] making a virtue of necessity." The next day, Watkins's company loaded the new boat and moved on; however, because the boat was poorly built, the group had to stop, unload, and camp while waiting for a second boat to be built. Near the campsite, Watkins obtained corn ("but not any for our horses") and pounded bread "to meal in a mortar as there were no other nor better conveniencey [*sic*] to be had in that country." On another occasion, he wrote, "Our diet chiefly consists of pounded meal, hominy, some milk and such meat as we can purchase of hunters. . . . [W]e have not the smallest prospects of being better provided for till we can arrive at Limestone." Complaining of the high cost of food, he wrote that corn cost four shillings (approximately sixty-six cents) per bushel, bear meat cost one shilling (approximately seventeen cents) per pound, and flour cost six shillings (one dollar) per hundred pounds.[42]

Virtually all travelers carried weapons and could have hunted food—and many did. But there were times when gunshots fired while pursuing game might have alerted Indians, and travelers were reluctant to use ammunition they might need to defend themselves. Sudduth and his companions traveling overland with horses nearly depleted their ammunition killing game before learning of Indians' presence. To conserve what was left for defense, they decided to "kill but one turky a day in October for five men and that rosted without bread or salt we continued to travel . . . on a Turky a day for eleven days."[43]

Scarcity of provisions meant that many traveled hungry, and one reason for hunger, as Arnow suggests, was that some, especially migrants from towns and farms far from the frontier, lacked the requisite hunting skills.[44] Those traveling in large companies were most vulnerable to food scarcity. Samuel and Jean Shannon, who wrote to their son Thomas of overtaking companies of 500, 400, 130, 120, and "another large one" on the wilderness road, said one company traveled "not more than eight or nine miles a day, and we thought if we could not travel faster we must suffer, for a number . . . had not more than four days provisions, and were 130 miles from the first station." The Shannons moved on and joined another company, but, they wrote, "There were several . . . in a suffering condition . . . for want of provisions."[45] Daniel Trabue, on a 1778 trip along the wilderness road, wrote of running out of food: "We could get nothing to eat. Thursday morning . . . our provisions consisted of one rasher of hog bacon to each man and not another mouthful did we get until Sunday[,] which was Ester Sunday[,] about 2 o'clock [when] we got to Boonsborough. . . ."[46]

Moses Austin recorded his shock at how inadequately equipped for travel were migrants he met on the wilderness route as late as 1796.

I cannot omitt Noticeing the many Distress.d families I pass.d in the Wilderness nor can any thing be more distressing to a man of feeling than to see woman and Children in the Month of December Travelling a Wilderness Through Ice and Snow passing large rivers and Creeks with out Shoe or Stocking, and barely as maney raggs as covers their Nakedness, with out [*sic*] money or provisions except what the Wilderness affords . . . to say they are poor is but faintly express'g there [*sic*] Situation.[47]

Many travelers became ill from inadequate food and exposure.

William Christian's mother was forced to turn back because of illness on the Wilderness Road in 1785. Christian's company continued, but he worried about her, writing to a friend after arriving near Louisville, "I long much to hear from my poor Mother and how she got back, if she is alive. I have a great many fears that she is not alive, as she was so low when she turned back, and I hope to hear how it is soon by some of the movers."[48] Joel Watkins wrote in 1789 of "being unwell since the morning after I arrived at the Kenhaway" [three days], and noted later that in fifteen days on the trip, he had lost eighteen pounds.[49] James Smith became ill after his company in the fall of 1785 traveled through a rainstorm so severe that "the amazing quantity of trees . . . continually falling round us rendered our riding extremely dangerous." He wrote on 19 October:

> I was also still very unwell, after one of the most disagreeable nights lodging that I ever had in my life; for the ground being wet all our bedding wet, the wind all night blowing exceeding hard, and either rain or snow frequently beating in upon us, was the cause of my being seized with a shivering ague. . . . I had little expectation of ever surviving . . . even were I at home where I might lie at ease on my bed with proper attendance. But here I was in a wild uninhabited part of the world having near 150 miles to travel without any proper nourishment, under an absolute necessity of traveling and without so much as an acquaintance except my brother and two or three others (whom I but barely knew by sight) from whom I could reasonably expect any thing of consequence in my situation.

Disregarding his brother's advice to turn back, he continued and "was again taken with an exceeding hard ague which on its going off was succeeded by as hard a fever." He suffered daily, writing that he "seemed to be in a Kind of insensibility and blindness." His illness slowed travel, and when the group arrived at "Bro. George's" on 24 October, he was "confined almost entirely to the house and chiefly to the bed" until 21 November.[50] Dewees became ill the first day of travel and wrote three days later that she "Lost all the fine prospects [scenic views] the first days oweing to my sickness . . . being Obliged to be led from the Waggon to the bed, and from the bed to the Waggon."[51]

Accommodations were generally available only in towns. Only in the last years of the century might a traveler expect to find accommodations along the entire route. Drake wrote that the few taverns between Philadelphia and Pittsburgh in 1788 were expensive and crude:

Aside from affording shelter from the elements, the taverns . . . offered little in the way of comfort. Many of them consisted of a single room which served all purposes. The few beds available in even the more pretentious ones usually had cornshuck mattresses. It was customary for men, women and children to sleep, rolled in their blankets, on the floor of the public room which was heated only by a fireplace.

Drake explained that travelers generally cooked food when they stopped at night and before starting out in the morning.[52] Often, they sought accommodations in homes, where they existed along the route, and some people living on or near the frontier used their homes as inns, or "ordinaries." But many travelers complained of dirty hosts and surroundings. Indeed, the kind of accommodations Dewees wrote of one day could have aggravated her illness:

put up at a Cabin at the foot of the hill[—]perhaps a dozen logs upon one another, with a few slabs for a roof and the earth for a floor & a Wooden Chimney Constituted this extrodnary [sic], ordinary. The people were Kind but Amazing dirty[;] there was between twenty & thirty of us all lay on the floor. Except Mrs. Rees[,] the Children and your Maria, who by our dress or Adress or perhaps boath were favoured with a bed and I assure you we that [sic] thought ourselves [lucky] to escape being fleaced alive.

Dewees also often praised accommodations and kind hosts, as did other travelers, but gratitude simply for shelter and a bed may have led to overstatement of qualities more often than not. After one especially tiring day of walking, Dewees wrote, "Believe me my dear friends the sight of a log house on these Mountains after a fatiguing days Journey affords more real pleasure than all the Magnificent buildings your city contains."[53]

Many travelers slept under the stars, in makeshift "tents" contrived on the spot, in caves, hollow logs, or other natural shelter. One migrant described deep snow when his company moved in the fall of 1791; they camped "behind an old log," and, after arriving at their destination, "rived clapboards, and made a shelter" until they could build a cabin.[54] During especially severe weather, some travelers died from exposure. During the winter of 1779–80, for example, when severe cold weather paralyzed Kentucky "from the middle of November to the latter part of February," many migrants died en route and "more than 500 cattle perished while being brought in over the Wilderness Road." A family named Davis, marooned by rising water while camping near Rockcastle River, froze to death en route to Kentucky via the wilderness road.[55]

Although many lives ended during passage, some began. Nicholas

Meriwether wrote to his father on 25 February 1784 from the North
Branch of Potomac River that he was en route to Kentucky, but his
wife's "situation" would "retard the voyage" since she would "lie in
in about a month." On 20 May he wrote "from on Board my boat lying
at the mouth of Georges Creek . . . in Monongahela," of plans to
press on to Kentucky in time to plant crops." The letter did not
mention the birth of the child, which, if living, would have been
approximately two months old, according to the expected birth date
given in his earlier letter[56] W. Warfield wrote to John Breckinridge on
11 February 1793 of fears about his wife's tolerance of the trip to
Kentucky. She was in "the fifth month of pregnancy," he wrote, "and
from repeated disasters that have attended, when in a similar situation, she takes very little exercise." But he wrote that "Capt. Sorrell," whose wife was "in a similar situation," was "determined to
go."[57]

Moving meant a protracted journey that was difficult and dangerous
for even the heartiest adults, but what did it mean for children?
Although thousands of children migrated in the late eighteenth century, few diaries and letters mention them. Stories of settlers' children
carried off to Indian villages are legion, so migrants probably feared
for their children's safety. Dewees occasionally referred to two daughters and other children, always in a lighthearted tone. Once, writing
of a treacherous mountain road, she added, "You would be surprised
to see the Children, Jumping and Skiping, some times quite out of
Sight some times on horseback sometimes in the Waggon." Another
day, apparently alluding in jest to her youthful looks, she intimated
that people assumed her children belonged to "Sister Rees" and that
she was a "Miss from Philad." She didn't bother correcting the
misimpression, she wrote, unless her daughter cried out for her
"mar." She added that the "Children are very hearty and bear fatigue," and that "Rachel mostly passes half the day in Spelling and
Sally in Singing."[58]

In addition to the unusual hazards during such a journey, children
were more prone than adults to accidents. Hickman wrote that his
second oldest son, Thomas, about fifteen, "got kicked by a horse the
second morning [of travel], which laid him up several days."[59] Drake,
who was under three years old when his family migrated to Kentucky,
wrote that, according to stories told him, while his family's wagon
climbed the steep, rocky Allegheny Mountain, "[I] clambered over
the front board of the wagon, and hung on the outside by my hands,
when I was discovered & taken in, before I had fallen, to be crushed,
perhaps, by wheels."[60]

Mishaps ranging from comical to tragic were commonplace during trips. For example, nineteen of twenty-three in one boat on the Ohio River drowned when a horse kicked and broke off a side of the boat, causing it to sink. Another boat was driven against a log and sank, drowning a woman and three children.[61] When Sudduth and four men set off overland with horses taken off the company's overloaded boat, it was agreed that the boat was to wait if it passed the men at night. The men came to a creek so swollen that they had to go far inland to cross it, and when they returned to the river, the boat had passed, but, believing it still behind them, they traveled forty miles before they stopped and waited a day and a half for it to catch up. Deciding to swim across the river, they made a raft to carry baggage and guns and towed it behind them. Sudduth, who could not swim, writes comically of trying to ride a horse across ("nearly drowned the horse") and then clinging to the raft as the other men towed it. Continuing down the river, the men found a note stuck to a tree by a member of their company, telling them to continue by land and that "the danger of Indians was so great that the boats crew thought it was imprudent to wait" for them.[62]

During Nourse's trip on the wilderness road, the severity of the winter of 1779–80 often delayed travel. Members of the company suffered frostbite, halting travel for four days at one point. One horse sickened and died, despite Nourse's ardent efforts for several days to save it, and a mare gave birth. Horses wandered so far from the camp during one night of heavy snow that they could not be tracked by hoofprints or the tinkle of the bells attached to their harnesses. The travelers' food supply dwindled, forcing hunting excursions, one of which took them onto ice so thick that they feared the crackling sounds of walking on it might alert Indians.[63]

Despite the difficulties, travelers often jotted down impressions about the countryside, historical sites, and other observations and often expressed delight in what they saw. During the overland portion of her trip, Dewees noted passing the field "where Braddock fought his famous battle," the site of General Grant's battle of 1758, Indian mounds, and several forts; and in Pittsburgh, she was especially impressed with "Capt. Oharras Summerhouse . . . on the Banks of the Aligahany river which runs about a hundred yards from the Bottom of their Garden," from which one could "at one view behold the Alligany, the Monogahela, & the Ohio rivers." Excitement about the future, too, ran high for many travelers, as perhaps best expressed in Dewee's descriptions of her young daughter's attitude: "Every house we stop at she enquires if it is not a Kenty. house and seldom leaves it 'till she informs them she is a Kenty. Lady."[64]

Migrants generally complained about the wait at Pittsburgh, but the Dewees family passed the time with visiting that seemed only slightly hampered by their having left most of their clothes at McKee's Ferry. On 21 October Dewees recorded declining several invitations to go ashore, "as the trunks with our cloaths is not come up, and we in our travelling dress not fit to make our appearance in that Gay place." She added:

> Just received an Invitation from the french lady we traveled part of the way with. . . . Mr. Tilton call'd on us with Mrs. Tilton's Compliments [and] would be happy to have us to tea. He gone and three french Gentlemen and an Englishman came on board and expressed a great deal of pleasure to see us so comfortably Situated. In the afternoon Mr. and Mrs. Oharra waited on us at the boat and insisted on our going to their house, which in Compliance to their several invitations we were Obliged to Accept.

On 22 October Dewees wrote that she "engaged to tea with Mrs. Tilton," and "Mrs. Oharra waited on us to Mrs. Tiltons to Mrs. Nancarrows & Mrs. Odderongs." Also, "Col. Butler and his lady" visited with the Deweeses and "took a bit of Biscuit and Cheese with a glass of wine." Dewees then "spent the afternoon at Mrs. Tilton with a room full of Company, and received several invitations to spend our time with the Ladys at Pitts." She also "Called on Mrs. Butler and saw a very handsome parlour, Elegantly papered and well finished . . . more like Philad. than any I have seen since I left that place," she wrote. On 25 October the Deweeses tested the water but moved down the river only a short distance, where the visiting continued. Although visiting, reading, strolls, parties, and excursions whiled away time, Dewees fretted about the lack of rain, writing that she feared the family might have "to winter among the rocks."[65]

On 18 November the family moved on despite the lack of rain, probably fearing worse conditions should the river freeze. An item in *The Kentucky Gazette* in 1791 suggests the dilemma posed by low water in winter weather: "We are informed that at least 100 families are at Redstone and on the river destined to Kentucky. That the water was so low that they were 14 days . . . from Pittsburgh. We have every reason to suppose they will suffer in their passage from the uncommon inclemency of the season."[66] Ice delayed the writer of a letter published in *The Pittsburgh Gazette* on 15 May 1788: "As there were very hard times this winter here, we left Redstone the 2d day of March as the river then opened, we got about 30 miles down the river[;] it was frozen across, and there we lay 15 days on ice, we were all but perished."[67] Winter travel also risked ice damage to boats.

Baldwin relates a traveler's report of "five boats with fifteen hundred bushels of corn that were crushed in the ice in December 1792; and eleven years later, there were said to have been two hundred boats that passed the mouth of the Kentucky in floating ice, some of them containing frozen corpses. . . ."[68]

Literature about the migration to Kentucky concentrates on Indian warfare and those who died during sieges, and although conclusive figures of the numbers of migrants who died en route are not known, some estimates are instructive. Historian Dale Van Every wrote that most contemporary estimates placed the number killed annually on the wilderness route at 100, and evidence indicated that as many as 450 died violently each year on migration routes and frontiers in the late 1780s. He added that Reuben T. Durrett concluded, after a study of Indian wars, that 3,600 Kentuckians were killed in the twenty years after the first settlement.[69] Kentucky District Judge Harry Innes wrote to Secretary of War John Knox in 1790 that "since my first visit to this District [1783] . . . I can venture to say that 1,500 souls have been killed & taken in the District & migrating to it—that upwards of 20,000 Horses have been taken . . . & other Property . . . carried off and destroyed . . . to at least £15,000."[70]

Those who read newspapers saw almost constant reports of deaths. A 15 May 1788 newspaper reported a letter excerpt from Lexington that told of several deaths on the river route:

> after we left Pittsburgh, we came to Limestone in four days, in going down the river we run on the point of an island, in the night close upon the Indian shore, but nothing was hurt; I and two more men went out of the boat next morning, and shoved her off with ease; the Indians were very troublesome, they killed and robbed all that came across, there was Mr. Ryecout, Mr. Pricinse, Mr. Ferguson and Mr. Black, went in our boat from Limestone to the Falls, and two more boats in company with them; unluckily they were taken . . . and killed at the Miami; Coming to Lexington we lay at John Keyser's and the Indians stole four horses from the inhabitants, within half a mile from this place, there were two families killed close by.[71]

On 19 June 1788 *The Pittsburgh Gazette* reported, "By a gentleman from Kentucky we learn, that scarce twenty four hours pass but some murder or other depredation is committed," and added that "about twenty men with as many pack horses, loaded with goods were attacked" on 14 May on the wilderness route. One man was killed; the others escaped but lost all their goods to the Indians. A 9 July news item reported that twelve on the wilderness route were attacked on 22 May; five were killed; the others escaped but lost all their horses except two to the Indians. The same newspaper reported "an intoxicated party of Indians having decoyed some persons, lately passing down the Ohio . . . to the shore, under assurances of friendship, and then barbarously putting them all to the tomahawk." The next week, an item reported that "Scarce a boat can pass below Limestone but what is attacked by Indians." An item in *The Kentucky Gazette* in 1790 reported that Indians attacked a boat on the Ohio River and captured the whole company (six men, three women, and six children). They sunk what property they could not carry and, as they marched the prisoners away, one of the women gave birth the second evening "and marched next day."[72]

The possibility of violent death haunted all who migrated through 1793, the year the Breckinridges moved, and the decision to move across the mountains meant preparing to face that terrifying prospect—in addition to travel difficulties, scarce food, and illnesses. William Calk wrote in early 1775 of fear causing some in his company to turn back when news came from Daniel Boone of Indian hostility. The following day, Calk wrote of meeting "a good many peopel turned Back for fear. . . ." The next day, two more of his company turned back, and they met "another Company going Back." Calk wrote, "they tell such News Abram and Drake is afraid to go aney farther. . . ." And the following day, he wrote of meeting "about 20 more turning Back."[73]

Many, of course, experienced real fear for the first time. The diary of Daniel Trabue, who first went to Kentucky via the wilderness route when he was eighteen, reveals his feelings. "Travelling along Powel's Valley," he wrote, "where the Indians had broke up some places[,] seeing waste *dessolate cabbins*[,] I began to feel strange. . . ." Daniel's older brother James apparently led the company. When they saw "fresh indian tracks," Daniel wrote that "James Trabue ordered us everyone to alight and primm our guns afresh and put two bullits in each man's mouth and if we come up with the indians we must fight our best." James and another went ahead, leaving instructions that, should they see Indians, they were to jump behind trees as a signal; the others should then "dismount and run up and fight and the negro boy stay and mind the horses." Daniel wrote that "one man . . . named Lucust said he wished he could come up with the indians[;] he wanted so bad to have a chance of killing them, he said he knew he could kill five himself."

The company moved on, expecting an Indian attack at any moment, and Daniel wrote that as they moved down the mountain, "it looked like I was going out of this world." James sent Daniel to scout for Indians, and he wrote that when he saw three trails he "began to feel chicken hearted" and to fear "I should be killed in this dreary howling wilderness." He never mentioned it, he wrote, adding, "I thought if I could have courage like Lucust I would be glad. . . . I then wished I was back in old Virginia."

When the attack came, Lucust showed little daring, however. After the skirmish, James, discovering the slave in the front line, reprimanded him: " 'I thought I told you to mind the horses'[;] the negro boy says 'Lucust is there. . . .' " Daniel wrote, adding, "we could see him behind a tree near the horses. . . . James would swear when he was angry, [and] he cursed him for a damed coward."[74]

Preparing to move over the mountains meant confronting fears, but it also meant preparing to face hardships and danger after arriving in a wilderness, isolated from neighbors and assistance.[75] Thousands who survived the trip did not live to enjoy life over the mountains. One woman, deranged after seeing her husband killed and being captured herself and taken from her three children, rambled aimlessly after escaping later. The children's grandfather, in the meantime, had raised them after coming from Virginia to retrieve them from the wilderness. Years later, one of the woman's sons, then grown, found her and took her home, where her sanity gradually returned.[76] Death by violence came so frequently, transportation scholar Seymour Dunbar reported, that natural death elicited awe. He cited a passage from Bogart's *Daniel Boone* about "An old lady . . . describing . . . her residence in Kentucky" during those years:

the most comely sight she beheld, was seeing a young man dying in his bed a natural death. She had been familiar with blood, and carnage and death, but in all those cases the sufferers were the victims of the Indian tomahawk and scalping knife; and that on an occasion when a young man was taken sick and died, after the usual manner of nature, she said the rest of the women sat up all night, gazing upon him as an object of beauty.[77]

Despite the fears and hardships, however, the overwhelming message in the letters and diaries is of courage, fortitude, and concern for fellow migrants. One woman told of her company stopping to console a family whose four children had been tomahawked and scalped. Their aunt, she said, "sat on a stump . . . and cried all day." Another migrant years later described sojourners who were "literally starving . . . without a mouthful to eat for two days. Their feet blistered, and legs & thighs raw with the scratches of the Green briars in the midst of a world of cragged rocks & cliffs, under a broiling sun . . . exhausted by fatigue, hunger, and despair." He averred, "it ought to be

remembered by their children, until the third and fourth genera-
tion."[78]

In addition to living with the dangers of travel, moving meant
giving up the familiar for the unknown, security for insecurity, comfort for discomfort. It meant resigning oneself to never again seeing
neighbors, old friends, relatives, and even parents and siblings; it
meant exchanging all that had structured one's daily routines for a
new structure dominated by uncertainty. Those left behind also suffered losses, and references to the pain of final separations in a few
extant letters and diaries are poignant. Sarah Wigginton, writing from
Stafford County, Virginia, to Mrs. William Calk in Kentucky in 1783,
yearned for communication with her, acknowledging that the two
would not see each other again: "I remember your last charge was not
to fale writing to you every convenient opportunity. . . . I should be
mighty glad to hear from you, but much moreso to see you; but the
distance is so great that I never expect [to] see you, again."[79]
Hickman's statement about the effect on his wife of his plan to move
typifies the sadness of women migrants: "I knew it would be a Killing
stroke to my wife when she heard of my determination, for she was so
attached to the church and neighbors that she could not give them
up. . . . I told her what I had concluded on, when she burst in tears,
and begged me to decline but it was in vain."[80]

Not only did migrants face the possibility of not seeing relatives
and friends again, they could not count on hearing from them because
circulation of information was severely inhibited. Communication by
letter and newspaper to and from the Kentucky country was directly
tied to waterways and overland routes and therefore was an integral
part of all the difficulties associated with moving. The full import of
this may be lost in an age when long-distance telephone conversation
is taken for granted as almost as good as being there, when a homesick
son or daughter wishes to talk to parents, or when one simply yearns
for a heart-to-heart talk with a friend who lives far away.

Maintaining ties to the familiar support system—church, school,
friends, and relatives—was difficult for eighteenth-century migrants.
Letter exchanges took months. In isolated communities far removed
from long-settled areas, news from "home" and from other frontier
communities was a precious commodity. Chapter two describes the
mode of letter communication that linked friends and families in
older, settled areas of the East with the pioneers "gone over the
mountains."

2
Sending Letters over the Mountains

During Kentucky's earliest settlement, relatives and friends had no systematic way to keep track of people who went into the wilderness.[1] Through the 1760s, the earliest venturers—hunters, traders, and explorers—generally were not heard from until their return. Those who did not return within a reasonable amount of time were presumed dead. As late as 1774, Virginians exchanged anxious letters about Daniel Boone, who had gone to warn surveyors on the Ohio River of an impending Indian war. They worried about his long absence (sixty-two days) and fretted indecisively about sending someone to see what had happened to him.[2]

As the Kentucky country became settled, travelers carried letters to and from the area. Sending mail with travelers had long been customary because the American colonial postal system, which began in 1692 and did not link all colonies until the 1740s, was inefficient, hampered by problems, and served only coastal towns.[3] The one postal route hugged the Atlantic coastline until the 1780s—after trans-Appalachian settlement had begun—and then extended westward only in short links between neighboring towns. After 1786, several New England cross-routes began. But it was not until 1788 that the first truly westward route crossed Pennsylvania, linking Philadelphia to Pittsburgh via Lancaster, Yorktown, Carlisle, Chamberstown, and Bedford. Mail went once weekly from Philadelphia to Chamberstown and once in two weeks from there west to Pittsburgh.[4]

Despite developing cross-routes, the entire postal route grew by little more than 300 miles from 1749 (1,541 miles) to 1790 (1,875 miles).[5] Except for the Philadelphia–Pittsburgh route, the whole country west of the Atlantic coast lacked postal service in 1790, although the states then had seventy-five post offices. When the Kentucky settlement began in 1775, the westernmost post office was in Fredericksburg, Virginia, a few miles from the coast.[6] When Kentucky became a state in 1792, the westernmost post office was in Pittsburgh, Pennsylvania, some four hundred miles from the new settlements.[7] The federal postal service did not reach Kentucky until

59

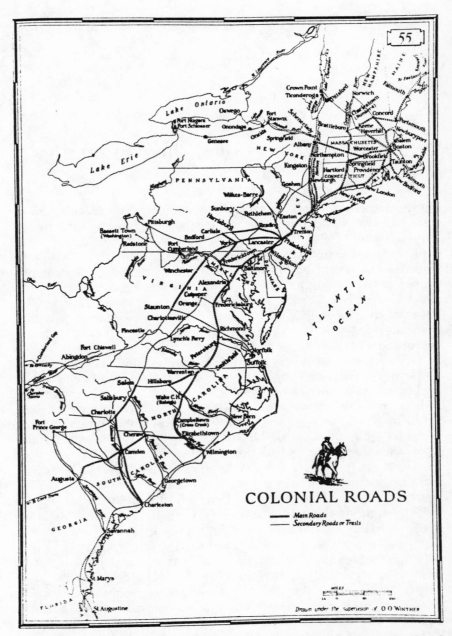

Colonial Roads circa 1775. Reprinted with permission of Charles Scribner's Sons, an imprint of Macmillan Publishing Company, from *Atlas of American History* by James Truslow Adams and R. V. Coleman. Copyright 1943 by Charles Scribner's Sons, renewed 1977.

1794, a year after the Breckinridge family moved there and two years after statehood.[8]

Problems plaguing the postal system until reorganization in the 1790s entrenched the practice of private mail delivery.[9] Bad roads, inadequate travel accommodations, and sheer distances between offices made postal schedules unreliable. The 343 miles from Philadelphia, Pennsylvania, to Jamestown, Virginia, for example, took two weeks in good weather.[10] To get from Newport, Virginia, to Williamsburg, Virginia, where mail arrived every other Saturday, took two to three days.[11] The estimated 480 miles from Williamsburg to Charleston, South Carolina, took two weeks under the best conditions. Few towns along the way had post houses or good inns, and a rider often rode the same horse 200 miles.[12]

The best travel conditions rarely prevailed, and irregular mail delivery was the rule throughout the colonial and early-nation years. In the 1750s Virginia Lieutenant Governor Robert Dinwiddie complained that a letter took five to six weeks from New York City to Williamsburg. In 1762 North Carolina Governor Arthur Dobbs complained that a letter took three or four months (and often twelve) to reach him from New York City. In 1769 a new monthly service from North Carolina to South Carolina failed soon after it began.[13]

The most serious problems hampering the postal service were inadequate financial support and nonchalant post riders. Ferriers, required to carry post riders free, often delayed a crossing until enough other passengers appeared to make the trip across a waterway profitable. Post riders often contracted to carry mail privately at lower rates than the system required;[14] and many used their trips to conduct a variety of private business activities along the way.[15] Furthermore, people often refused to pay postage and generally found private means to send mail.[16]

Given such problems with the regular postal service, it seems remarkable that letters reached the Kentucky country at all. The western country was far west of the one mail route along the coast. The distance by land and riverway from Philadelphia to present Louisville, Kentucky, via Pittsburgh (one thousand miles) amounted to two-thirds the total colonial American post road mileage in 1775. Overland from Philadelphia to present Louisville via the Valley of Virginia (eight hundred twenty-six miles) was more than half the total post road mileage.[17] And, of course, travel accommodations became scarcer as a traveler moved westward.

Ship captains regularly delivered mail from port to port by sea, and, generally, three categories of people carried overland mail throughout the colonial and early-nation years.[18] Urgent messages required drafting the most convenient person, usually a servant, family member, friendly Indian, or expess rider.[19] A second kind of carrier was anyone who traveled anywhere with any regularity, if at least once or twice a year. This category included merchants' wagon boys, newspaper carriers, and legislative representatives.[20] Finally, anyone who went anywhere any time served as mail carrier and news source. People often detained travelers while hastily preparing messages for them to deliver, or sent letters with carriers to catch up to a traveler already departed.[21]

Letter exchanges between Kentucky frontier settlers and eastern Virginia settlements took many months, especially in the earliest years considered here. After the end of the War for Independence, as migration increased, the time required for letters and word-of-mouth news to travel between the areas decreased. By 1787 Mary Howard wrote from Botetourt to John Brown in Danville, "I have the happiness of hearing of your health and welfare almost every week."[22] She probably referred to word-of-mouth news that she learned more by chance than by design, for people could not expect news on any regular basis, despite the increased travel to and from the West.

When travelers could not deliver letters to final destinations, they left them at courthouses, taverns, printing offices, residences, or with other travelers. After John Bradford began publishing the *The Kentucke Gazette* in 1787, a list of unclaimed letters in his office became a regular column in his newspaper, as it was in most eighteenth-century newspapers. The rider Bradford hired in 1790 to deliver newspapers also carried letters.[23]

Many letters were lost en route. Furthermore, the customary letter delivery hardly allowed for privacy in correspondence. Most letters fell into many hands in their passage, and the carriers read them eagerly; on occasion, carriers copied letters entrusted to them and sent the copies to friends and relatives.[24] Kentucky settlers' isolation and distance from settled areas meant that news circulated slowly, so people eagerly sought and shared any information. They shared letters en route and upon arrival at destinations and often gave them to printers, who published excerpts in newspapers.

Letter style increased the likelihood that many people would share any letter's contents. Letters were usually written on long sheets (approximately what is now called legal size), although many paper sizes existed.[25] The back of the sheet, when folded, became the address space (see figure). The back lower left corner indicated the carrier, usually written as "Honoured by John Doe," or "Favoured by John Doe." Most letters traveled simply folded and unsealed, and any curious individual into whose hands they fell had only to unfold and read. Writers who could afford sealing wax impressed a thumb-nail-size seal at the flap closing. Wax, however, as well as paper, had to be imported and was sufficiently expensive to cause most people to forego the seal. Although the seal, which appeared on military and government letters, increased chances for privacy, the curious usually broke it. Complaints about the lack of privacy appear frequently in letters. For example, David Campbell wrote to Arthur Campbell in 1787, "[Y]our letter was not only broke open before it came to me; but almost thumbed to pieces."[26] Similar complaints appeared in Breckinridge letters throughout the years under study.

The nature of the letters differs dramatically from that of *friendly* letters of today; some of the differences may be attributable to circumstances surrounding transporting letters, but probably most flow from the value system governing people's behavior in the eighteenth century. A special politeness underlies the letters' messages, particularly in salutations and closings. Messages almost always begin, "Dear Sir," or "Dear Madam," even when addressed to family members. Closings are always deferential, including such phrases as "Your most obedient and humble servant," and "Yours affectionately." Generally, what would today be called *intimate* letters either have not survived or were not written—perhaps the latter because of the public nature of letter delivery. Some letters do make clear the writers' choice not to mention certain matters. For example, Rev. John Brown, in a letter to William Preston, says he could not write why he has not written but would tell Preston when they met.[27]

Letters show the closeness of family members. Even members of an extended family provided support and other forms of nurturing and sustenance through letters. Advice was sought and freely given on education of children and youths, business ventures, political issues—virtually every sphere of life. This was particularly true—and remarkably so, considering the distances and communication facilities—when deaths left spouses with young children. Education was a prevalent topic in the Breckinridge family correspondence, particularly during the 1770s, for lack of schools was a problem. After the death of John Breckinridge's father, William Preston's letters often dealt with John's education.[28]

Letters also give insights into the writers' anxieties at times of tragedies and occasionally when they were far from home and old friends. At such times, letters seemed to serve as psychological releases, especially in the latter instances, when writers, on rare occasions, poured out feelings of loneliness distorted by months of isolation.

Primarily, however, the letters served to convey information. Of

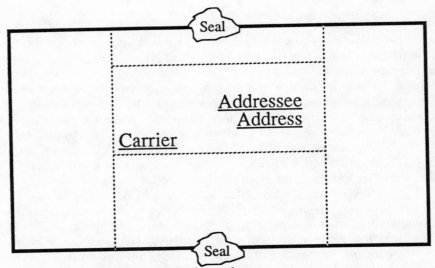

Type A Letter: Legal size sheet

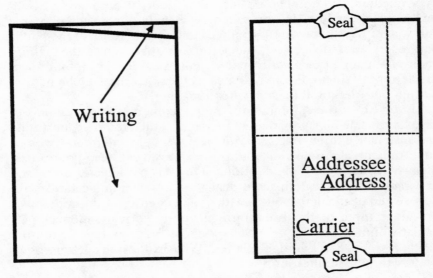

Type B Letter: Legal size sheet folded

Letter Styles in the Late Eighteenth Century.

particular importance in their contents is instruction on migrating—best routes, best times of the year to move, degree of Indian threat, availability of accommodations, sources of food for livestock, costs of various items, and the best lands or areas for settling.

Preparation of letters required careful planning. People often put much effort into finding out who might be traveling in what direction at approximately what date. They prepared as many letters (depending on writing supplies and time available for writing) as they could,[29] and then they often had to draft a carrier to take the letter to the traveler.

No evidence was found that either these short- or long-distance letter carriers were paid. The consistency with which carriers were named on the "envelope" backs of letters suggest purposefulness. Possibly, the name was provided to try to assure privacy, for the recipient always knew at least who started out with the letter. But the name may have been provided because someone, very likely the recipient, paid the carrier—unless the latter was a servant or immediate family member; one paid for service rendered, and if a letter never arrived, one had not paid in advance for unsatisfactory service. Such does not, of course, explain how carriers may have been paid for letters left at public places. (Notes in this book give carriers' names where provided and legible, in part to show the consistency and in part to show who was traveling where in the period under study.)

The first Breckinridge family letter references to the West appeared in 1769. By early 1784, some family members had been in the Kentucky country for some time. The letter excerpts, set in the context of newspaper reports about the West, show the family members tracing out the first migration stages—that is, visiting and assessing the land.

3

Assessing the Kentucky Country

John Breckinridge grew up in a society based primarily on face-to-face communication, where rumor (labeled as such) was as faithfully conveyed as fact because the irregularity of information circulation meant people could not rely on getting later reports. In such a society, Breckinridge grew to maturity during the years the first Kentucky settlements began and struggled amid crises propelled by the American Revolution, Indian hostilities, and harsh winters. Family ties provided him with most of his earliest information about those events.

Family members and relatives, who held important positions (including membership in the Virginia Assembly) and were privy to official information before it circulated widely, drafted messengers to carry letters among relatives. During John's youth, his uncle, William Preston, was central in circulating such information. After John's father died, shortly before John's twelfth birthday, Preston oversaw his education and employed him in the Fincastle surveying office, a position that kept him in contact with reports about western land.

When John went from that office to the College of William and Mary and also gained a seat in the assembly, opportunities for information about the West increased and probably took on greater significance for him. By that time, his older brother had spent time in Kentucky and was seeking a surveying job there. And a short time later, four brothers were writing letters from Kentucky, urging John to join them. This chapter follows John's life as it related to the West from 1769 through the spring of 1784, a period that encompasses the first stage in the migration process, of assessing the land.

John Breckinridge was a few days short of his ninth birthday in 1769 when his uncle William Preston wrote to his father, Major Robert Breckenridge, in Augusta, about a division of the territory from which the state of Kentucky later came. Preston, Virginia Assembly representative from the sprawling frontier county of Augusta, wrote from Williamsburg to Major Breckenridge about the passage of the bill that divided Augusta County:

The county is Divided by the North River and the Bill is to be read a Third Time to Day or To Morrow when it will be proposed. The new County is Honoured with the name of *Botetourt*. I can't stay to have a Commission of the Peace and other officers appointed but will endeavour to get Mr. Wilson to stay a day or Two after the House breaks up for that Purpose.[1]

The tramontane region, however, continued to be known as "the backcountry," "the westward," "over the mountain," "the western waters," or "on the Ohio."

Most of the news from "over the mountain" in 1769 was not good. At age eight or nine, John Breckinridge may not have read newspapers. But he probably heard talk among those who did, or among relatives who sat in the Virginia House of Burgesses. During 1769, John's relatives could have read seventeen items in Virginia newspapers about the western country. Dominant among those were reports of Indian hostilities that gave graphic details of Indians literally chasing settlers from their homes. At the time, Fort Pitt (Pittsburgh), claimed by Virginia, represented the westernmost English settlement, and individuals on duty there served as principal western news sources.[2] In the early summer of 1769, items such as the following extract of a letter from Fort Pitt appeared in Virginia newspapers:

The Indians daily increase in their insolence and threatening to the inhabitants of the country hereabouts, and have already robbed them of every way of subsistence; they steal their horses, plunder their houses, and threaten themselves; so that there is greater probability of an Indian war . . . than there has been . . . since I came to this post.[3]

Another Williamsburg newspaper of the same date contains a letter extract from Fort Bedford, Pennsylvania, dated 2 August, reporting all settlers west of the Allegheny Mountains had fled, and "not a white man to be seen in the woods at Red Stone creek, nor between the Forts Pitt and Legionier, but what are in motion. . . ." A Fort Bedford letter, dated 31 August, reported that "Indians commit great mischief on the Green Briar and Holston rivers, killing and driving away cattle and horses, and even went so far as to tie a woman neck and heels and threw her into the river, by which means she was drowned. . . ."[4]

John Breckinridge's elders probably read with equal interest other news concerning land and surveys over the mountain in late 1769. The Treaty of Fort Stanwix, in November 1769, theoretically ceded some tramontane land to Virginia,[5] and the House of Burgesses asked that Virginia boundaries be extended beyond the mountains. In December 1769, about the time Major Breckenridge received Preston's letter about creation of Botetourt County, the Virginia governor reported that he had asked the king to grant such an extension. The king had agreed to extend the boundaries into the mountains, the governor reported, if Virginians would bear the expense.

The governor's speech to the Virginia Assembly drew a lengthy protest from the Burgesses. They agreed to raise the necessary money if the boundary could be extended *beyond* the mountains, but they argued strongly against a boundary *in* the mountains and expressed fear that the king had not "yet been made properly and fully acquainted with the true Situation of our Frontiers." A line through the mountains would be expensive and difficult to establish and maintain, they argued. It would be dangerous, incense the Indians, expose western settlements to attack, and cut off the Indian trade. Militia could not be kept in the mountains, the burgesses said, and a line there would separate soldiers' land grants (awarded for service in the French and Indian War) from the colonies. They repeatedly stressed that Virginia would lose a valuable area if the boundary was not extended *beyond* the mountains:

> a great Part of that most valuable Country, lying on the *Ohio*, below the Mouth of the great *Kanhaway*, lately ceded to his Majesty by the Northern *Indians*, would be separated and divided from the *British* Territory, on the upper Part of *Holston's* River, the great *Kanhaway*, and the *Ohio*, which your Memorialists humbly conceive must greatly impede, and may totally prevent the Settlement of that fertile and extensive Country, which, from its Situation and many natural Advantages, would open the fairest Prospect of a very Beneficial Commerce to our Mother Country, by securing to his Majesty's Subjects a new and extensive Trade with the several Tribes of Western *Indians*, which has hitherto been almost engrossed by the Subjects of France.[6]

While such news circulated, the next week's newspaper carried an advertisement that soldiers of the French and Indian War had been granted two hundred thousand acres near the Great Kanhawa River. George Washington, who signed the advertisement, asked soldiers to notify him of their claims.[7]

After Preston's 1769 letter to Major Breckenridge about the creation of Botetourt County, Virginia, the next extant Breckinridge family letter about the western country is dated in 1774. In the intervening years, news items reflected Virginians' growing interest in the West. During 1770–71, ten newspaper items about the West appeared, five of which concerned settled Botetourt County areas. Items related to the Kentucky country were about land surveys. Thomas Bullitt, for example, advertised a surveying expedition "on the Ohio" and asked nonattending soldiers to appoint agents to see their claims surveyed.[8] And Washington again advertised, calling on soldiers who had land grants to meet in Winchester, Virginia, on 4 March 1771.[9]

The one newspaper item during the years up to 1774 that described western land, and that might have motivated people to migrate, appeared on 29 July 1773. Washington announced that he was dividing twenty thousand acres "on the Ohio" into "tenements":

> As these Lands are among the first which have been surveyed in that part of the country, . . . it is almost needless to promise that none can exceed them in luxurancy of soil, or convenience of situation, all of it lying on the banks either of the Ohio or Kanhawa, and abounding in fine fish and wild foull of various kinds; also in most excellent meadows, many of which (by the bountiful hand of nature) are, in their present state almost fit for the scythe. From every part of these Lands water carriage is now had to Fort Pitt by an easy communication, and from Fort Pitt up the Monongahela to Redstone, Vessels of convenient burthen may, and do pass continually; from whence, by means of Cheat River, and other Navigable branches of Monongahela, it is thought the portage to Potomack may, and will be reduced within the compass of a few miles, to the great ease and convenience of the settlers, in transporting their produce of the lands to market.[10]

Other newspaper items about the West during 1772 and 1773 told of a proclamation prohibiting settlement beyond the mountains, of people moving to the "western waters,"[11] and of the king's terminating all land grants and surveys and closing all land offices[12] (in 1774 newspapers reported reopening of the land office).[13]

Most newspaper content regarding the West during these years, however, focused on the British plan to establish a colony "on the Ohio." This news first appeared in a late 1771 newspaper, followed by thirty-two items about it over the next two years. The proposal, according to an item on 4 October 1771, was on the verge of being implemented:

> The Plan of a new Town which is to be settled on the junction of the Ohio at present engages the Attention of many persons of Distinction, Lord Eglington is to be the Director, as his Lordship is possessed of vast Tracts of Lands in those Parts. Several Families are ready to embark, and those not of the meaner Kind. It is to be formed into a regular Government. It is expected it will be as flourishing a City as any in the World. Several Persons of Rank are making interest already for Posts in this proposed Establishment for their Dependents.[14]

Other items were reported: the petition for the patent; the grant; government structure, that Benjamin Franklin and other Pennsylvanians owned part of the proposed colony; preparation of people abroad for migrating to the new colony;[15] and proposed boundaries.[16] In another item, George Washington, advertising his own western land holdings, noted that the new colony would enhance their value. "And it may not be amiss further to observe," he asserted, "that if the Scheme for establishing a new Government on the Ohio . . . should ever be effected, these must be among the most valuable Lands in it. . . ."[17] A report of the Indian attack on the first six families to attempt to settle in the Kentucky country in 1773 noted that they had been on their way to "settle in the limits of the expected new government."[18]

The initial item about the proposed colony may have prompted an advertisement calling for a Williamsburg meeting of the Ohio Land Company, which purportedly owned land where the proposed government would be established.[19] Notices of such meetings continued through early 1774, when the plan for the new colony was abandoned. Lord Hillsborough, secretary of American affairs in England, opposed the colony from the start; newspapers reported the running dispute between him and members of the Board of Trade, as well as Hillsborough's subsequent resignation over the issue.[20]

No Breckinridge family letters refer to the colony, but family members involved in government knew about it, no doubt. Virginians might have been incensed that land granted in their original charter had been "sold" to Pennsylvanians, but they more likely welcomed the proposed colony. Only three newspaper items suggest attitudes about it, and these indicate acceptance. One letter to the printer criticized Hillsborough and his followers' opposition and vowed that settlers would not be barred from western land:

> Little do they know, Mr. Rind, that not even a second Chinese wall, unless guarded by a million of soldiers, could prevent the settlers of the lands on Ohio and its dependencies. . . . When the people of North America, finding themselves too much confined to the sea coasts, are for spreading over a fertile, unpossessed country, for the purpose of better pursuing their plan of agriculture, they are then following the peaceful directions of nature.[21]

The writer darkly hints that war might erupt over any attempt to prevent settlement "on the Ohio." Nevertheless, a March 1774 newspaper item announced that the plan for the new colony had been tabled because General Gage, after a trip to America, "assured the ministry that . . . a new colony on the Ohio would inevitably involve America in an Indian war."[22]

While news of the proposed colony held Virginians' interest, news of Indian hostilities in the west continued. Although no such news appeared in 1770 newspapers, early 1771 items reported that one thousand Cherokees had attended a meeting with the superintendent of Indian affairs and agreed to the boundary between Virginia and the Cherokee nation.[23] But late 1772 newspapers reported that Indians killed the officials who went to view the ceded lands.[24] Through 1774, Indians intensified the fight against encroachments on their land by murdering, scalping, and capturing settlers, and by destroying livestock, homes, and crops. The following items are typical of those that thirteen-year-old John Breckinridge might have read in 1774:

> Williamsburg, June 16 [1774]. On Monday evening late an express arrived from Hampshire, with letters from Colonel Abraham Hite . . . who reports . . . that on the 4th instant, some people going to or by the house of one William Speir, they discovered him, his wife, and four children, murdered and scalped, with a broad ax sticking in the man's breast, and his wife lying on her back entirely naked. At another place they found a man's coat, with a number of bullet holes in it, and a child murdered close by the same. The cattle have likewise been killed.[25]

> Philadelphia, June 20 [1774]. We hear from Fort Pitt that the Shawanese have lately murdered 18 white people, within nine miles of that place, and that several parties of Indians have gone . . . to war against the defenceless inhabitants of the frontiers of Virginia and Pennsylvania; that it is supposed all the English traders in the Shawanese towns are killed . . . and about 1500 families, *settled to the westward of the Allegheny* mountains, have deserted . . . and fled for relief to the more interior parts . . . and that the traders at Fort Pitt are about leaving . . . as soon as they can form a party strong enough to venture forth.[26]

During 1773 and 1774, seven such dispatches came from Fincastle County, which then included the Kentucky country. One 1774 newspaper reported Indians had murdered about forty Fincastle County families.[27] And on 8 September 1774, the first Virginia newspaper mention of the word *Kentucky* appeared in news of Indian hostilities against surveyors in the Kentucky country.[28] That item was signed by William Preston, who had become chief surveyor of Fincastle County when it was carved from Botetourt County in 1772.

During John Breckinridge's thirteenth year, an October 1774 letter from Preston to John's mother alluded to the impending war that would open the Kentucky country to settlement. John's father had died in 1772, and his mother, forty-four-year-old Lettice Breckinridge, Preston's sister, was running the farm and caring for four of six children who were still at home. John was the middle child, with three older brothers. Alexander, nineteen, and Robert, eighteen, were half-brothers—sons of Major Breckenridge's first wife—and were carpenters' appentices in Hanover Court House, Virginia. Next came William, who was fourteen. The three younger siblings were ten-year-old James, seven-year-old Betsy, and Preston, only three.[29]

On 9 October, the day before the battle of Point Pleasant in Lord Dunmore's War, Preston wrote his sister that he had hoped to see her and other relatives in Botetourt that week, "but the bad News from Holston and Clinch with the Expresses that come here daily from all Quarters render the agreeable Journey Impossible at this Time." He wrote of a neighbor, Mrs. Ingles, "who with her two Daughters are very bad." They had sent for "Dr. Floyd," who apparently lived near the Breckinridges, for Preston wrote that he wished "Johny could come up with him," adding, "perhaps it might hurry the poor Body along."[30]

The Indian war Preston alluded to ended in a treaty promising tramontane land to Virginia. However, Daniel Boone—with Richard Henderson's help—began a settlement in the Kentucky country the following spring despite English and Virginian proclamations banning such activities.[31] Newspapers, although not reporting the settlement, reported two official condemnations of Henderson and his followers.[32] The Boone settlement caused consternation among Breckinridge relatives who served in government positions. Preston, in whose jurisdiction the settlement lay, wrote letters apprising the Virginia governor and other officials of events leading to, and including, the settlement's establishment.[33]

The colonies' War for Independence from England began almost simultaneously with the first Kentucky settlement, and government affiliations changed as Virginia Governor Dunmore was forced to flee Williamsburg. Breckinridge family views of the "illegal" Kentucky settlement apparently also changed in conjunction with such power shifts. Preston's deputy surveyor, John Floyd, assisted in building a settlement in the Kentucky country while on a surveying trip in the spring of 1775.[34]

Although a few settlers held Kentucky settlements against Indian raids and an Indian-British alliance, the years from 1775 through 1780 yielded few Virginia newspaper accounts of the area. Of nineteen items during those years, twelve concerned Indian hostilities, four advertised land for sale, and three concerned surveying. By June 1781, Fincastle County had been abolished to create Kentucky

County and two others in 1776, and in 1780, Kentucky County also had been abolished and divided into three others—Lincoln, Fayette, and Jefferson.[35]

The years between the first Kentucky settlement and 1781, when the Revolutionary War ended, were very hard for the settlers. In May 1777 the total population in the Kentucky country was 280; only three forts existed before 1778, when settlement began at the site of present Louisville.[36] Still, only eighty persons lived in Louisville in April 1779,[37] when settlement began at present Lexington in Fayette County. Louisville, in Jefferson County, was incorporated in April of 1780.[38]

The winter of 1779–80 was especially severe. William Fleming, who visited the Kentucky settlements from 10 November 1779 through 27 May 1780, wrote of illnesses, starvation, and death in crowded, unsanitary forts. At Louisville he wrote of inhabitants using filthy water and "a great number . . . complaining of the fever and Ague and many Children dying."[39] On 25 December 1779 Fleming wrote of people arriving "hourly" from the wilderness route "with accounts of the distresses of Families on the road," and on 31 December he noted that "people moving out to this Country . . . were in the utmost distress[;] numbers . . . not being able to get in were building huts on the road to winter in." On 9 January he wrote of as "severely cold as ever I felt in America, the People . . . all sickly from colds and hardships they endured in the Journey and the Change of Air[—]the most of the Settlers moving from S. Carolina[.] [T]wo young men died yesterday."[40] On 6 February he wrote:

Kentucky [River] was frozen near two feet thick . . . the snow was two inches thick on the old snow . . . the people in general sickly[,] seized with pains in their head, back and breast attended with a looseness in the beginning which continued with some through the whole course of the disorder[,] voiding a green or black bilious matter[;] the blood taken was black and Vicid or highly inflamed with a tough buff skin[;] having no assistance many died in ten[,] twelve or fourteen days.[41]

And on 20 March, Fleming wrote:

Last night it was cold and froze hard, the effects of the severe winter was now sensibly felt, the earth for so long . . . being covered with snow and water entirely froze, the Cane almost all kiled, the Hogs that were in the Country suffered greatly, being frozen to death, in their beds, the deer likewise not being able to get either water or food, were found dead in great numbers, tirkies drop dead of their roosts and even the Buffalos died starved to death.[42]

Fleming himself became ill several times and suffered frostbite during the winter.[43]

It was a time when Kentucky settlers contemplated death. An unknown author of a poem about death that winter later said, "The hazardous situation in which I passed a considerable part of the winter of 1780 in the wilds of this district produced" such thoughts. The poem, which reflects its author's expectation of death any day and his struggle to rationalize away his fears, reads, in part:

> To the air of Rosalind Castle
> Death's wintry hand has slain the year,
> And laid the vernal nations low,
> Made loftiest Oaks his trophies wear,
> And hangs a shroud on every bough. . . .
>
> . . . .
>
> Vain! vain are thrones, or softest down;
> Death humbles all the high and proud;
> Laughs at the idle pomp of crowns
> And wraps his victim in a shroud.
>
> . . . .
>
> Then why should we the tyrant fear,
> Since death but leads us to repose,
> Wipes from our cheeks the falling tear,
> And makes us conquer'rs o'er all our foes. . . .[44]

Virginia newspapers did not report Kentucky settlers' hardships that year, so the Breckinridges may have known little of them until Fleming returned to Virginia in the spring of 1780. John Floyd, William Preston's former deputy surveyor who had moved his family to the Kentucky country in late 1779 or early 1780, relayed information about the severe winter, indicating that he and his family nearly starved during those months.[45]

But 1780 put a new face on the settlements. George Rogers Clark's defeat of the British in Illinois in 1778 and 1779 had secured a measure of safety, and as the spring of 1780 came, people moved out of the forts and began to incorporate towns and establish churches and schools. The three counties carved from Kentucky County were organized into a district, and a land office was opened. As the country took on the character of permanent settlement, migration mushroomed. In the spring of 1780, Floyd wrote to Preston of three hundred large family boats arriving at the Falls of the Ohio, and of ten to fifteen wagons departing daily for interior parts of the Kentucky country.[46]

But the Revolutionary War had not quite ended, and one of its final events involved a twenty-year-old John Breckinridge in the life of a leading Kentucky settler. Daniel Boone, a Kentucky district representative to the Virginia Assembly, was captured by the British as the members, meeting in Charlottesville in 1781, abruptly adjourned to flee the approaching British and reconvene in Staunton, Virginia. John, attending his first session as an Assembly member, wrote to his mother on 7 June 1781 of these events.[47]

John, no doubt, heard news of the Kentucky country from representatives such as Boone. For, despite the distance and travel difficulties and the inevitable pressing responsibilities at home in the wilderness, the Kentucky district representatives faithfully attended sessions and kept Kentucky country affairs before the legislature. Such firsthand accounts, added to knowledge John had gained in the Fincastle surveyor's office from 1774 to 1779 and accounts brought back by surveyors and soldiers,[48] must have intensified his interest in the western country. Breckinridge family members moved ahead with investments in Kentucky land. John's brother William, who was perhaps a soldier in the Kentucky country during the summer of 1780, had written to his uncle William Preston from "Bear-Grass, Fort William[,] Kentucky County," giving information about land tracts on Elkhorn and near the Falls of the Ohio and mentioning a deputy surveyorship he hoped to get.[49] He returned to the West soon after the Revolutionary War ended, and his two half-brothers soon followed. The three, working as surveyors, began to amass Kentucky land.

During 1781, John had additional opportunities to hear news of the West in Williamsburg, where he was a law student in the College of William and Mary from late 1780 until 1784.[50] His frequent trips between Williamsburg and Richmond (which became the Virginia capital in 1780), surveying excursions, and visits to his Botetourt home presented increasing occasions to encounter people bearing western news. During 1782, while his brother William was in the Kentucky country, he surely followed newspaper accounts about the West, which that year included news of surveying, land sales, and Indian hostilities.

Through the summer and fall of 1782, the Richmond newspapers conveyed fear of an imminent Indian war abetted by the British, although the War for Independence had ended in October 1781. On 11 May, an item reported, "We are sorry to inform the public, that all our accounts from the frontiers . . . afford a gloomy prospect; scarcely one of the Counties along the Alleghany, that has not had some of its inhabitants massacred by the Savages." On 8 June another item said, "Our accounts from the Westward mention the continuance of hostilities by the Indians, who give out, that the British expedition from Detroit against the Kentucky Country, will be executed in August. . . ." A week later the printer announced, "Our last accounts from the westward announce with certainty the designs of the enemy against the Kentucky Country and the Spanish Illinois settlements. . . ."[51]

It would seem that such news might discourage travel to the Kentucky country, and it surely caused concern among Virginians who had relatives there. A letter from John Breckinridge to his mother on 22 and 23 June 1782 reflects concern for his brother William. From Fort Chiswell, John wrote that he would not write "Billy till he condescends" to write, and that lack of paper would be a good excuse. But he must have heard more news of the Kentucky country while seeking a carrier for his letter, for he wrote in a second postscript that he would write William soon and tell him to "come in" from Kentucky. Perhaps trying not to alarm his mother, he added, "I saw a letter from Mr. Floyd to Mr. McGavack a day or two ago, he has no news but what is common here. . . ."[52] (The reference probably was to John Floyd, Preston's former deputy surveyor, who became Jefferson County lieutenant and justice of the peace in 1781.)[53] John's third postscript, dated 23 June, said, "Since I wrote the foregoing . . . a Gentleman that came from Kentucky tells me that Billy intends in in [*sic*] a very Short time, & that he would have come in with them, but had some Business . . . which detained him a Day or two longer."

The same letter said John had written to his mother "Some time ago . . . favor[d] by Captain Quirk," but he suspected she had not received the letter since Quirk "did not go as low down as he expected." John assured his mother he had received the money she sent by "Mr. Preston," and his comments provide insight into means and frequency of circulation of information:

> I entirely forgot when I left home to bring any paper . . . there was not one inch to be had at this place, & if I had not luckily got a few sheets from Uncle I should have been entirely idle. I have now finished that, & am obliged to write upon old Copy Books & News Papers. And[w] Armstrong I suppose has some yet, & if he has, pray send me two or three Quires at least—opportunities daily offer, that it may soon be conveyed to this place. . . .[54]

Western news during the early summer of 1782 may have caused concern in Virginia, but later reports from the Kentucky country were surely alarming. The date of William Breckinridge's return to Virginia in 1782 is not clear, but he apparently was not in the West during one of Kentucky's most tragic summers. Early August reports of the grim fate of Colonel William Crawford were but a prelude to later news. Through the summer months, newspapers reported Crawford's defeat, his agonizing death and the torture of those taken prisoner with him. "Doctor Knight," who escaped, brought the news, which appeared in the Richmond newspaper on 3 August 1782. In part, the report said:

> [Doctor Knight] says that . . . they were carried to an Indian town, stripped and blacked, and forced to march through the Indians, who beat them with clubs, sticks, &c. in the most cruel manner. Col. Crawford and the Doctor were confined together all night, and the next day were taken out, again blacked, and their hands tied, when the unfortunate Colonel was led by a long rope to a stake, to which he was tied, and a quantity of red hot coals laid around, on which he was obliged to walk bare-footed, the Indians at the same time torturing him with squibs of powder and burning sticks for two hours, when he begged of Simon Gurty (a white renegade who was present) to shoot him; his [Gurty's] reply was, "Don't you see I have no gun." He [Crawford] was soon after scalped and struck several times on the bare skull with sticks, till being exhausted, he laid down on the burning embers, when the squaws put shovel-fulls of coals on his body, which made him move and creep till he expired. The Doctor was obliged to stand by and see this cruelty performed; they struck him in the face with the Colonel's scalp, saying "this is your great Captain's scalp, to-morrow we will serve you so."[55]

Reports of this and related events continued for sometime, including a 17 August report of murder of other members of Crawford's group:

> After the barbarous massacre of Col. Crawford . . . the Delawares demanded his son in law, Col. William Harrison and his nephew, ——— Crawford, of the Shawnese, by whom they had been taken. . . . They both experienced the most horrid tortures till they were dead. Col. Harrison was then quartered and stuck on poles. One slave was to have been put to death in the same manner; the fire had once been kindled for him, but a heavy shower of rain falling saved his life then, and before the next day he fortunately escaped.[56]

A few weeks later news came that Indians had defeated Kentuckians at the Battle of Blue Licks. The first report appeared in a 28 September newspaper but gave no details, noting there was "reason to doubt the truth of the report."[57] But a week later, the 5 October 1782 newspaper reported:

The unfavourable reports mentioned in our last *from the Kentucky Country,* we fear, are likely to prove true. It is now said with confidence, that in the beginning of August, a body of Northern Indians, were discovered in Lexington Settlement, upon which Col. Todd, the County Lieutenant, assembled about 100 men and went in pursuit of them, but finding them [, he was] desirous to wait until the arrival of Col. Logan, who was then advancing with 600 men. Some of his inferior officers, however, urging . . . that the attack should be made without delay, he unfortunately consented to it, and the consequence was that the whole party was entirely defeated, & Col. Todd, Col. Trigg, several officers upwards of forty men, were left dead on the field—after scalping and mangling their bodies, the Indians retired.[58]

Deaths of many early Kentucky leaders in this battle devastated the country; had the Indians continued the offensive instead of retreating to revel in victory, the western settlements might have been demolished. Their retreat, however, gave Kentucky settlers time to organize an expedition against Ohio Indian towns, where they destroyed buildings and crops—actions that intimidated the Indians for a time. Then, in November 1782, the peace treaty between England and America meant the English would no longer assist Indians in raids against settlements.[59] Raids continued throughout the frontier years, but no other Kentucky battle matched the disastrous magnitude of that at Blue Licks.

Settlers rebounded from the defeat and resumed the business of building a future state. In July 1782 the Virginia legislature passed acts to establish a district court in Kentucky and a town (Lexington) in Fayette County. November newspapers reported appointments of Harry Innes, a Bedford, Virginia, lawyer, as chief justice and Samuel McDowell, a Rockbridge, Virginia, lawyer, as assistant judge of the Supreme Court of the Kentucky district.[60]

By November, Alexander Breckinridge (and probably Robert and William) seems to have been en route home from the Kentucky country. Alexander wrote to William Preston on 21 October from "4 miles west of Rock Castle Ford" that not much had happened since his party of nineteen men had set out. Sixteen of the men carried arms, he wrote, adding:

we passed many familys on the way that appeared to be very helpless in case of an enemy, but we apprehended no danger until we came to Laurel River, where we found two advertisements informing the Travelors to Kentucky to be very careful as the Indians were on the road and have killed nine men at the big flat rock[?] and one more about six miles on this side of the Lick and four within six miles of Ingles[?] Station, all which happened on the 11th and 15th Inst. on the same evening we overtook Mr. Todd with 20 armed men and 72 women and children and a great number of stock, we joined parties and moved on tho' very slow, not exceeding fifteen miles a day, we are within 20 miles of Ingles's Station which will take us two days more before we get in.[61]

The party had arrived home a month later, when a note signed by William Breckinridge indicates that he sold his mother a "Negro Man and Woman" for 1,000 acres in Jefferson County, Kentucky country.[62]

In early 1783 came news of the treaty of peace.[63] John Breckinridge surely knew of the treaty, and he must have been optimistic—as were many—about the future for the West. Some eight thousand migrated to the Kentucky country in 1783, bringing the total population to an estimated twelve thousand that year.[64] William and Alexander, at home in Botetourt, made plans to survey Kentucky land. And John, then barely twenty-two, hinted in a letter to his mother on 28 January 1783 that he might also be planning a trip to Kentucky. Writing from "Uncle Prestons" of disappointment in a recent Guyandotte survey-ing trip (it seems to have been aborted because the area was unsafe), he said he would survey a month more, then "quit the Business, & make Preparations for the Journey" he had "so long been preparing for."[65]

Meantime, John's younger brother James was also contemplating a trip to the Kentucky country. Then nineteen or twenty, James had planned to survey with a company on Guyandotte, but, unable to go without his compass—which he blamed William for filching—he de-cided to accompany William and Alexander to Kentucky. He would wait at Preston's home (called Smithfield) for the brothers to arrive from his mother's and join them for the remainder of the trip to the Kentucky country. He wrote to his mother from Smithfield:

> I came here and met my Company in order to start the 5th Day of the Month[,] but when I came to hunt for my Compass I found Billey had not left it, but ment to disappoint me in going[;] the men could not detain but went Yesterday Morning. —I have concluded as I was so disappointed, to proceed to Kentucky, with my Brothers, altho I know it will be out of my power to make as much there, as I would have done if I had gone to Guyandotte. —[I]f Eleck [Alexander] should not be started[,] I would be glad you would send all my Cloaths out . . . by him as I am satisfied I have not near enough with me.

He added that he would also be "scarce of money" but was sure his mother could not spare any, and he urged her to hurry his brothers along. James sent the letter by an uncle, "Mr. Howard," who may have been passing Preston's on a return from the Kentucky country, for he would not tarry while James wrote a longer letter. James promised to write "more fully tomorrow by Johnny Smith as uncle [Howard] is in a great hurry to get home."[66]

James did not go to Kentucky that summer, however. He may have been dissuaded by his mother and brothers, particularly John, who assumed a fatherly authority over all his younger siblings. It may have been a summer of missed opportunities for James, for Virginia newspapers carried a relative abundance of news about Kentucky surveying and land.

The year 1783, in fact, represents a peak for such news. James' three brothers Alexander, Robert, and William went to the Kentucky country in the early spring, probably arriving about the time newspapers published a surveying advertisement by Kentuckians Daniel Boone and William Hays. In the notice, published on 3 May 1783, Hays and Boone announced they had "undertaken the location of lands in the Kentucky district for a number of Gentlemen," but the paper money paid them had "died in our hands before their business could be done." They requested "all those who have heretofore furnished us with paper money" and others who had hired them "to send us a sufficiency of money, without loss of time to defray the expenses of their land, as we shall think ourselves no longer bound than we are supplied with money to enable us to comply with our contracts." A week later, on 10 May, another surveying notice, signed by Thomas Marshall, "S.F.C.," directed those wishing surveys done in Fayette County to pay his sons, John in Richmond or Thomas in Shenandoah. Thomas Marshall would conduct the surveys after receiving receipts in Kentucky for such payment.[67]

By May 1783 John Breckinridge was back at law studies at the College of William and Mary in Williamsburg and attending Virginia Assembly sessions in Richmond. His servant, George, accompanied him to Williamsburg and carried letters from John home to Botetourt. Some time later, John wrote his mother, "When I wrote you by George I had not procured Lodgings nor was certain where I could." His previous letters had described inflated costs and financial hardships, but this letter, written at Richmond and delivered by "Mrs. Howard," an aunt, told of particularly trying financial stress. He said he would sell his "backcountry" lands for half their value, if they were worth anything, and advised his mother to sell hers if she could (he added that he had been unable to buy the cotton she requested but would "& send it up by some Waggon").[68] Expenses for John's studies, in addition to inflated wartime costs, drained him. A 1780 newspaper item noted that "attending two professors" at the College of William and Mary cost one thousand pounds of tobacco.[69]Lowell Harrison notes expenses for room, board and two lectures were estimated at 4,000 pounds of tobacco.[70] In November 1781 John wrote to William Preston, explaining that "a Person cannot live in Town [Williamsburg] one day, for less than two thousand dollars," and he had rented a room "in the Country . . . about five miles out of Town," where costs were less.[71]

While John contemplated selling some land to alleviate financial stress, others were successfully speculating in Kentucky land. On 24 May Samuel Meredith—a future Breckinridge in-law—advertised two thousand acres in Fayette County, "on the North Fork of Elk Horn creek, a branch of Kentucky river, adjoining the lands of Col. William Christian, and the Rev. John Todd." The advertisement said, in part:

> This tract . . . was surveyed the 11th of July, 1774, and is equal in quality to any . . . in that Country[;] it is also free from the disadvantages that attend many rich tracts . . . in that quarter, having . . . several never failing springs and streams. . . . It lies in an oblong square, and should two or more persons incline to join in the purchase, it might be laid off in such manner as would, in every respect, render it agreeable to each party. Cash, tobacco, hemp, or negroes, will be received in payment.[72]

John's brother Alexander was busily amassing Kentucky land. On 1 June 1783 James Warren assigned to him "half the land that he has located for me in the Kentucky Country, for his trouble of locating 4,000 acres." In addition, Warren paid Alexander six pounds and thirteen shillings "for Surveying fees and other expences attending a Survey of 2,000 acres to be made for said Warren . . . on the Waters of Floyds fork."[73]

On 28 June John May, whom the older Breckinridge brothers intended to work for in Kentucky, advertised that he "would sell or exchange for other property, near Richmond or Petersburg, a quantity of very valuable Kentucky Lands, conveniently situated, officers and other specie warrants and certificates will be received in payment." He recommended that those interested in more information apply to him in Petersburg.[74] From 26 July through mid-October 1783, John Mayo advertised 14,000 acres "of the first quality" in Kentucky and 3,800 acres in Virginia.[75]

Surveyors James Knox and Hancock Taylor gave notice in a 16 August newspaper that all who had hired them to survey Kentucky land should pay immediately because they would go to Kentucky in mid-September. A week later, surveyor George May announced to those holding Kentucky warrants that most of the surveys could be done during the coming winter. He warned that those "who fail to attend with money to defray the expences, will lose their lands" and gave surveying fees as five pounds per 1,000 acres—"except the locations are large, and in that case, they will be less." In the same newspaper, Cuthbert Bullett advertised "about" 24,000 acres "in several tracts, situate on the Ohio, Green River, and the waters of Kentucky." He added that the lands were located under military warrants, "under the King's proclamation of 1763," issued 15 October 1779. Purchasers, who must give "approved security for the money," could pay in three annual installments—"the first to be made at the end of 12 months from the contract." The same notice advertised 2,278 acres on the Great Kenhaway "at the mouth of Elk . . . at which place most of those, who remove by water from this State to the Ohio, must build vessels, and set out with their families."[76]

In October surveyor Thomas Marshall again advertised, directing that surveying fees be paid to his sons. The "business will not be compleated," he warned, unless he received receipts showing payment. He requested power of attorney from those who had asked him to survey so he could "comply with the contracts" he had "entered into on their accounts, and with money to make their surveys."[77]

Beginning on 1 November, another advertisement, signed by Isaac Hite in Kentucky on 5 August 1783, announced that "The obstructions which have hitherto impeded the surveying business in this Country, being now removed by a general peace," he would "proceed immediately to survey the lands of those gentlemen" who had hired him. Hite asked payment in advance, saying that many completed surveys could not be registered until he was paid. He called attention to the law governing land registration, warning that people could lose land not registered before the law lapsed. Further, he warned, "In many instances claims of those whose business is in my hands have been injured by persons whose entries were made long since theirs; caveats cannot be entered, nor suits commenced, until money comes to hand to pay fees." John May, in a 15 November advertisement, offered "20 or 30,000 acres of KENTUCKY LAND on short credit, very cheap," and said he "would receive in payment, tobacco, negroes, or Officers certificates."[78]

Such land and surveying notices probably kept the Kentucky country in the minds of Virginia newspaper readers, and John Breckinridge probably read them with special interest. The John May advertisement appeared the day before William Breckinridge, who planned to work for him in Kentucky, wrote to his mother about his own successful land deals. In a letter tinged with homesickness, he wrote from the "Wilderness, November 16, 1783":

Dear Mother

[I promised when I] left that I would write to you by every oppetunity [*sic*] that I should have during my stay in this Country, which I am still determined to do be my circumstances or Situation what it may, and the distances which Time may put between us. I must [be a] person void of all human feelings to forgit [*sic*] one of the dearest and most loving of Mothers that ever this world afforded; I shall rush out tomorrow in order to get out lands Survey [*sic*] on Besheers [*sic*] Creek after which I will proceed on to Fayette County to get our Lands Surveyed on Licking. Since I have been at this place[,] I have had an opportunity of getting locations for twenty thousand acres of my Warrants on good land and in a torable [*sic*] good part of the Country. The Remainder of my Warrants I shall keep and enter myself, while I am surveying. I was the other day offered a location of fifteen hundred acres ground[?] for my little Sorrell Mare which [is] about twenty miles from this place but in doubts whether I will take it or not, however I shall have a better oppertunity [*sic*] in [a] few day's [*sic*] of see^g. the land and then I shall have a better oppertunity [*sic*] judging what to do, I am determined to put her off to the best advantage I possibly can. . . . [I]f my Bay Horse is sent Home I would be exceedingly glad if it was possible to have him sent out to me this winter; horses sell[?] so well in this Country that I am well convinced I could get four hundred acres of first rate land, and in almost any part of the Country.[79]

It is unclear whether the twenty thousand acres William had gotten "locations for" were his acquisitions or merely surveys for others, but the latter seems more likely.

Advertisements through the end of the year show people continually amassing Kentucky land, and one may read in the surveying and other notices optimism about peace and better times ahead. In a 6 December advertisement, William Christian offered "for sale some of the prime Elkhorn lands in the Kentucky country." He described "a valuable tract near the Falls of Ohio, and Saltsburg, the lick upon Salt river, which now and for several years past, has supplied that country with salt," adding that the land, surveyed in 1774 under "old" military warrants, was "patented by the present Government." In the same newspaper, Neil M'Coull offered twelve hundred acres in lower Virginia and two thousand acres on the Ohio River, which, he said, was "located" in 1774 and adjoined Colonel William Henry's land. Another December advertisement may suggest optimism about Kentucky or simple interest in, and curiosity about, an area that had created a market for publications. The 13 and 20 December newspapers advertised "HUTCHIN'S MAP of the Kentucky Country" and "a pamphlet describing the quality of the soil, &c.," on sale in Richmond at William Peacock's or Henry Banks's stores.[80]

Optimism clearly permeated surveyor Richard Terrell's late December and early January advertisements. Dated in Kentucky, 24 November 1783, the advertisement said that since "the obstructions which have . . . impeded the surveying business" had been removed by a general peace, he would "proceed immediately to survey the pre-emptions given Messrs. Hawkins and Terrell." He asked claimants to accompany him to point out their lands. The 27 December newspaper carried two other official surveying notices. In one, George Rogers Clark informed that, pursuant to the law governing officers' and soldiers' warrants, authorized persons would "receive warrants . . . at Mrs. Younghusband's in Richmond" on 1 February and at Louisville from 10 to 15 March, and that "the drawing of the lots for priority locations" would be "at said town as soon as may be after the fifteenth." Everyone holding a warrant would be expected to, "upon delivering it, pay half a dollar per thousand acres, and so in proportion for a greater or less quantity . . . exclusive of one dollar per hundred acres, as prescribed by law." The other advertisement indicated that Richard C. Anderson was authorized to receive warrants "for military bounties . . . at Richmond, until February 1, and at Louisville" on 15 March. "G. Morgan," he said, would "receive such warrants in my stead at Winchester" until 15 February. The advertisement repeated fees given in Clark's notice.[81]

While Kentucky lands were being surveyed, divided, and sold, John Breckinridge continued to suffer hardships. On 26 December 1783 he wrote his mother from Richmond recounting financial difficulties and added, "Tell Jimmy the land office is shut, as to the issuing of Warrants, & he need not trouble himself to get any Money or certificates to procure Warrants, as they can't be had."[82]

Although no evidence suggests that John considered an immediate move west, surely his financial difficulties made Kentucky increasingly appealing while the general peace added to the area's attractiveness. During 1783 Indians seem to have left Kentucky settlers pretty much alone. The worst Indian news was three years old, appearing in a deposition by Isaac Ruddell, who was tried for treason after his post-Revolution release from two years' imprisonment by Indians and the British. Ruddell's account of a 1780 attack on Ruddell's Station in Kentucky and subsequent events appeared in newspapers in late 1783. The account explained how the fort was attacked on 24 June 1780 by "Captain Bird with 300 Indians, 150 Canadians, and 50 British, with two pieces of cannon and two howitz." Forced to capitulate that afternoon, Ruddell's people agreed to terms that permitted them to stay in the fort overnight before marching out in their "best cloathes" next morning to "be safely conducted to Detroit" while Indians would take possession of the fort and "plunder." However, Ruddell explained, as soon as his people laid down their arms, "the Indians rushed in, stripped and tied us, and murdered a man and a woman on the spot, besides several others whom they murdered on their way to the towns." The Indians divided the families, carrying off Ruddell's wife and children and burning one child.

The account continued that on 3 August Ruddell was taken to Detroit, where the commandant, displeased that the surrender terms had been violated, assisted in recovering his wife, four of his children, and some other prisoners from the Indians. The commandant then allowed Ruddell and his family to live on an island, where they raised corn and helped supply food for fellow prisoners, some of whom Ruddell said he helped to escape. In 1782 Ruddell and other prisoners were permitted to return to Virginia, where, Ruddell reported, he "was accused by some of my fellow prisoners as being inimical to the cause in which I had suffered so much; charged with treason, taken into custody and tried by the Court of Frederick County, by whom I was acquited."[83] Copies of the accusations against Ruddell and the court's statement of acquittal also were published in the newspapers.

News of more current Indian events in 1783 included a 14 June newspaper announcement that General Anthony Wayne had gone to settle a peace treaty with Georgia frontier Indians. The 12 July newspaper contained the Virginia governor's statement that he had abandoned plans for a war against Indians because the effort would be too costly at a time of need to "adopt the most prudent economy." A 23 August newspaper reported the arrival of the superintendent of Indian affairs for the northern district, Captain Dalton, from Canada with two hundred former prisoners of Indians. Dalton, who, with his wife, had "been many years prisoners," reported that Indians still held many prisoners, and he gave estimates of the "different savage nations they had to encounter with, the number of warriors annexed to each nation that were employed by the British, and have stained their tomahawks with the blood of Americans." Among the twenty-eight nations he enumerated, the "Uchipweys" had the largest population (3,000), and the "Suez and Sothase" had the second largest (1,300). His estimate gave 12,690 warriors among the twenty-eight nations.[84]

On 1 November 1783, newspapers published a proclamation designed to reduce Indian hostilities. All persons were prohibited "from making settlements on lands inhabited or claimed by Indians without the limits or jurisdiction of any particular State, and from purchasing or receiving any gift or cession for such lands or claims," without authority from the Congress.[85]

As 1784 began, John Breckinridge could continue to read newspaper accounts about Kentucky land and surveying, but he apparently heard little from his brothers there. On 10 January George Rogers Clark again notified claimants under military warrants to meet at Louisville by 1 April. And on 7 February he and Richard C. Anderson advertised that they had to be at Louisville by March, and, since bad weather might have delayed claimants, Samuel Jones would receive warrants in Richmond until 20 March. The next week's newspaper announced that Anderson and "Major William Croghan" had left for "the backcountry, being appointed by the General Assembly . . . to survey and lay off the Officers and Soldiers lands. . . ."[86]

The race to acquire Kentucky land led to corruption. On 28 February the auditors of public accounts announced that no more soldiers' claims would be settled until after the Virginia Assembly could meet. They said that "great impositions are practiced . . . in obtaining settlements upon forged certificates for military service," and, since they had no way to check "this growing evil," they would handle no claims until the legislature could authorize an effective procedure. They regretted "that many worthy soldiers may be subjected to inconvenience," but they hoped that "every honest citizen" would approve their decision.[87]

By this time, John's brother Alexander had spent nearly a year in Kentucky, and, on 4 March 1784, he wrote of land secured for John and of his own intentions to settle permanently in Kentucky:

Dr. Johnny,
   This is the only opportunity that has transpired since I came to this Country of writing you, this opportunity I am determined not to let slip, tho I have nothing to write about, more than to tell you all your acquaintances here are well.
   News there is none, Deaths, Births, and Marriages there are none, there is nothing a stir, only a most intolerable hard winter has just blown over, so hard that it has not been in my power to do but very little at surveying. . . .
   I have made a location of 4,000 acres for you . . . on Floyds fork and about ten Miles from this, a prety [sic] good piece of land about a second quality. . . . I have made an entry for myself of upwards of 2,000 acres, tho' I am not certain whether I shall get it all or not[;] it is land of the first Quality, and near the Ohio about twelve miles above the Falls, at which place if I shall be fortunate enough to get, there I shall lay my bones.

Alexander promised to write "every opportunity" and hoped John would, too. He said he would send his letter "by our friend B. Smith who left this a few days ago, but have an opportunity of sending it after him." He ended the letter, "Good night," at "about 10 o'clock," and went to the fort (on Beargrass Creek, near Louisville) to find someone to take the letter to Smith. But, at the fort, he met a man who, having recently arrived from Virginia, gave him a letter from John dated 11 December 1783 "at home." The letter, written three months earlier, detailed John's financial hardships. Overcome with homesickness, Alexander quickly added a note to his own letter that he "eagerly opened [your letter] and paused when I found your melancholy Situation." He wrote that he thought of John "Alone with only a Tender Mother and an Effectionate Sister" and added, "I believe I felt when reading your letter, as you did when a writing it[;] were it in my power to Erect a Hut that would contain us all, let it be in what part of the Globe was most agreeable, I care not where it is, so we could all be together." His postscript was cut short; he wrote, "I have not time my Dear Brother to say anything more to you as the bearer is waiting," and hastily promised, "I shall have an opportunity of writing you by the latter end of the Month."[88]

John's younger brother James in Virginia was perhaps stirred by news from Kentucky and the numbers of people moving there. Historians W. H. Perrin and others note that Kentucky's population by the spring of 1784 had reached an estimated twenty thousand and that ten thousand more moved there via the Ohio River during the year.[89] In any event, James again decided to go to Kentucky, and by March, John—then back at the College of William and Mary—had heard about it. He wrote to his mother on 17 March, "Brother Ja[s.] writes me he is going immediately to Kentucky. This I hope he has taken your advice in." Sounding more like James' father than his slightly older brother, twenty-three-year-old John approved since James was not "fond of confining himself" and had little to do. John added that the "Surveying business in Montgomery is now done, & I don't know what else he could employ himself about. His Brothers are all there to whom he is much attached, & I trust his own good Sense & their prudent Advice will enable him to conduct himself with Propriety."[90]

James, however, did not go to Kentucky that spring. Letters indicate a romance that perhaps kept him in Virginia.[91] But continued land news from Kentucky may have made him restive, for he continued talk of going. A 20 March newspaper announced cession to Congress of the "Western territory"; and an advertisement by Samuel Beall offered six thousand acres for sale at Louisville. A month later, in a 17 April newspaper, John Mayo offered fourteen hundred acres "of the first quality in the Kentucky Country" to be sold "on very reasonable terms."[92] A 3 May 1784 letter from "J. Preston" to John

Breckinridge at the College of William and Mary indicated James's continued talk of going west. The letter informed John that James had not yet gone to Kentucky, "but he will in a few—I don't know how long" (the same letter told of John's election as representative to the Virginia Assembly from Montgomery County).[93]

Still, James did not go to Kentucky that summer, and he seemed to make excuses in a 23 May letter from Botetourt to John in Richmond. James wrote that he had been "so often disappointed in getting a company and indeed my horses were rather too poor to undertake such a journey." He had decided to "stay at home this Summer" because, he reasoned, he could "not Survey any by the time I would get out, the season would be so far advanced, the Indians very Mischievous." Since there would be no other kind of work for him there, he said, he would wait until fall. He had promised to survey for James Madison on Guyandotte, "not far from Kentucky," he wrote, and he believed he could "get a small company to go to Kentucky" with him after completing that job. Anyway, he wrote, he expected he would not get enough business to do in Kentucky, "as the Surveying is nearly over." He commented also on some of John's land holdings in Kentucky, opining that two or three of his entries "near the Ohio" would be valuable "in time." He had not withdrawn those entries, nor did he intend to; one consisted of five thousand acres, the other of twelve hundred, and both consisted of very good land "within half a mile of the Ohio."[94]

While James tarried in Virginia, newspapers continued to reflect Kentucky land business. On 26 June J. Garland advertised thirty thousand acres on Green River, sixty miles from "the Falls of the Ohio"; another 26 June item announced that lots had been drawn for priority locations among officers' and soldiers' claims on 22 and 23 April, and that surveyors—who asked to be paid—were marking the tracts. In other news, a 3 July item announced a law for "the better support of the Supreme Court" in Kentucky; a 10 July article detailed a law governing surveying fees; and on 17 July, an unnamed advertiser offered five thousand acres on Green River—described as "near Pittman's Station, level and exceeding well watered"—plus one thousand acres "of the first quality on Elk Horn, near Bryant's and Lexington."[95]

A different entrepreneurial interest appeared in a 26 June advertisement. Clearly intended to capitalize on the market produced by westward migration, a business on the Monongahela River would serve virtually every need of those traveling westward via the Ohio River:

The subscriber begs leave to inform all persons who may hereafter move down the River Ohio, that he has erected a complete merchant and saw mill, with a good storehouse for the reception of merchandize, on the Monongalia River ten miles below the mouth of Redstone, and the same distance from Budd's ferry, on the Yohogania, where plank boats of all kinds, and provisions may be provided on the shortest notice, and most reasonable terms. Travelers who consult convenience and dispatch, must prefer this place of embarkation to any on the waters on the River, lying in the neighborhood of a large settlement, where every sort of accommodations may be readily provided. This landing is twenty miles from Mr. Thomas Gist's, and twenty five miles nearer Philadelphia than Fort Pitt, and is approached by as good roads as any in that country.[96]

In addition to such businesses that sprang up along routes carrying the westward migration, others had emerged in Kentucky by this time;[97] and eastern entrepreneurs transported goods to the western settlements for sale at auctions.[98] But by 1784 more permanent institutions (schools, churches, stores, and other towns), operated by residents to serve communities, had been established in the Kentucky country.[99]

With the Indian threat diminished, the development of such institutions and rapid land sales (which provided various jobs), the growing accessibility of commercial goods, and the attachment exhibited by settlers claiming a new permanent home, Kentucky must have appealed more and more to such families as the Breckinridges. Alexander, who had shown no inclination to return home from his year-plus sojourn, had vowed to settle permanently in the Kentucky country. And, indeed, the time had come when the whole family began discussing a move to Kentucky.

4
Discussing the Move over the Mountains

By the summer of 1784, the communication system affecting John's life included an information network of his legislative and college contacts, encounters during travels through Virginia, and his brothers in Kentucky, who kept him aprised of events there. After his uncle William Preston died in 1783, John had become a primary source of information for family and relatives. His responsibilities extended much further, however, as his mother, who had depended on him as he grew up, relied ever more heavily on him for advice, assistance, and emotional support.

On another level of the communication infrastructure, a passable road led to Kentucky, and many more people traveled there and back, affording more opportunities for information about the West. Newspapers reported more regularly about Kentucky and the increasing diversity of events there. In 1784 John Filson's history of the Kentucky country was published and advertised. That same year, John's brother James went to Kentucky shortly before the first statehood convention met in Danville. In 1785 two more statehood conventions met amid growing concern about absentee land ownership, developing legal problems regarding Kentucky land, and threats of an Indian war. In the same year, John left the Virginia Assembly, began his law practice, married, and moved into his own home in Albemarle. As his responsibilities grew, his interest in Kentucky seemed dormant for a time. In 1786 William and James returned home, and his sister, Betsy, married and settled in Virginia. By early 1787, John, enchanted with his first child, also seemed settled. This chapter follows events from the summer of 1784 through early spring of 1787, years marking the second stage of migration when family members discussed moving to Kentucky.

In the late summer of 1784, the Breckinridge brothers in Kentucky began a concerted effort to persuade John and his mother to move to Kentucky. On 8 August 1784 Alexander, then thirty-one, wrote from Beargrass to twenty-three-year-old John:

Dr. Brother,

I have set myself down with an intention to write you something, but I dont [sic] know what it will be about as Yet, I have begun with a preface, and believe it will end in one. As to your landed matters I dont know how they all stand . . . as they are not all Surveyed, I believe all except the late entry I made for you last Spring, if that Should all be got it will be valuable, or any part of it. . . .

Lately in an evenings conversation with Mr. Daniel[,] our attorney Genl. He mentioned your name in the warmest terms and seems desirous of your coming to this Country if you have any intention of practicing the law and seems desirous of an acquaintance with you; I do not undertake to give my advice but am this far satisfied that there is more money in circulation in this Country then [sic] in that, at least the part where you would practice; and a great deal of business in Court, and much more will be.

I have nothing to write to Jemmy as I have for some time past expected him out. . . .[1]

On the same occasion, William, then twenty-six, also wrote from Beargrass, adding his own plea for John to move:

Dear Brother:

I have long waited for a line from you but to no purpose. the reasons of your silence I can not account[,] unless it is for want of Oppertunity which cannot be altogether the case, as I am certain that in the course of twelve or fifteen Months you certainly might have had an oppertunity of writing me a line[;] nevertheless I shall not omitt every favourable Oppertunity of writing to you though at Present I am not certain wither [sic] you are in Botetourt or at Richmond or in Williamsburg. this letter however I shall direct to Botetourt[;] perhaps it may find you there in case it should I would be glad to hear from you by the first chance you have and let me know your Intentions wither you Intend Staying another Year at Williamsburg or whither you intend turning to practice immediately. if you Intend [illegible] would be happy to see you in this Country as this will be a most excellent Place for your business, as the Attorneys are but few, and the business very extensive, and Money fully as plenty if not more so than it is in the Interior parts of the Country; the business is daily a growing, and the land disputes, in, are almost Innumberable. These advantages . . . with having a satisfaction of living on some of your fine rich soil in this Rich and extensive Country will add greatly to the happiness of this life.

William asked John which year the act passed for reserving officers' land on the northwest of the Ohio River. He added that "Mr. Bullitt" had made a good offer for John's Brashear Creek land, but he assured John of his best bargaining in any such sale. He concluded by asking for news and indicating plans to survey on Green River, a dangerous area, he said, because of Indians.[2]

Also writing to James in Botetourt, William said he would have written earlier but had expected James daily in Kentucky. He hoped James would not stay longer in Botetourt "unless you are determined to make true the Report which prevails against you in this Country; and that is your getting married. . . ." William surmised that event would keep James in Botetourt "for sometime on account of your lady." He assured James, "We all wish much for your Company. . . . We have fine Corn field & Plenty of Meat & Milk." He urged James, if he did plan to come to Kentucky, to arrive early in September before William went on a three-month surveying trip to Green River.[3]

Only a week later, the murder by Indians of Walker Daniel, the attorney general for the Kentucky District, led Alexander to again raise the issue of John's moving. On 14 August 1784, he wrote to John about Daniel's death and added:

> probably it may suit You to avail Yourself of this opportunity, and with the Interest you have in the House may get the appointment Mr. Daniel held. . . . Mr. Bullett [*sic*] is here and lives with me, I have mentioned the matter to him, He would be glad you would make a tryal for the appointment and is satisfied you may succeed, indeed he rather mentioned the matter first and seems very desirous you may succeed; he intends in to the fall session [of the Assembly] and will give you what Interest he can have. . . .

In a final note, Alexander added that Robert, then thirty and also in Kentucky, would start to the Mississippi River with officers to survey in early September, and that he (Alexander) would leave on May's Green River surveying business at the same time.[4]

August newspapers reported a bill in the Pennsylvania legislature for raising 250 men from the state militia to help protect the "Northwestern frontiers," in compliance with a federal law to place 700 "non commissioned officers and privates" on such duty.[5] And on 18 September the Virginia newspapers reported Walker Daniel's death:

> By a Gentleman immediately from the Kentucky country, we are informed, that the depredations of the Indians is not yet at an end in that country; that on the 12th ult. As Walker Daniel, Esquire, the State Attorney in that District, Mr. Keightly of Philadelphia, and a Mr. Johnston, were going from the Falls of Ohio to the Salt Works, about six miles from the works they were attacked by a party of about seven Indians, when Daniel and Keightly were shot dead on the spot; and Johnston wounded across his breast with a ball, though fortunately

effected his escape. The dead bodies were scalped, and stabbed in a very barbarous manner, but the Indians did not plunder them of their money and cloathes [*sic*].[6]

A few days later, John Breckinridge learned that brother James was on his way to Kentucky. On 20 September 1784 John Brown wrote from "Mr. Craigheads" to John in Botetourt, "Cousin James in his way to Kentucky call'd upon us yesterday, his Company had gone before which put it out of his power to delay more than two or three Hours, he was in great Spirits & his Journey thus far had been prosperous."[7] On 5 October William wrote to John from Kentucky that James had arrived safely and brought family news, "the first Satisfactory Account that I have had since I left Home." He said James had come at "an exceeding lucky time" because he and Alexander had "undertaken John Mays [*sic*] business." There will be the greatest Plenty of work for us all this Winter," he wrote, "and perhaps if we keep our Health and Scalps, something may turn up . . . . Against Spring." News, he said, was so "triffling that is hardly worthy writing," but the chance to send a letter to John was "so favourable that I can not help writing something. . . ." William detailed planned work, surveying progress, general land business, and then launched into another appeal for John to move to Kentucky:

> I am in great hopes from what Jemmy tells us that we shall have the Pleasure of your Company in this Country this Winter which I much rejoice. I am in hopes that in case you should come you will have no reason to repent. But it is more than Probable that as you have diped so Deep in State affairs it will be hard to get & you at the same time think you can be of more Service to yourself and Country than by coming. . . .
>
> There is one matter for which I am over-antious [*sic*] for which I would wish you to come so soon as I do and that I want my Mother very much to come next Spring; and I [illegible] that your either Staying or coming will very much sway as her Affections are very much sett upon [you], if I thought she would come[,] I would rent her a piece of clear land for two or three Years and would come in for next spring and bring her out then or next fall which she Might think proper.[8]

James had, no doubt, carried letters from Lettice Breckinridge, for the day after writing to John, William wrote an equally long and impassioned plea to his mother and referred to a letter from her. He mentioned her regrets that she had no clothes to send him and reassured her that "I have the greatest Plenty of Cloths and can at any time get what I have not Money for . . . at Present. . . ." After assuring her that James was safe and in good time for work, he wrote:

Jemmy tells me that you appear to be very anxious about coming to this Country next year perticularly . . . if Jonny [sic] should come . . . you mention in your oun letter that Jonney intended coming out this Winter[.] [I]f you are fully determined to come out next year—and will write me fully on the Subject[,] I can get you a place with sixty acres of clear land, for [sic] Mrs. Floyd and will raise you a good Cabbin . . . this Winter and go in myself for you next Spring.

This place . . . I can get for two or three years until you can have an Oppertunity of making a settlement of your own lands . . . if you fully determine to come the sooner you come the better. And as to the Clear lands . . . I could this day get from Mrs. Floyd in case you were certain that you could come out. Mrs. Floyd appears . . . very antious [sic] for you to come and says if you will only write that you will come she will keep the place for you in preference to any person living. I have also engaged a good Carpenter for seven Years to live in my lands on Harrods Creek and to do whatever building we shall stand in need of.[9]

Approximately two weeks later, William again wrote to his mother urging her to move. He began by writing that he had expected to be at "Green River at this time but it has so happen'd that we are not as yet sett out on account Mr. William May's having lately received a new Commission." This, he explained, had ended surveying "until next Court in order that we may be again sworn in." This would occur in a few days and then they would "go immediately to the Woods," and he would not have another chance to write to her until his return. The business would take two or three months and pay them five hundred pounds each, besides providing a chance to get warrants on vacant land. He added:

I do [not think] it my duty [to urge] you to come to this Country as you are tolerably agreeably fixed in that Quarter . . . and in some Measure all your Friends[?] around which perhaps you might have [illegible] in this Country. At any rate for some time to come—together with inconveniences which are to [be] encountered in removing to a new Country, as also the disagreeable Neighbours which you might have . . . with the inconveniences of living in a bad house. . . . However, my dear Mother, if you are desirous of coming . . . I will endeavour to make the Country as agreeable to you as I can by having you a good piece of land and as good a House as the Country affords at this time, besides I will go in and help you out at any time you will write after I come back from Green River . . . you may rely on my doing everything to have you agreeably fixed in this Country. . . .

Asking his mother to write and let him know if he should keep the Floyd lands, William concluded, "There is no news worth relating but what Mr. buchanan [*sic*] can inform you . . . who will hand you this."[10]

James also took advantage of Buchanan's trip to Virginia to send a letter to John. He opposed his mother coming to Kentucky, but he said he would return to assist her if she insisted on moving:

> Dear Sir
>
> It is not long since I last wrote you but having so favourable an opportunity by Mr. Buchanan that I can not help writing something . . . as it is more than probable that it will be the last Chance . . . until I shall have the pleasure of seeing you in this Country which I hope will be against we return from Green River; if we have the good fortune to get safe back with whole bones . . . after which time if it should so happen that you should not come out I propose returning Home as I shall not have any thing particular to detain me . . . and the more particularly if my Mother should let me know . . . that she is desirous to come . . . next Spring or fall—but as I before mentioned that her coming . . . greatly depends on you as her expectations are altogether from you that of course the place which you chuse she will endeavour to be as near you as possible. [F]or my own part I will not undertake to advise my Mother ever to move from where she is tolerably well fixed and is now growing old and feeble and perhaps is not able to withstand the difficulties which attend people removing to a New Country. However, if she will come . . . I will doe everything that lies in my Power to make the Country agreeable to her by fixing her on a good piece of land and getting a good House built [mss. torn] and go in order to remove her.

James then turned to John's own possibilities in the Kentucky country, writing, "I am well convinced there is no Part of this State that you can so soon make a fortune." He asked John, if still in Richmond, to send warrants for "one or two hundred thousand acres to be laid on the half," and promised his own reliability in handling any of John's Kentucky business. He concluded, "There is no news in this Part of the Country worth relating."[11]

The coaxing of John and his mother to move continued unabated for sometime, and a 6 November 1784 letter from Alexander indicates John considered a move. Apparently, he had written to ask Alexander's own opinions of the Kentucky country and his future plans. Alexander, who earlier had vowed to settle permanently there, now seemed less decisive:

> You requested in your last to know whether I intended to Settle in this Country or no; that matter is still undetermined with me as Yet, tho' extreamly fond of the Country and have some fine land, yet there are other Materials wanting, such as a Wife, Negroes, etc. etc. These articles

are very necessary towards house-keeping & I have none of them[;] must consequently get someone who has them, or wait and Struggle on till I can make them myself; and as for my lighting the Hymenical torch[,] at present I have not yet obtained my own consent[;] neither do I know when it may be the case. But I shall be able to tell you more about the matter when I see you[,] which I hope will be in a short time. Attorneys here are much wanting & a great deal of business to be done, more probably then [sic] you have any idea of.

Alexander complained of the work facing him. "After one twelve months confinement in this Country," he wrote, "with a determination to get my business done before I left, . . . I find there is a probability of near twelve months more. . . ." He had brought warrants "to the amount of 200,000 Acres," had entered 100,000 of those and surveyed only a small part of the total. He said he had to enter the remainder and survey all of it before he could think of leaving Kentucky.[12]

Alexander's reference to the "Hymenical torch" may have been a response to rumors about a romance between him and the widow of John Floyd, who was killed by Indians in the spring of 1783. Despite his coy denials in this letter, Alexander married Mrs. Floyd a few weeks after writing it.[13] Klotter reports that relatives in the 1840s related that Mrs. Floyd was betrothed to Robert when she married Alexander, and that Robert's disappointment may have been responsible for his later "habits of intemperence." One version held that Mrs. Floyd was pregnant and Alexander married her after Robert was believed killed by Indians. Letters over the next year do not mention a child, but Alexander refers to his "handsome son" in an August 1786 letter (see n. 48). The letters, however, make it more believable that William was in love with Mrs. Floyd, for his later life was erratic and caused the family concern, while Robert was involved in politics, served as a delegate to the Virginia ratifying convention, was Kentucky's first Speaker of the House of Representatives, and held civic posts.[14] Robert was, however, away the fall of 1784, and letters show concern about lack of news from him. He supposedly left on a surveying trip in early September; on 24 October William Croghan wrote of meeting "Capt. Brackenridge [sic] surveying on the north side of Cumberland" and appears to have stayed with him until 20 December, when, he wrote, "Brackenridge & party" went on to "Red River Station."[15] William returned home a year later, and then seems to have drifted. John worried that he settled on no productive pursuit, and his mother, particularly, worried about what might become of him. In 1788 James complained of having to bail him out of debt in Williamsburg, where he had run up a large tavern bill.[16] Of course, other factors may explain his behavior, but his letter's references to Mrs. Floyd stand out because men rarely, if ever, mentioned "unattached" women in letters, and the letters were written "at Mrs. Floyds."

Less than two weeks after Alexander's November 1784 letter, James wrote to John from Beargrass, this time earnestly urging him to move to Kentucky. He said he needed John's advice, which he sorely missed from so great a distance. He had no one in Kentucky to turn to but Alexander, "who is always consulted in any of my most trivial transactions," he wrote. But he hoped this would not long be the case, "as I flatter myself you consider your interest more immediately in this country than to think of staying in that country any longer than you can possibly help." He continued:

> the business of them Counties I hope you will by no means think of engaging yourself in; This I believe is the third I have writ you pressingly on this Subject, which would not have been the case had it not have been from a suspicion I have & will have until I see your face, that perhaps M. Madison might persuade you to undertake his business, in deed as well as I recollect he and you intimate as such. This resolution I hope D[r.] Johnny you have resigned before this time.—Col. Fleming is now in company who I have consulted on that score and he desires me to write you most pressingly to come out, indeed he has promised to write you himself on the Subject, who is much more capable of giving you a detail of the affairs of these Counties.

James added that idleness since his arrival had made him "quite disatisfied." He had waited to go to Green River to survey for John May "for some time & was prevented . . . by a letter from John May until he comes out which is very uncertain. . . ." However, he and William had "been about bargaining" ever since he arrived, he said, and "I would mention every particular . . . but Col. Fleming is in a hurry." Still, there followed a very long essay about land interests and a final postscript: "Tell Cousin Johnny Brown I would have writ him if I had a minute . . . the Col. is now Ready to mount his hourse [sic]. . . ."[17]

Colonel William Fleming, who visited Kentucky during the severe winter of 1779–80, visited again the winter of 1782–83 and had become a prominent citizen there by late 1784. He probably carried James's letter only to Lexington.[18] On 27 December, he was elected president of a convention in Danville,[19] and it is unlikely that he could have gone to Virginia and returned between 18 November (the date of the letter) and 27 December.

Shortly after James's November letter to John, William wrote to his mother from Lincoln County, pleading innocent of neglecting her:

> I was the other day at Col. McDowals [*sic*]. Mr. John McDowall [*sic*] informed that you requested him particular if he should see me that he might inform me that you were very desirous to hear from me by the first Oppertunity; dear Mother I am sure I have not been negligent in that respect for I have wrote you by every Company that has gone in this fall and now am embracing this Oppertunity of writg· . . . again though I have nothing particular to write you. As I have often wrote you . . . this Year of my Intentions of going to Green River but have been from time to time been [*sic*] disappointed though I expect that we shall go in . . . a few weeks in case we hear from Mr. John May who is daily expected out. . . .

He added that whether May came or not, he planned to go immediately after returning to Beargrass to do his own business on Green River. He had waited so long for May, he wrote, because he wanted that work to defray his own surveying expenses, "which woud· save my Paying money into the Office as money is hard to be got in this Country." After the surveying, he would return to Virginia, he said, especially if she planned to come to Kentucky. He asked her to tell John, if he were at home, that he "would be glad he would come out as soon as possible." He reported that James and Alexander were well when he left Beargrass and that Robert had not returned from Cumberland.[20]

On 22 December 1784 William again wrote to his mother, this time from Beargrass, "to be as good" as his word and "not omitt writing." But he said he had "nothing particular to write" because he had written to her only a few days earlier. John May had written the Breckinridge brothers not to proceed "to his business until he came out," William explained, and the waiting kept him in suspense. Meantime, he added, the Indians had become "troublesome," and he was not anxious to go. "Take it for granted," he wrote, "that I prize my life above Kentucky lands." He would survey her four thousand acres that Alexander had located on "floyds forks," he assured her.

In a terse statement, William reported that Alexander had married Mrs. Floyd "a few days ago," and that he had received news from Robert, who was well and would return soon. William complained of having received no letter from John since James arrived in Kentucky and excused himself for not having written to John because he said he did not know where to send a letter. "[T]he Boys [James and Alexander] will both write you by this Oppertunity," he wrote, adding, "tell Sister Betsy . . . I am in hopes that she will be married against I go Home."[21]

Weeks passed, and the brothers in Kentucky heard nothing from John. Virginia newspapers carried no Kentucky news the next few months. Possibly, travel had been reduced because people chose not to migrate in the harsh winter months or because some autumn news, such as William's, implied that Indians were "troublesome." Reduced travel, of course, reduced opportunities for news to pass between the Kentucky country and the East.

In the meantime, Kentucky settlers entered upon a new phase—seeking statehood. They had long been dissatisfied with government by long distance, first from Williamsburg and then Richmond, as attested to by petitions sent to Virginia. On 27 December 1784, seven years before ratification of the then unwritten United States Constitution, thirty-seven Kentucky settlers met in a convention in Danville to formally exercise a presumed right to petition their government for redress of grievances.

The meeting, which lasted until 5 January 1785, became the first of ten conventions that met during the next seven years to advocate statehood. The members resolved that "the inhabitants of this District have a right peaceably to assemble to consider their grievances, and adopt such measures as they shall think prudent for redress." Foremost, they abhorred their lack of authority to deal with emergencies. Further, they protested "the law imposing a duty on merchandize brought into the District by way of Pittsburgh," because "such goods having paid a duty on their first importation, are again subject to an additional duty on their advanced price, when they arrived here." Among other grievances, the members argued that some taxes raised in the district should go to Kentucky's Translyvania Seminary (incorporated in 1780) in Lexington instead of the College of William and Mary in Williamsburg. And they protested "the law restricting the payment of Judges salaries here to certain duties and taxes arising within the District, and not out of the common Treasury" because Kentucky settlers paid "not only . . . their own Judges, but also their proportion for the support" of those for the "Eastern part of the State."

Regarding land claims, Kentucky settlers were especially bitter. They protested grants to anyone who did not plan to settle his family on them "because it is subversive of the fundamental principles of a free republican government to allow any individual, or company, or body of men, to possess such a large tract of country in their own right, as may, at a future day, give them an undue influence[;] and because it opens a door to speculation, by which innumerable evils may ensue" to less fortunate people. Finally, they protested the "non-residence of those . . . who hold lucrative offices in this District. . . ."[22]

News of this convention did not appear in Virginia newspapers for six months—until 4 June 1785.[23] Meantime, word of the resolutions filtered back to Virginia via letter and word of mouth. John Breckinridge, having left the Virginia Assembly with the last 1784 session, probably heard of the resolutions from former colleagues who considered them in the legislature. As an absentee Kentucky district landowner and someone who had suffered financial hardships, he must have been concerned about the resolution against absentee ownership. His brothers in Kentucky, not having heard from him, worried about his absentee land claims. William wrote him, alluding to the problem, on 7 February 1785, a month after the Danville convention adjourned. Perhaps with greater urgency than in previous pleas, he again encouraged John to move to Kentucky. Cautious about stating the problem, perhaps for fear of calling attention to John's absentee ownership to any who might come across the letter in transit, William casually referred to non-news and buried his pointed warning in brief, veiled phrases deep in the letter:

> I have sett down with an Intent to write . . . and know not about what. our Country is so peaceable that it affords no news. . . . you are determined I immagine [*sic*] from your very long silence not to let us hear any thing from that Quarter as you have not wrote me a line since Jimmy came [six months earlier]. . . . However I will excuse if you will be a good Boy for the future and write me first oppertunity after the recep$^{t.}$ of these few lines though from what you informed me in your last concerning your coming to this Country in the Spring its more than probable that you will be coming so shortly . . . that it may be convenient for you to bring the letter yourself. [F]or reasons which I have before given together with the very precarious Situation that your land matters stand in at present makes me the most anxious that you should come out as soon as possible at which time it will be in your power to settle your land disputes more to your own Satisfaction than it will be possible for me to do for you. Therefore let me advise to be as expeditious in coming out as possible—as I am well convinced all that you could gain by staying in that Country for a few months longer than you have done would be more loss to you than you can at present possibly immagine.

Apparently, William had not heard how the Virginia legislature reacted to the Danville resolutions, for he asked John to send him "a Couple Copies of the two last Sessions of Assembly," complaining that "we are amazedly at a loss for them in this Country." He said he had "scarcely seen one Act of Assembly" since he came to Kentucky, "but them that we brought out ourselves." The Kentucky delegates, he complained, either didn't know that they "ought to bring them or they think themselves above doing it and by such like doings as these the Country is in a manner left without laws." Repeating his appeal to John "not to let Slip the first favourable chance of coming out in the Spring," he warned that he lost by each day's absence because there was "such a multiplicity of business to be done." Clearly, William wanted news of state affairs, for, in asking John to write by the "first Oppertunity," he specifically asked for "news of every kind both foreign and Domestic,"[24] and this may indicate some anxiety about what might transpire regarding absentee land claims in the Kentucky district.

Still, efforts to coax John to Kentucky brought no immediate results. And evidence suggests that, more than thinking of migrating, he was settling into life in Virginia. After leaving the Virginia Assembly at the end of 1784, he began law practice in early 1785. In addition, he had a more compelling interest in his familiar home environment: In the summer of 1785, when John was twenty-four, he married sixteen-year-old Mary (Polly) Cabell, daughter of the prominent Joseph Cabell of Albemarle County, Virginia.[25]

While John made these transitions in his life, hints of legal snarls over Kentucky land began to appear in newspapers. The first problem explicitly related was that claimants, after duly registering entries, delayed surveying the land to avoid paying surveying fees and taxes. On 2 April 1785 newspapers reported "An ACT concerning EN-TRIES and SURVEYS on the WESTERN WATERS," which was designed to remedy this problem by setting deadlines beyond which claimants could lose any land not surveyed.

WHEREAS several persons, having early entries and locations for large tracts of land, in order to procrastinate the charge of surveying and the payment of taxes, refuse or neglect to survey them, while others who have adjacent entries and locations of a later date, are desirous to sue out grants and pay taxes on for their land: In aid therefore of the present means to compel surveys upon the said entries,

Be it enacted, That all entries made in the County Surveyor's books on the Western Waters, other than the entries made by virtue of Officers and soldiers claims for military services, before the passing of this Act, shall be surveyed, and the surveys thereof returned as the law directs, on or before the first day of February, One thousand seven hundred and eighty-six; and that all future entries on the said Waters, shall be in like manner surveyed and returned within one year after the date of every such entry. If any entry shall not be surveyed and returned within the terms aforesaid, it shall be lawful for any person to enter for and [illegible].

The same newspaper contained another official notice—this one from the United States Congress—indicating another land problem: Some people were altering officers' and soldiers' certificates by erasing the numbers of acres granted and writing in much larger numbers:

> WHEREAS information has been received from the Comptroller of the Treasury, that various certificates of final settlement issued by the Commissioner for settling the accounts of the army, to the Officers and soldiers of the United States, have been counterfeited by some fraudulent and wicked persons, by erasing the sums for which they were first given, and inserting others to a much greater amount . . . the United States in Congress assembled, have deemed it necessary to offer . . . reward of FIVE HUNDRED DOLLARS to any person or persons, who shall discover and make known the person or persons guilty of said forgery, or his or their accomplices.[26]

The growing pall over Kentucky land speculation caused many people to be wary of any business involving the West. An estate executor warned creditors "that their debts are yet more desperate" because the estate included "lands on the Western waters." The value of that land, he announced, "must depend on opinion, the art of speculating, and long credit. . . ." He explained that he was anxious to finish the business soon and "not leave law suits to my children."[26a] Another newspaper item indicated that in the wake of growing unease about stability of land claims, Henry Banks sought to sell his western land to his creditors, "either for what they [the lands] may be now valued by reputable men, or to give security on them, to be sold in two years."[27]

Finally, another of the recurring notices about delinquent payment of surveying fees appeared in a 14 May 1785 newspaper. "M. Carrington" warned that claimants who did not pay promptly would lose their lands:

> THIS method is taken, to inform all those interested in the Military Claims for Lands, in the late Virginia Continental line, that . . . last Fall, a considerable part of their claims were surveyed, and that the surveys on the S.E. side of the Ohio will be nearly compleat in . . . the present Spring and Summer. The claimants having failed to transmit to the principal Surveyor the money necessary for the purpose, has subjected the business to many difficulties and inconveniences, it is requisite that they transmit as early as possible, the sums necessary for clearing out their lands, otherwise they will . . . be lost; the expences of surveying was ascertained in only one district, at the time I set out for this country; but to be certain of securing them in time, I would recommend the sum of twenty-two dollars per thousand acres, and in proportion for a greater or

less quantity, which will be sufficient to take the platts out of the Surveyors, and lodge them in the Registrar's Office.

Carrington, who also advertised "a considerable quantity of LANDS in the Western Country," noted that a copy "of the Lottery, with a list of surveys made and returned" before the previous 18 February—plus a list of all entries made but not surveyed—was available for inspection in Richmond.[28]

As John Breckinridge's 30 June marriage date approached, newspapers published, on 4 June, the resolves of the Danville convention the previous December and January, and, on 9 July, an excerpt of a letter from Danville that told of a second convention. The writer complained that several recent Virginia laws that were disadvantageous to the western country had caused Kentucky settlers to seek statehood earlier than planned. The new state's name had been selected, he wrote, but he noted that the current population of thirty thousand must be greatly augmented before the area separated from Virginia:

> Our second Convention has met, and now sitting. They have resolved on making application to the Legislature of Virginia for an Act of separation at their next Session; and a petition is now drafting for that purpose, which will be read in the Convention this day. An address will also be handed out to the people, on the expediency of the measure.
>
> Several late Acts of Virginia Assembly which operate grievously in this district, have anticipated the application at an earlier period than was generally thought of; though perhaps it may be better for us in the end.
>
> This new State is to be called "THE COMMONWEALTH OF KENTUCKY," and by computation contains at this time 30,000 souls; but before a separation can take place must be vastly increased.[29]

During the early months of 1785, the newspapers published little news of Indian hostilities. The presence of troops guarding the western country may have reduced Indian raids. A brief notice in a 9 April newspaper told of a Frenchman being murdered "as he was returning from Kentucky to Philadelphia." But the man carried a large sum of money, and the item said that "10 or 12 other adventurers" traveling with him were suspected of the murder. The body was found in the river, "but no account can be given of the money," the item reported. An item in a 2 April 1785 newspaper hinted at lawlessness among the western troops. Virginia Governor Patrick Henry announced suspension of an act, "past at the last session," for regulating discipline and preventing insurrections and invasions in the western militia until 1 January 1786. At the same time, Henry warned "all Officers and others of the militia of those Counties" to "perform their respective duties."[30]

The writer of the news about the Danville statehood convention, as was usual in letters from Kentucky, gave Indian news. "The savages still continue to do mischief, though chiefly about the Ohio river," he wrote, but added, "it is not of any considerable consequence." However, a letter from Philadelphia, published in the newspapers two weeks later, suggested a serious Indian threat. "All things combining, seem to indicate a general discontent among the Indians," the author wrote, and added that "a Gentleman from Pittsburgh" had reported that Indians were "by no means satisfied with the late treaty, and will not . . . give up the territory ceded." The writer emphasized that "Indeed, this seems to be the general opinion of the people from the back country, who all say that the British take great pains to excite in them a jealousy of us," and reported that "Six or seven regiments are ordered from Ireland to garrison the British posts on the lakes." Explaining that he had "been at some pains to inform" himself, the writer said he was convinced "that what has happened is not a partial affair, nor a mere sally of their [Indians'] disorderly young men," but was part of "a regular digested plan." His "strong evidence," he said, was that the Indians had "begun at Kentucky, on Scioto, on Hockhocking, and near Wheeling, about the same time, and a Mr. Walker just arrived in town from the East branch of Susquehanna, informs that some people have been killed on Tioga, a branch which falls into the Susquehanna about eighty or ninety miles above Wyoming."[31]

As it turned out, the Philadelphia letter writer's warnings were well founded. As the summer of 1785 progressed, news of Indian hostilities grew more alarming. An item in 16 August newspapers reported the brutal murders of Thomas Lewis and others who had gone to negotiate the treaty with the Indians:

> On Wednesday evening last, an express arrived from the Western Country to our Governor, advising that about the first of this month, a treaty was to have been held between some of our people and the Indians; that upon their meeting, about twelve miles from Point Pleasant, on the other side of the Ohio, the Indians, instead of entering into negociations [sic] as proposed and expected, did, cruelly and savage like, kill four of our party—Colonel Thomas Lewis, Capt. Lockhart, Capt. Lamberton, and another gentlemen [sic].

Eleven days later, on 27 August, still another report told of Indians' anger about the treaty and their determination not to comply with its terms. The person reporting blamed the British for inciting Indians with hints of improprieties on the part of settlers regarding the treaty. Indians' objections to the treaty included that they had not been fully represented, they understood certain lands were to be set apart as hunting ground, and they had never been conquered and therefore would not yield their land:

> Very recent accounts from Kentucky confirm reports hitherto received from that quarter, that the Six Nations have expressed the greatest dissatisfaction of the late treaty, alledging [sic] that the British Officers at Niagara and Detroit, had informed them that our Commissioners had imposed on them, in asserting that those lands were ceded to us by the British, and that we were to take possession of the above-mentioned posts— That the celebrated and noted Brant had arrived from England, who united with them in the same sentiment and opinion— That in consequence of this information, a council had been held at the Shawanese town, where several other tribes, besides the Six Nations, assembled; the result of which we are unable precisely to ascertain and determine; but as two Chiefs viz. Cornplanter and another, with thirty warriors, have since been at Fort Pitt, and presented papers, exchanged at the treaty, to Col. Harmar, our commanding officer there, it is conjectured, and reasonable to suppose their intentions hostile and unfriendly. Col. Harmar, after having a talk with them, declined receiving their papers, and observed that those persons gave them such intelligence with a view to excite their jealousy, and to make them uneasy, and that they were enemies both to them and to us. The Indians said they always understood that the lands contracted for by the Commissioners from Pennsylvania, were to be set apart and considered as hunting grounds for both parties, and not to be surveyed and the trees spotted for . . . settlement and cultivation. They likewise observed, that as only a few of their Chiefs were at the treaty, they had not been fully and regularly represented. In their drunken frolicks they have also declared, that they had never been conquered, and would not give up their lands. They seemed the more inclined to believe the stories imposed on them by the British emissaries and incendiaries, because we had not taken possession of Niagara and Detroit, agreeable to the representations of our Commissioners. These are the principal arguments now urged by the Indians, for not complying with the terms of the treaty. And we understand that an express has been sent from Fort Pitt, with this intelligence, to Congress.[32]

In the midst of such events, the third Kentucky statehood convention, meeting in early August, produced and circulated a document that reflected deep anger and frustration about Indian hostilities and Kentuckians' lack of authority to deal with them. Convention members demanded of the Virginia Assembly "that an act may pass at the ensuing session . . . declaring and acknowledging the sovereignty and independence of this district," and defiantly assuming their own authority to call western troops into action against the Indians.[33]

Although widely circulated, the convention document was not published in Virginia newspapers. John Breckinridge probably got news or a copy of it, however, for his next letter to his mother begged for news from his brothers in Kentucky. Whether or not he had seen the document, he had probably read newspaper accounts of Indian activities; and this alone would have aroused concern for his brothers. After an apparent long lapse in communication with them, he wrote to his mother on 12 November 1785 from his father-in-law's home, "pray have you heard from my Brothers, James & Robin since I left Home?" He pleaded, "If you rec[d.] any Letters from them, or from Billy, send them to me. —I am uneasy to hear from Billy. If you have any thing particular from them; be sure to let me have it. . . ." John informed his mother of plans to move to the Glebe, the four-hundred-acre farm in Albemarle County, which Joseph Cabell had given him and Mary as a wedding gift:

> I expected when I saw you, to have been settled at the Glebe before now, but being desirous to attend Amherst & Buckingham Courts, I have been detained here, on that Account two Weeks longer. Every thing however has been ready for our reception this Fortnight, & we shall without Accident move down there in three Days from this time.

He continued with other news, explaining that he had not made an intended trip to Richmond and didn't know whether he would go before Christmas because the business there that he thought would require his attendance the last time he visited with his mother could be "dispensed with." In a few days he would know whether he or his father-in-law would have to go, but his wish to get fully settled before "the hard weather sets in" made the trip less important to him— unless it was absolutely necessary either for his mother or himself that he go. He asked his mother to let him know when she sent her tobacco "down" (to market) and explained that tobacco was selling low—for "28. s.3d. at most"—and said he would have none [to sell, presumably]. Because county courts had "adjourned all Business of consequence 'till March," he would be "without Business of that kind" during the winter, he wrote, and assured his mother she could "depend on" seeing him in January. He would write to her as soon as he and Polly moved to the Glebe; he was not yet certain when that would be but was anxious to "be comfortably fixed," he wrote, and commented extensively on his in-laws' kindnesses:

Col. Cabell & Mrs. Cabell, seem willing to lend us every Assistance; and am satisfyed will not let us want anything they can furnish us with. I still continue to experience from them every parental attention, that I could desire even from yourself. Every Day's tryal of their Affection increases my respect for them, and am pleased with the prospects, of my situation being rendered as comfortable with them as it could possibly be elsewhere, when [away] from you.[34]

No letter indicates whether Mrs. Breckinridge could give John news of his brothers, who had perhaps accepted that John's marriage would alter, or at least delay, his plans to move to Kentucky. In any event, they ceased their direct appeals for him to move, although they continued to write of their own love for the Kentucky country. Their letters, however, did not directly refer to the statehood issue or the agitation it created in Kentucky.

Division of opinion about statehood became apparent in Kentucky during 1785. Some chafed at delayed statehood while others feared destroying future relations with Virginia by overly precipitous actions. On 9 December James Madison wrote to George Washington of Kentuckians' formal application for statehood and their impatience at having to wait for congressional actions concerning their affairs. Madison informed Washington that the issue had been considered, "and the terms of separation fixed by a committee of the whole." Kentuckians, he added, "dislike much to be hung on the will of Congress," so conditions stipulated that Congress must give assent before 1 June 1787. One Kentucky faction sought immediate separation and complained of delay after three conventions had already appealed for, and expressed the urgency of, statehood. Others, however, not wanting to antagonize the Virginia Assembly and risk future relations with Virginia, favored moving slowly. The different views gave rise to heated dissension, electioneering for convention delegates, and some rumored heavy-handed tactics using the army to ensure votes for the "right" delegates. Ultimately, voters decided that a fourth statehood convention would meet in September 1786.[35]

The Breckinridge brothers in Kentucky seemed cautious in taking sides and were otherwise untouched by these events. John, however, wrote to James in January 1786, warning him of potential problems with Kentucky land entries.[36] On 8 March 1786, twenty-three-old James, who had been in Kentucky for a year and a half, wrote from Lincoln County, thanking John for his advice and noting that he had "formed so great attachment for the place [Kentucky]" that he had decided against settling all his lands. He was about to purchase four hundred acres on Beargrass, which he believed would be his "seat in this Country, if I chuse to ever settle on it, tho," he wrote, "I assure you I am very undetermined where to fix myself."

Acknowledging John's advice and noting his own caution regarding Kentucky land deals, James wrote that "Mr. Brown" delivered John's letter, "the contents of which I must confess myself under obligation to you for, it has been hitherto a fixed Resolution with me to be particularly cautious in making conveyances for land in this Country." Brown, he wrote, had also shared one of his letters from John, in which James found "you are somewhat uneasy about your Brashear's creek land," and said he promised Brown to correct the survey and "endeavour to discover who interferes with you" so that Brown could "proceed as he then may think most proper." John Brown, a cousin of the Breckinridge brothers and attorney who would soon become Kentucky's representative in the United States Congress, was handling cases involving land disputes in Kentucky, and John Breckinridge had entrusted to him some of his own legal questions about his land affairs. James wrote of others of John's and his own land affairs in Kentucky and of his intention to return to Botetourt as soon as he finished his work:

> Squire Boone has surveyed a Preemption of 1000 acres on that place [Brashear's Creek?] which is at least three miles distant from where he ought to have Surveyed; this claim I think you need not be under any apprehension from, I will mention the matter to Mr. Brown when I see him & its [*sic*] more than probable he will make up the matter without the cost of a suit. There are no other claims that Interfere with you but what are much Younger, therefore I don't think you need give yourself any uneasiness about it. I am now about to bring my business to a close in this Country, my surveying I expect to have finished by the sixteenth of May next and my Platts all returned to the Registers office. [S]hould this be the case I will endeavour to see you against the last of May, but untill my business is finally settled or will not suffer by my absence I am fully determined to continue in this Country[.] My lands are all very clear of disputes & I am in hopes will be able to obtain patents for them immediately.

Continuing with other news, James wrote, "The Indians have been doing mischief lately near the falls & people in this Country appear to be very apprehensive of a Troublesome summer." He could not write more because he was "so indisposed" that he could "scarcely set up to read over" what he had written, he explained and said he "caught a most Violent cold" a week before "& after getting almost clear of it was obliged to attend the G. Court," had "since caught a fresh cold," and feared it would be hard to get rid of. "Pray write me every opp^{y.}"

he pleaded, and added in a postscript, "The Residue of Carrington's debts after you & Maj^r Lockhart are paid, you may either make use of yourself or lay it out in any way you think most proper for me."[37]

Virginia newspapers published very little direct information about Kentucky land disputes, but occasional items implied their existence. For example, summonses, such as the following, appeared in newspapers:

> The Commonwealth of Virginia. To the Sheriff of Nelson County [Kentucky], greeting:
> We command you, as we have hereto fore [sic] commanded you, that you summon Henry Funk to appear before the Judges of our Supreme Court for the District of Kentucky, at the Courthouse, in Danville, in the County of Lincoln, on the 9th day of the next November Court, to shew cause why five hundred acres of land, surveyed on Nolin Creek, a branch of Green River, or so much thereof as interferes with John Handley's entry of one hundred and fifty acres, as assigned of John Paul, may not be granted to the said John Handley, who hath entered a caveat against a grant's issuing therefor to the said Henry Funk: and have then there this writ. Witness, Christopher Greenup, Clerk of our Said Court, at the Courthouse aforesaid, the the [sic] 27th day of September, 1785, and in the 10th year of our Commonwealth.[38]

William Breckinridge returned to Botetourt sometime in late 1785 or early 1786. A 19 March 1786 letter indicates that he was at his mother's home.[39] An 8 May letter from his aunt Mary Howard to John expressed pleasure that "Billy is in his mother's House again," but she commented at length on William's lack of judgment and distressed sojourn in Kentucky. Mary Howard also informed John of her husband's plans to go to Kentucky, plans she fretted about and characterized as insane. Then, in a postscript, she added that she had just learned (via a letter from John Smith in Richmond) that her husband had already "sett off to go to Kentucky by Pittsburgh."[40]

Howard, who may have been an alcoholic, was unpredictable, and his instability was probably the chief source of his wife's concern.[41] But news accounts from the West gave her reason to fear for his safety, regardless of his ability to cope with life. In the spring of 1786, Indians killed William Christian, a Breckinridge friend and one of the Kentucky country's most respected leaders. The news reached Mrs. Lettice Breckinridge in Botetourt County before newspapers published it. In a letter to John, dated 11 May 1786, she fretted about her "Sons in Kenetky," writing that since hearing of Christian's death, she was "very much Concerned for the Famely," adding, "they are all greatly scytred" and she was afraid it would "be the fait of Some of my D^r· Sons to fall into the hands of their Enemies."

At the time, the only family member with Mrs. Breckinridge was her youngest, Preston, then about sixteen (her letter implied that she did not know where William was). Her only daughter, Betsy, had gone to assist John's wife, Polly, as she awaited her first child's birth.[42] Mrs. Breckinridge had not heard from Betsy and wondered about her trip to Albemarle. "I am very uneasy to heare how my Dear Polly is and Betsey (how she got down?)," she wrote, after complaining that she had not heard from John "since you left me."

Mrs. Breckinridge wrote of health and farm problems. She said she had been very sick but seemed to suggest that anxiety about her "Sons in Kenetky" may have been the cause. Despite the fact that her oldest son, William—unoccupied since his return from Kentucky—and her youngest, Preston, were available, the letter reflects her dependence on John:

> As there is no overseer Come I expect it is out of your Power to get me one at this time[.] I think it is Best to Plant the new Ground with Corn[,] but I shall wait till the 18 of this month and if none shou^d· Come I will do the Best I can[.] I am afraid it will not be in your Power to come up at this time to see me but if you Cou^d· Spear the time I should be very glad to see you if you wou^d· only stay 2 or 3 Day with me[.] Tell my Dear Polly and Bettsy I intend to write to them, but has not got one bit of paper[.] I will writ to them the first good opportunity I have & Expect Bettsey will stay with her brother till sometime in June[,] as I hope by the Last of June my Dear Polly will be over her Difficulty and perfectly Recovered[.] I hope you have your Family in your own House[?] [I]f that is the Case I think Bettsey may stay with more Safety on account of her health[.] I beg you will writ if you Cannot Come your Self and Let me now [*sic*] when I may Expect to see you.

Mrs. Breckinridge concluded the letter, saying Preston "sends his best Compliment to his Dear Sister Polly and Bettsey and would have write [*sic*] to them but had no peperr[*sic*]"; a postscript said she expected her "dear son Billey is gon to Richmond before this."[43]

The Breckinridge brothers still in Kentucky—Robert, Alexander, and James—escaped harm, but news reports suggest that their mother's fears were not unfounded. A week after her letter to John, newspapers reported Christian's death, general news of Indian hostilities, and that Kentucky settlements faced danger of serious Indian uprisings. The item, on 17 May 1786, reported:

Extracts of letters from the Western Country, to his Excellency the

Governor, dated Lincoln county [Kentucky], April 18th and 19th, 1786.

The Indians have been very troublesome this spring, and of late have invaded the county of Jefferson, and are almost every day committing depredations there. Our spirited, generous-hearted friend, Col. William Christian, and a Captain Kellar, have lately fallen a sacrifice to their barbarity; and it is to be feared, if measures are not speedily pursued for the support and defence of that part, the country will break up, and of course the people be greatly distressed. The Indians that invade Jefferson, live on Wabash, and not more than 150 miles from the Ohio, and might be attacked with success. We are not troubled with the Wabash Indians; but the Chicamagies, a part of whom have lately settled over the Ohio, on a creek called Point-Creek; they are said to be about 70 warriors, who have stolen almost all the horses from Limestone and Licking settlements. Those of the Tenasee [*sic*] disturb our Eastern and southern frontiers, and about 10 days since have killed Col. Donnelson, on his way to Cumberland from this country. Several settlements are evacuated in this county, with the loss of different people; There is a compact between the Southern and Western Indians, and it appears that they intend to cut off this country.

All the Indians on and about the Wabash are out for war; and news is just received that there are several hundred of them at this time out at war, which is highly probable, from the circumstance of their being at this time in almost every part of our Western and Southern frontiers. They had been frequently on Beargrass; and Col. Christian, in order to induce others to go in pursuit of them, has upon every occasion gone himself;—and last week, he, with about 20 men, crossed the Ohio and overtook 3 Indians, whom they killed; but his men not rushing upon them altogether as he had ordered, he with 3 others only, came up with them. It is remarkable there were only two guns belonging to the Indians, both of which did executions, although one at the time firing his gun at Kellar, lying on the ground totally disabled in one arm, and unable to rise up.[44]

Indian hostilities, particularly Christian's murder, prompted John Brown to write to John Breckinridge from Danville on 20 May 1786. And he took the occasion to report other news—especially about John's Kentucky land holdings:

Dear Sir

I should have written to you long since had an opp°· of Conveyance offered but can assure you that it is a more difficult matter to send a letter to your part of the Country than I expected. This I write by Col. Knox in his way to Staunton, he promises to give it safe conveyance. I lately saw your Brother James, & enquired at him about your land on Brasheers Creek. [H]e informs that he is well acquainted with the Situation of your Claim & of those [?] adjoining & that there is not the least danger that you will loose [*sic*] the land[;] expect he has written to you upon the Subject &

given you a full State of the Case[.] I examin'd the Office of the Supreme
Court for this District & find that there is no Caveat on that Dockett
against Barn's land on Elkhorn, this being the case I have procured a
Certificate thereof which I have sent inclosed; your presenting it to the
Register will be sufficient authority for him to issue your Patent. Mr. Craig
inform'd me that he has a Patent for part of Barns Survey & expects at
least to hold the Surplus lands as his Entry Survey & Patent on all prior to
issuing of Barns Patent. I expect to obtain Judg$^{t.}$ should he fail in that
quarter I fear we shall not gitt it shortly as his property here is very small.

I have very little News to inform you of from this Country that is worth
your notice. The Indians have been very Troublesome to our Frontiers
this Spring, and have killed several of our most useful Citizens, among
whom were Col. Christian[,] Col. Donelson & Capt. Kellar—they have
also stolen a great number of Horses. All the Wabash Indians appear
disposed for War; as also part of the Shaneese & Chickamaga's.

Continuing to draw a graphic picture of the threat to Kentucky
settlements, Brown wrote, "Our Situation at present is truly distressing. The Indians can at any time with ease make incursion upon our
Frontier & can in almost every instance repass the Ohio with their
plunder before they can be overtaken." He complained that "our
officers have no authority to lead men out upon an Expedition . . .
over the River" and "neither can a sufficient number of Volunteers be
raised for that purpose."

Echoing Kentuckians' dissatisfaction with government from a distance and lack of confidence in the Richmond administration, Brown
added, "A Representation of our Situation has been laid before the
Executives of Virginia[,] but [we] do not expect that any measures of
consequences will be adopted on our behalf." He continued, providing his evaluation of the status of the statehood movement:

Many are the difficulties & grievances which this Country labours under,
that arise in a great measure from our total Situation & in my opinion are
only fully to be removed by a Separation from Virg$^{a.}$ The distance is too
great from the Capital to suppose that the Executive can take effectual
measures to guard the Banks of the Ohio. However[,] our Western Politicians are much divided in Opinion as to the propriety of a Separation, & at
present it is a very doubtful matter whither the public Voice will decide for
or against it; but I rather think it will be in favour of it.

Ending the letter with details of his own life, he wrote that he had
"set up an Office . . . where I live in perfect security, enjoy a good
State of Health; & have a good share of business." But he added that
money was "extremely scarce[,] being carried off by the northward

merchants," and "unless we have a Supply of paper money the next Session of Assembly[,] people in this Country will be ruined." He appealed to John to write to him; "I wish you would make it convenient to write to me by every opp[y,] as it would afford me the greatest Pleasure to hear of your welfare," and he concluded, "Give my best compl[ts.] to Mrs. Breckinridge[,] also to Col. Cabell & family & believe me to be with Esteem your most Affect[e.] Cousin. . . ."[45]

John Breckinridge probably received this letter about the time his first child, Letitia Preston, was born on 14 June 1786.[46] James Breckinridge was still in Kentucky, although his February letter had said he would return to Botetourt in May. John's uneasiness about his brothers' welfare probably intensified as the summer passed, for Indian hostilities in Kentucky worsened. A 19 July newspaper reported "a severe conflict" between Lexingtonians and Indians, in which "17 whites and 14 Indians" were killed "and a number wounded."[47] Within a couple of months after this publication, however, John received a reasuring letter from Alexander.

Writing from "Jefferson Office" in Kentucky on 21 August, Alexander dealt mostly with land business and asked John to handle some legal matters for him in Virginia; but he took occasion to describe his "handsome son." He promised to write again "by our Delegates, and then fully."[48]

Meantime, John's law practice absorbed, and even drained, him. On 21 August he wrote to his mother from the Glebe that he could not visit her because "My Horse & myself are so much fatigued, from the last Circuit, which is now just over, that I find I cannot with any Convenience go up to Botetourt myself." He added that "Brother Billy," who had been visiting him, "left Col. Cabells about a fortnight ago upon my Horse," but "No body knows where he is gone. . . ." Despite the strain of his work, John reveled in his young family, and his letter continued with news of his two-month-old daughter. His growing responsibilities for his own family in addition to his workload perhaps made him weary of his mother's continued dependence on him. He chided that she could more easily visit than he:

> Polly and your little Grand daughter are both well. Your grandaughter grows finely, & is very healthy, but much afflicted with the Belly ach. We wish & hope to see you down here this fall. It is impossible for us to go up. If we could visit with only half the convenience you can, we would certainly be in Botetourt this fall.
>
> Col. Cabell & his Family are well as yet but fear will not continue so long. The People on the River begin to be sickly. Young Mrs. Cabell had a son a few Days ago; and all things are well.

John added that he was sending some money, collected from a debtor, and apologized because it was "scarcely better than nothing"; but, he wrote, "the Daily demands that are made for my little family, & my Bacon to buy, keeps me from collecting any sum together of consequences." He concluded, "Write to me if you please & make Preston write also. . . . I really have not time to write."[49]

Unhappy about John's refusal to visit her, Mrs. Breckinridge responded immediately, insisting that he come. She reminded him that she had sent William to stay with John's family so that he could come, but William had been there and gone, and John still had not come to Botetourt. Betsy, who had returned to Botetourt after assisting John's wife through the final weeks of pregnancy, was contemplating marriage. William had told John this news, and Mrs. Breckinridge was peeved that he seemed unconcerned about it. She did not approve of Betsy's suitor, and she needed John's advice, she wrote, pleading for his support in the matter:

My Dear son
    I am very sorry it was not in your Power to come up to see me when I sent Billy down in order to stay with his Sister till you wold return[.] Your not comming at that time made me certain of your Comming at this time as you promised in your Letter to me by Betsey[;] but after all my Expect[at]ions you Seem to think it impossible to come up this fall. but I will not be put off in that maner[,] for you must Try to Come as soon as you possibly Cann as thear is a matter of importenes waits for your advice[.] I Expect Billy Let you know that Mr. Meredith is Paying his respects to your Sister Bettsy[,] and Col. Meredith has wrot me a Letter about this affear[;] he Seems much Pleased[.] I will Send you a Copy of his Letter that you may See what he intends to give his Son and what he wants me to give my Daughter. I have not wrot him an answer to his Letter as yet for I waited for your Comming[.] I beg you will inquear into his Character[.] Mr. Meredith Seems to wish to appoint the 2d of Next month to be marred. I woud not have [MS torn] appointed till he came from Richmond.
    I am very happy to hear that you and [MS torn] Dear little famly is in good health and that my Little Grandaughter is growing so fast[;] you cannot conceive how much I long to Se her and what fears I have had about her since Betsy Left you as I have not heard a single word from that tim till now.

Expressing anxiety about James in Kentucky, Mrs. Breckinridge wrote, "I am much Concerned for my Boy Jammy," and "I expected him before this . . . but is almost out of hopes . . . as there is Expedison going out against the Indians and I am affraid he will goe."[50]

No response came from John, and Mrs. Breckinridge, apparently refusing to discuss Betsy's marriage without him, informed Betsy's suitor, young Samuel Meredith, that he must have approval of John, who would soon come to Botetourt to discuss the marriage. But John did not arrive, and two weeks later, Mrs. Breckinridge wrote to tell him that Betsy's suitor, after waiting vainly for John, was on his way to the Glebe to consult him about the marriage. Resigned to the marriage by then, however, she sought John's help in obtaining items Betsy needed for the wedding:

My Deare Johnny
　　I teack this oppertunity of writing to you by Mr. Meredity [*sic*] as he intends to be at your House in a fewe Dayes[;] he has waited to heare some time. Expecting to have Seen you but as you have not Come[,] I could not insist on him Staying any Longer as he Seemed Uneasy to goe Down to his fathers in order to Prepare for his Marriage as he Expects it will be in a verey Short time[.] I have Done all I cann to put it off, a Little Longer but the bouthe Seems to wysh it some time this Month[.] I cannot say that feal Happy on the Occation[.] But as my Deare Betsy Seems Determined in Her Choise I have Left here to act as she thinks fit[.] I have given her my advice on the matter and has tould here Every thing I heard concerning hime[,] but She is so fixed in her mind that She gives very Little attention to any[thing] she heares to his Disadvantage[.] She is very uneasy that she Cannot git any thing hear that she wants on this Occation[.] I thought to have got her some things in Col. Lees[?] Store but Did not get any thing that she wanted.
　　You will se the memoranda I sent by my Cousin Johnny Preston to Mr. [illegible] in Richmond[;] thear is [illegible] yeards of pinck [illegible] that Betsy wants put in the [illegible]. I thought to have got it in Col. Lees[?] Store but was Dysappointd. Betsy is in some feares that she will be disappond. about her Cloaths as she wants to mack a gentile appeareens among her [illegible]. I could wysh it was in my Power to get her every thing that she stands in need[.] I hope my Dr Johnny that you will Doe all you Can to get her all the things I wrot for by Directing my Cousin Johnny Weare he will get in Case Mr. [illegible] would disappoint me.[51]

She abruptly ended the letter, saying she had no more paper.
　　While Mrs. Breckinridge prepared for Betsy's wedding, James returned from Kentucky. A letter to John from Alexander in Louisville, dated 22 September 1786, said he wrote last "by James in July." Alexander, who wrote news of land business, Indian hostilities and expeditions, again sent John some business to be handled in Virginia. Sending the letter by "Col. John Campbell . . . who sets out tomorrow Morning for the Assembly," he wrote that Indian actions in Kentucky foretold war:

Our Country is all in Arms and a continual bustle for War, on Sunday the 14th Inst. about 1200 Men well equipped marched under the Command of Gen[l.] Clark against the Wabash Indians. There is now another party on foot and will March in from this on Tuesday next under the Command of Col. Logan against the Shawnee's, since our Troops marched, a certain Col. Legraw at the Opost having intelligence of the march dispatched an express informing the Indians there was an army coming against them, this I had from Mr. J. May who came from Louisville last evening and saw the letter sent to Gen[l.] Clark. The express from the post missed the army and came to Louisville which gave the opportunity of knowing the contents. Twas immediately sent after them and the messenger has returned & informs the army will be at the post this evening or tomorrow morning. . . . I shall ride to Town some time today, should there be any further news, I will give it to you.[52]

Three weeks later, on 11 October 1786, Virginia newspapers reported Indian news, but the information, dated 10 August, was older than that in Alexander's letter.[53] During the ensuing months, little news of Kentucky appeared in Virginia newspapers. The fourth statehood convention, which met in September 1786, had no quorum because so many members were away on expeditions against Indians. Those attending adjourned from day to day until a quorum appeared in January 1987. Then, the second Act of Separation arrived from the Virginia legislature, and the members referred it to a fifth convention to meet in September 1787.[54]

Meantime, despite the Indian hostilities and statehood limbo, rapid migration continued to the Kentucky country. An official at Fort Harmar on the Ohio River recorded passage of thirty-four boats in thirty-nine days at one point in 1786.[55] But Breckinridge correspondence during the winter and spring months of 1786–87 shows no hint of the lower Virginia family members' plans to join the trek. Letter references to Kentucky concerned land primarily, suggesting that speculation may have become the only interest the Virginia Breckinridges had in Kentucky. Alexander had settled in Kentucky, and Robert seems to have also, although correspondence rarely refers to him.

Betsy Breckinridge married Samuel Meredith, Jr., in October 1786. Her in-laws hosted a formal get-together for the Breckinridges, and William, John, and James attended.[56] John later visited the newlyweds and reported to his mother that they were fine, that Betsy appeared "very well Contented; & pleased with her new Acquaintances."[57] Both William and James seemed to experience a lost sense of purpose after their sojourns in the Kentucky country; William, who had been back for some months, had not settled into any meaningful pursuit; and James, more recently returned, seemed equally at loose ends. Both became students (apparently of musical instruments) for a short time.[58] Then, in early November 1786, James enrolled in the College of William and Mary because, as he wrote to John, "I am entirely out of business & know not what to apply myself to that would be of so much advantage." He said he would study "natural & moral Philosophy & probably attend the Lectures" and asked for John's opinion of his plans.[59]

John continued riding circuit for court duties. Apparently following Betsy's marriage, her mother suffered an illness, which may have been caused by what is today called the "empty-nest syndrome." John's wife alluded to such a possibility in a letter written on 19 November 1786 and sent by John on one of his circuit trips. Sure that Mrs. Breckinridge was lonely, Polly pleaded with her to visit:

My Dear Madam
    Mr. Breckinridge sits out to morrow for Stanton [*sic*] and from there he intends to Botetourt, and I am in hopes my Dear Madam that he will find you Perfectly recovered of your late Illness, I hope it was nothing More than your being So lonesome and that of cours Would mack you very low Spearted [spirited], I am convinst Company would be of Serves to you, I think if you would Come down with Mr. Breckinridge and Spend this Winter in Amherst and Albemarle it would be of infinit Services to you, I can assure you my Dear Mother there shall be Nothing wanting That [is] In my Power to do to mack the place Agreeable to you, I wish it was in my power to go up Now to see you, but it is So bad travailling in cold Weather with a young Child; that I shall be deprived of the pleasure of seeing you untill next summer if you Dont come down with Mr. Breckinridge, Mr. Meredith and my Sister has been with us a week[.] Betsy Says if you cant come down with her Brother that she will go up very Shortly, and I am in hopes if you Cant come now you will with her.[60]

Such exchanges about family, without references to the western country, suggest that life was settled for the lower Virginia Breckinridges. John was settled with his young family in his own home and ensconced in his law practice, and with Betsy also married and settled, James in college, and Preston still at home with his mother, only William remained unsettled. But he gave no indication of a desire to return to the Kentucky country.

Although the Breckinridges no longer wrote of moving to Kentucky, some relatives did. On 24 March 1787, Mary Howard wrote to John of her determination, "if I live[,] to move to kentucky next fall." However, she said she was "in great distress for money to fix my famaly for the Journey," and she planned to sell property to raise the needed funds. She already had sent slaves ahead to clear land and build fences, and John Brown had written to tell her that "our negros is making a fine improvement on our land," she added.[61]

By 1787 such migrants as Mary Howard might expect a comfortable sojourn in Pittsburgh. After the summer of 1786, when *The Pittsburgh Gazette* began publishing, advertisements reflect rapid development of stores, trades, and professions there. Some catered especially to the increasing flow of migration. On 9 September 1786, John M'Don announced boat transportation from Pittsburgh to Washington, saying this provided the best means to transport merchandise, produce, and *The Pittsburgh Gazette*. He added that he planned to build a large storehouse to receive produce and other baggage on his landing. And on 4 November 1786, A. & J. Tannehill (in an advertisement dated 15 September 1786), announcing plans to open a "PUBLIC HOUSE in Pittsburgh" on 16 October, hoped the news would reach prospective migrants:

> It may be necessary to inform those at a distance, who travelling this way, may wish to be well accommodated: having the advantage of a convenient building with a number of apartments & separate lodging rooms, with proper furniture, it will be in our power to give satisfaction to those who may favor us with their company. We will endeavour at all times to be provided with the best liquors, and with good water, having a well in our yard, and not being under the necessity of sending for water at a distance. Our stable is good, and we shall be provided to take the best care of horses, well knowing this to be a point not less material to a traveller than the accommodation of himself.[62]

As spring 1787 came, the Pittsburgh newspaper announced openings of still other businesses to accommodate the swelling tide of migrants through the small town that had become a busy gateway to the West.[63]

If John Breckinridge saw *The Pittsburgh Gazette* advertisements, he may have been torn between his apparent settled life in Virginia and the vision of opportunities to the west, for surely communications from others—such as Mary Howard—who were joining the westward migration kept alive in his mind the possibility of following.

5

"I Find Myself Determined [to Move to Kentucky]"

By 1787 news traveled frequently between eastern Virginia and the Kentucky country. Companies left Kentucky via the wilderness road every two weeks after 12 April 1788, when *The Kentucke Gazette* began publishing routine announcements of such trips, and the pattern had probably begun earlier. Trips began on Monday mornings from Crab Orchard, near present Stanford, Kentucky. After the summer of 1789, occasional notices announced trips via the Ohio River (travelers met at Limestone) or via the "new road" (travelers met at Strode's Station). At times, different companies traveled the separate routes at the same time.[1]

The establishment of a newspaper in Kentucky in mid-1787 helped disseminate more organized information about such trips and western events. News from Kentucky increasingly reflected divisive political issues in which Breckinridge family and relatives participated. John very likely kept abreast of the issues, but his information about the area had always been secondhand. In 1787 he resolved to go see the Kentucky country for himself and buy land in preparation for moving there. He was impressed with what he saw. Although many tried to dissuade him, he was determined to migrate, and the issues dividing Kentuckians seem to have been inconsequential to his decision.

While Kentuckians had been debating statehood, the Mississippi-navigation issue emerged to engage attention and become bound up in the statehood struggle. These twin issues grew heated and, on occasion, led to serious talk of Kentucky's secession from the union. The first news of the navigation issue appeared in newspapers on 12 December 1786—two years after the first statehood convention met. Westerners had sent a petition to the Virginia Assembly, asking consideration of their rights to the Mississippi River. The House, as a committee of the whole, resolved that the navigation of the Mississippi River should be considered nature's gift to the United States—secured by the American Revolution—and referred the petition to the Virginia delegates in Congress, with the resolution

> That the Delegates . . . ought to be instructed in the most decided terms, to oppose any attempt that may be made in Congress, to barter or surrender to any other nation whatever, the right of the United States, to free and common use of the River. . . . And that the said Delegates ought to be further instructed to urge the proper negociation [*sic*] with Spain, for obtaining her concurrence in such regulations, touching the mutual and common use of the said river.[2]

Kentuckians did not wait for official channels to clear their rights to the river, however. A 31 January 1787 item reported that the Spanish had attacked a Kentucky boat going down the river. The boat had been sunk and several people on board killed outright or drowned, "the rest saving themselves by swimming." The report added that "Soon after[,] a Spanish batteau arrived at Kentucky to purchase flour, when a number of the inhabitants, in revenge, attacked the Spaniards, killed several, and forced the others to fly." The item omniously warned that "these quarrels may be attended with serious consequences."[3] An 8 March 1787 item, taken from a Philadelphia newspaper and dated 17 February, reported:

> The report in our paper of Wednesday last, relative to the people of Kentucky having captured a small Spanish vessel on the Ohio, probably took its rise from the following circumstances which we are assured may be credited, viz. That some time ago, two boats belonging to some of the inhabitants on the banks of the Ohio, went down the Mississippi, and were seized as soon as they had reached the jurisdiction claimed by the Spaniards—And that some short time afterwards, in order to retaliate, General Clarke, seized on two Spanish boats, which came up to Fort St. Vincents. Within the jurisdiction of the United States, for the purposes of trade. It is said they had furs and cash on board to the amount of near 20,000 dollars.
>
> We are informed that General Clarke has sent a person to Congress to advise . . . thereof, and to solicit permission to raise a regiment . . . for the defense of Fort St. Vincents. . . .[4]

Newspapers did not report the outcome of Clark's plans nor how the Spanish conflict reached a temporary peace. Subsequent newspaper content about the issue, nearly a year later, indicates some trade between Kentuckians and Spaniards.

In the meantime, the statehood issue received passing notice in Virginia newspapers. At about the time John Breckinridge received

Mary Howard's letter telling of her plans to move to Kentucky, *The Virginia Gazette and Weekly Advertiser,* on 5 April 1787, carried a Philadelphia newspaper report—excerpted from a Danville, Kentucky, letter dated 16 January 1787—that the fourth convention had just met "to decide on the great question—Whether we shall separate from the government of Virginia or not?" The letter writer, referring to the statehood convention only after relating various Indian "depredations" in Kentucky, said convention members "seem divided and no certain conclusion can be made."[5] A fifth convention was planned, but a year passed before another Virginia newspaper wrote about the statehood issue and it was nearly as long before another item about Mississippi navigation appeared.

Although Virginia newspapers gave slight attention to these issues, *The Kentucky Gazette* contained lengthy discussions, especially of the statehood issue. Former surveyor John Bradford, at the request of statehood convention members, began the weekly newspaper in Lexington in August 1787 to publicize, and mobilize public opinion about, statehood efforts;[6] and the subject dominated early numbers in essays that often filled three of the newspaper's four pages.

John Breckinridge probably had more opportunities to follow the statehood discussions than a reading of Virginia newspapers indicates. Given the custom at the time of passing newspapers around, travelers very likely carried copies of *The Kentucky Gazette* to Virginia. By late 1787, there seemed no scarcity of such travelers. Even while the press and type, brought from Pittsburgh, were being readied for the first issue, James Breckinridge wrote to John from Smithfield of plans to send someone to negotiate some business in Kentucky—in "time enough to return before I go to Wms[burg.] . . . the first day of October." James asked if John also had business that the man could handle for him in Kentucky.[7]

Kentucky's fifth statehood convention met in September 1787 as the new Federal Constitution was adopted in Congress and submitted to the states for ratification. The Virginia constitutional convention, in which Kentuckians would participate, was scheduled for the following summer. The fifth statehood convention members unanimously approved the Act of Separation, petitioned Congress for statehood, designated 31 December 1788 as the date of separation from Virginia, provided for a subsequent convention to draw up a state constitution, and petitioned the Virginia Assembly to authorize election of John Brown as representative of the District of Kentucky in Congress.[8]

In the meantime, perhaps believing Kentucky statehood imminent, thousands migrated through the wilderness and down the Ohio River. *The Pittsburgh Gazette* reported that records kept at Fort Harmar on the Muskingum River showed 177 boats, bearing 2,689 people, 1,333 horses, 766 cattle, 102 wagons, and 1 phaeton, went down the Ohio River between 10 October 1786 and 12 May 1787; and additional migrants passed unnoticed during the night. The newspaper also reported on 24 November 1787 that since the previous Sunday, 120 boats bearing an average of 15 persons each had passed on the way to Kentucky. These numbers, the item noted, would add "1,800 inhabitants to that young settlement," and more than that number waited on the Monongahela River to depart for Kentucky (the report attributed the numbers migrating, in part, to poor Virginia crops—which had produced less than a fourth the expected yield). An observer at Pittsburgh in the spring of 1787 noted fifty flatboats departing within one month.[9]

John Breckinridge's friends still expected him to join the throng of migrants. Roger Thompson wrote from "Kings Ford" on 17 January 1788 to thank John "& Lady" for caring for his daughter and added his thoughts about John becoming a Kentuckian. He would "Set out the 1st of Feb[y.] for Kentucky," he wrote. "What hurrys our march is that Col. G. Thompson is a Candidate in Kentucky for the Convention." He continued:

> Should the Weather Continue Very Cold we Shall go by land[;] if so will Call by & Shake You by the hand. [I]f we go by Water & I live to return will Call on you if possible . . . Col. Nicholas has taken his leave of Albemarle, as a publick man after the Convention (then for Kentucky g——v——r[;] will you ever go there, shall I be so happy to have you for a Neighbour[?] if so, we will live on the fatt of the land.[10]

While the prospect of statehood probably encouraged migration, a "truce" in Kentucky-Spanish relations may also have helped. Some credited James Wilkinson, who ingratiated himself with the Spaniards, with helping bring about the new cordiality, although newspapers gave no information about the events involved. Wilkinson appears as a hero in a letter extract in *The Kentucke Gazette* on 12 February 1788 and published in Virginia newspapers on 12 March. Dated at the Falls of the Ohio on 26 January 1788, the letter reported:

> Our friend General W——k——s——n has fitted out a small fleet, for a second expedition to New Orleans; it consists of 25 large boats, some of which carry 3 pounders, and all of them swivels, manned by 150 hands, brave and well armed, to fight their way down the Ohio and Mississippi into the gulph of Mexico.
> This is the first armada that ever floated on the Westtern waters—and, I assure you the sight of this little squadrun [*sic*], under the Kentucky

colours, opens a field of contemplation—what this country may expect from commerce at a future day.

The cargoes consist chiefly of tobacco, flour, and provisions of all kinds—some of which has been packed up in ware houses these three or four years past; and where it certainly would have remained, had not the General through his indefatigable entirprise [*sic*] and genius, opened the too long barricaded gates.

He has been very unjustly censured, by the inconsiderate part of mankind, for having monopolized the Spanish trade,—but the more expanded mind acknowledges, that to his penetrating genius, Kentucky stands indebted for having procured its citizens a market from which the jealousy of our neighbours excluded us these many years past.

Mr. B——n, our late negociator, and a Spanish gentleman, Son-in-law to the Governor of Louisiana, are to accompany the general on this commercial (or as some will have it a political) expedition. Our politicians seem silently contemplating the conduct of the Atlantic States and wait to hear the fate of Kentucke pronounced by your new Congress.[11]

Three weeks later, another newspaper item included a letter excerpt about the fifth Kentucky statehood convention. Dated 17 September 1787 and published on 3 April 1788, the letter noted that Kentuckians had resolved to void all Virginia laws on 31 December 1788, and that a convention would be elected with "full power and authority to frame . . . a fundamental Constitution of government" and to enforce the laws.[12]

Despite the apparent calm in Kentucky-Spanish relations and the firm resolve on statehood, all was not well. John Brown, representing the District of Kentucky in Congress, found that body lethargic. Lack of a quorum meant the session could not be called to order before spring of 1788.[13] Frustration over the inaction of Congress coupled with the navigation issue led to talk of Kentucky seceding to join Spain. In late spring 1788, the Virginia newspaper reported a letter extract from Philadelphia, dated 9 June, which said a man just arrived from Spain en route to Kentucky intended to buy thirteen thousand or fourteen thousand hogsheads of tobacco, as part of an agreement with the Spanish government, and deliver them to New Orleans. The letter writer said the man reported that Spain would grant Kentucky rights to navigate the Mississippi River "so soon as we shall have established a permanent government to form a treaty with them."[14]

Brown, finally able to present Kentucky's petition to Congress on 3 July 1788, found indifference. The sixth statehood convention members, meeting that month in Danville, received an unexpected blow that was sure to intensify secession talk. The members, who had met to draft a constitution for what they believed would soon be the new state, received news that Congress had tabled the statehood matter until after ratification of the new United States Constitution. The message endorsed statehood but said Congress "think it inadvisable to adopt any further measures for admitting the district of Kentucky, because that body was unwilling to act until proceedings could begin under the new federal constitution."[15]

Many Kentucky settlers felt betrayed and were outraged. They saw the statehood movement as being turned back to the beginning, and some believed working toward statehood was now hopeless. A little more than a month later, their impatience came through in a Virginia newspaper report that Kentucky was seeking to join Spain. The reporter of the news told of learning "through several channels" that Kentuckians had petitioned the Spanish King "for protection in the government of that country, as Congress, they say, will not, or cannot, afford them such accommodation as to them appears satisfactory." The report said Kentuckians expected that, by being part of Spain, they would enjoy "the free navigation of the Mississippi, which is the only and most likely means of establishing them as great and happy people."[16]

John Breckinridge became a leader in the navigation movement after moving to Kentucky.[17] In the meantime, his cousin John Brown, whose disgust at congressional indifference to Kentucky matters may have led him to consult Spanish Minister Diego de Garadoqui, became embroiled in the issue. The volatility of the situation led to rumors so rife that it remains difficult to sort out facts in the records, but some Kentucky dissenters called Brown's actions treasonous.[18]

Although letters do not indicate how closely John Breckinridge followed these activities, he surely knew of them—from newspapers, his cousin John Brown, travelers to and from Kentucky, and his brother Robert, who returned to Virginia in the summer of 1788 as a delegate to the constitutional convention.[19] James Breckinridge, who was studying philosophy at the College of William and Mary, sat in on the constitutional convention proceedings in Richmond. During the previous fall, he had repeatedly written to ask John's opinion of the new constitution, and on 25 January 1788, John finally responded that he was "for it and against it." He wrote, "I sufficiently despise the present and think the one proposed has some Fundamental Objections," but he said he was "so much a Friend to it" that if he could be satisfied "from the Mouths of some . . . who assisted in forming it, that no amendments could be expected from a second Convention," he would choose it over the old one. He could see nothing resulting from a delay except time for "the British or some other Nation to intrigue with some of the little States" and thus "be enabled hereafter to dissolve the Confederacy." Nearly all the states would meet before June, he wrote, and predicted, "this State will agree with the Majority."[20] On 13 June 1788, without mentioning his step-brother Robert, James wrote to John disapprovingly of the Kentucky delegates' attitudes and behavior at the convention:

> The Kentucky members (upon whom the fate of the constitution seems greatly to depend) are obstinately determined to continue the opinion which was impressed before they left their country: they think the adoption of the constitution would have a direct tendency to produce their eternal ruin and destruction; the powers of the federal court in calling them to a distant part of the world for the trial of their land claims; the obtaining the navigation of the river Mississippi they suppose would be rendered entirely impracticable by the constitution; which they think would occasion a combination of the northern states whose interest it would ever be to deny them the acquisition of that desirable an object; & many other imaginary dangers which are painted to them in the most alarming and terrifying colours by Mr. Henry, whose eloquence and oratory far exceed any conception; In such an assembly he must to be sure be better adapted too carry his point & lead the ignorant people astray than any other person upon earth; Madison, plain, ingenious, & elegant reasoning entirely thrown away and lost among such men. . . .

James said he would write more, but "M. Malloy who had heard more of the Debates" and "promised to . . . give every particular" to John, would be a better informant. Further, James added, he was in a "great hurry" and wished John would "find time to write."[21]

Also attending the convention, Archibald Stuart, an old college friend of John's, wrote to him on 19 June, "Yr. Brother Jas. has been here from College as well and he is a flaming federalist"[22] (James indeed became a Federalist while John became an anti-Federalist).[23] Stuart wrote that the convention outcome hung "suspended upon a Single Hare" and among twelve doubtful votes was Robert Breckinridge's. Ultimately, the Kentucky contingent gave the constitution the most opposition; Robert Breckinridge was one of only three of the fourteen-member Kentucky delegation to vote for it.[24]

Just how the statehood, navigation, and constitutional issues may have colored migrants' expectations of life in Kentucky is not clear. But the lure of the West intensified as the year wore on. In November the *Columbian Magazine* reported a list from Fort Harmar records showing that 850 boats, 600 wagons, 7,000 horses, 3,000 cows, 900 sheep, and 20,000 people had passed by between October 1786 and 15 September 1788; in December the magazine reported that "a gentleman who left Kentucky the 18th of September" said he met

"1004 people in one party, bound to Kentucky." Fort Harmar records show that 10,000 migrated via the Ohio River during 1788 alone.[25] Among those who made plans to follow was Samuel Meredith, John Breckinridge's brother-in-law.

Meredith wrote to John on 4 July 1788 of plans to go to Kentucky in August or September. At the same time, Betsy wrote that she would travel to Botetourt with her husband and stay with her mother until he returned from Kentucky.[26] The same July, John and Polly Breckinridge welcomed their second child, Joseph Cabell.[27] Perhaps contemplating the opportunities for his growing family, within a month after Samuel's letter, John announced plans to go to Kentucky.

From Charlottesville, Virginia, to James at Williamsburg on 17 August 1788, John wrote, "I have it in Contemplation, (Indeed firmly fixed on it) to become an Inhabitant one Day or other not far Distant of Kentucky." He said he would visit Kentucky for two months beginning 25 March 1789. "I am daily making my Business way[?] to that point and have, in the Conduct of my Affairs, a constant View to my future residence," he wrote. "A Violent Effort will be necessary to start me; but having the Consent of certain persons, whose Happiness is my greatest Object, I find myself determined." He asked if James knew of any good Kentucky land owned by nonresidents, speculating that such land would sell "on good terms." He would like to "view" such tracts during his visit.[28]

James responded ecstatically twelve days later from Williamsburg. After earnest, coaxing letters through 1784 while he was in Kentucky, and then seeming resignation to John's remaining in Virginia, James could not hide his delight about John's news. However, he cautioned that perhaps John should not move until the country was more settled and safe:

I cant [sic] but be agreeably astonished at your late determination to become a resident in the Kentucky country; I always knew you had a great propensity for it yourself but was apprehensive your own assent was all that could be had—I hope when you come to explore that country you will become more fixed and determined in your design. That being the country in which I at present design *burying my bones*, makes me the more anxious that you and some more of the family should move out; your going will no doubt be a means of taking others; I hope so at least. I wish you had mentioned to me what time you think there will be a probability of your moving out. I think you had better, should you be pleased with the country and make a purchase, defer moving out for two or three years until the country becomes better settled and less harassed by Indians; the settlements on the other side of the Ohio will soon become pretty formidable & will be able to repell the attacks. . . . I am anxious that you should make your purchase about beargrass; the Quality of the land is unexceptionable & its local situation must ever make it the most valuable and convenient. . . .

Describing several tracts John might wish to see, James added that he also planned to move in a year or two and would like to be John's neighbor.[29]

Although the Mississippi-navigation and statehood issues captured equal, and at times greater, attention of people interested in the West than Indian problems, the latter remained the running news story in Kentucky until after statehood. From the mid-1780s until 1791, most such news reported intermittent raids by small bands. And while John planned his trip, increased news of Indian hostilities came from north and south. The Cherokees had grown antagonistic toward the new state of Franklin (Tennessee). On 9 October 1788 the Virginia newspaper published congressional resolves intended to temper their threat:

Extracts from the JOURNAL of Congress, MONDAY September 1, 1788.

Resolved, That the secretary at war be, and he is hereby directed to have a sufficient number of the troops in the service of the United States in readiness to march from the Ohio to the protection of the Cherokees whenever Congress shall direct the same; and that he take measures for obtaining information of the best routes for troops to march from the Ohio to Chota, and for dispersing among all the white inhabitants settled upon or in the vicinity of the hunting grounds secured to the Cherokees by the treaty concluded between them and the United States, November 28, 1785, the proclamation of Congress of this date.

The document showed further resolves that copies be sent to Virginia and North Carolina governors, who were charged to see that "peace and harmony" be restored "between the citizens of the United States and the Cherokee" and to prevent "any further invations [sic] of their respective rights and possessions . . ." and that the states should cooperate if Congress sent troops to enforce the treaty provisions.[30]

While such attempts were made to placate the southern tribe, news came of northern Indian hostilities. A 16 October newspaper reported that "A letter from a gentleman at Muskingham, to his friend in Pittsburgh, dated September 11, says 'An express has just arrived here from the falls of the Ohio, with an account that Lieutenant Peters, with a party of 30 men, going down the river, had been attacked by the Indians, and . . . had 8 men killed, and 10 wounded.' "[31] Another, in a 4 December 1788 newspaper reported:

By a person who past through Winchester on Saturday last, from Kentucky, we are informed, that he with some others, coming down the Ohio, discovered something on the banks, which they supposed to be flour; on going on shore it prov'd to be heaps of feathers, and appeared to have been emptied from beds; upon further search, to their great surprise they found at a little distance, three fresh scalps, a plough, share &c. It being evident that the savages had lately perpetrated a murder on some unfortunate persons going down the river, and our informant with his companions, not being in a situation to stand a contest with the enemy, thought it most prudent to come off. No certain information could be obtained who the above devoted victims to savage barbarity were, but it was conjectured they belonged to a boat which had left Red-Stone about three weeks since[,] loaded with arms, &c. and was not afterwards heard of.[32]

Such news of Indian hostilities threatening the Kentucky country was continual, and Kentuckians' frustration at inabilities to deal with the threat and congressional inaction on statehood kept alive the specter of secession. Back in Kentucky by fall of 1788, John Brown offered a resolution at the seventh statehood convention meeting in November that the Kentucky district "separate from the State of Virginia and . . . be erected into an independent member of the Federal Union." The resolution was defeated, but separatists continued to clamor, and some, particularly James Wilkinson, continued to court Spain.[33]

Virginia newspapers, however, continued to emphasize Indian hostilities and occasional lighter news. No Virginia newspaper items gave glowing accounts of Kentucky land before the end of 1788, although other newspapers had. An item, labeled "ANECDOTE," published on 11 December 1788, satirized such accounts:

A GENTLEMAN, lately returning from the western country, who had been visiting the fertile banks of Muskingum, was asked by a friend . . . whether he really believed all those sublime things were true, which had been spoken concerning the goodness of that promised land; whether ten penny nailes did indeed sprout up from a crow-bar, after being planted *only* twenty-four hours; or whether the streams of Lethe and Castilla are branches of mighty rivers in that paradise of pleasure, and sipping the waters of the former, the adventurers *forgot* their old language, and tasting of the latter, have it prevailed with that of the classics? Why no! says the gentleman, I can't for my life see how upon earth they can be. But this I can assure you I can bear witness to, however it may fail of belief with some incredulous persons, that just before I left Muskingum, one day, being on horseback, having taken some pumpkin seed into my hand, at the door of a house, several of which I dropped, turning about to speak to a person then passing, so instantaneous was their growth—so surprisingly rapid their extension and spread, that before I turned back, the seed had taken root in the earth to such a degree, that I was dangerously encompassed about with enormous serpentine vines, which threatened keeping pace with my utmost exertion to escape being tied in, as I immediately clapped spurs to my horse, and with difficulty was disentangled.[34]

Although this item amused, most readers probably were more impressed with rumors in early 1789 of a British-Indian conspiracy. Those interested in the western country saw Kentucky as the most vulnerable territory. A 12 February 1789 newspaper reported that "the British government of the Bahamas has lately sent, and caused to be landed on a certain point in Georgia, a supply of powder, arms, and a few small field pieces, which stores have been delivered to the Creeks. . . ." The report again raised the specter of Kentucky secession, suggesting that the British and others were prepared to help in that effort: "From Kentucky we are informed also, that offers of a similar nature from Canada, have been made to the most influential characters of that country, should they think of asserting and declaring their independency without waiting for the consent of Congress. . . ."[35]

The Spanish issue intensified in Kentucky as John Breckinridge's departure date approached. News of his plans had spread, and people wrote asking him to conduct business for them in Kentucky.[36] Robert, who remained in Virginia after the constitutional convention, would guide John through the wilderness. On 6 March 1789, James wrote from his mother's Botetourt home to John that "Robert is now in Readiness for the Kentucky Journey & will expect you on the 25th inst." He added that he was trying "to have Preston fixed to go with you which I hope will be in my & his mothers power to effect—he is doing nothing here. . . ."[37] Robert also wrote that he awaited only John's arrival. "The rout by Kelleys" was the "most eligible" for their trip, he wrote, and asked John to bring copies of the debates of the constitution. Saying he expected to see John on the 25th, Robert repeated, " 'Tis for you I wait."[38]

While the Breckinridge men were enthusiastic about John's impending trip, the women mourned. Whether John's mother, mother-in-law, and wife had read news of Indian hostilities or not, they surely knew of them. Close friends had already died in Kentucky, and although the women seemed to have no comprehension of the geography, they knew well how perilous the journey was. John's mother-in-law wrote a letter on 23 March, which she sent with John to his mother as he departed. Her intent may well have been to induce Mrs. Breckinridge to dissuade John from the trip, for she emphasized that his own health and that of his children was bad, and that Polly was beside herself with grief about his going:

> i hope my Dear maddam you in joy perfect helth and that you are more a filosifier than to form Such dierfull apprehentions of the dainger of your Son's journey to Kaintuckey as we Have[,] for i declare to you i am very much distrest for fear he should be assaulted by the savages in the next instance[.] i fear he is in a bad State of helth and if he is exposed he has so Bad a cough now i dout he will Not get rid of it Soon[.] both of his dear children are poorly and his poor little wife never hears the mention of his Siting out but her eyes fill up brim full of tears[.] i tell Her i dont conceive any dainger but at the saim [time] i am trewly distresst[.] i wish you my dear friend would come Down and comfort all the mourners after your much Esteemd Son. . . .[39]

Indeed, none of the mourners suffered as much as Polly. Only nineteen or twenty, with two children under three to care for and facing two months of anxiety about John, she gave way to her fears in a letter to her mother-in-law:

> My D[r.] Madam,
>   I sit down tho very reluctantly to write by the bearer Of this letter. I thought for some time[,] indeed untill very Lately[,] that Mr. Breckinridge intended journey was all talk. But it has become a very serious matter with me[,] I assure you. Monday next is the appointed day for his departure and the Lord Only knows wheather I am ever to lay my eyes on him again. If I do not I am Convinc'd all my happiness will be done away at last. On this earth, the very thought is Insupportible, However[,] I put my Trust in that Supreme Being[,] the director of all things[;] his will Must be done[,] I know[,] and I hope he will arm me with patiens and Fortitude to bear with it all, I should be better satisfyed if he was Well but he is very far from being that, indeed[,] I thnk he is to blame To undertack So long a journey in the situation he is in, If he is Not better I hope my D[r.] Madam you will not let him go at least For some days. I think he has the worst caugh that I ever knew any Person to have, I am very happy to here the other day that Mr. Meredith is going to Kentucky and more so as she is very willing[.] I conceive a very triffling Idea of the distance[,] tho there must be a great Deal of Danger[,] and I know to my sorrow that Mr. B is very Ventersom.

Polly would go to her father's house but did not expect to stay until John's return. The house was small, she wrote, and usually filled with company. Further, her "sister Harrison" probably would be there to "lie in" [for the birth of her child]. She wrote that she would tire of being there and would get someone to stay with her at home. Needing comfort, she was perhaps hinting that her mother-in-law should come to keep her company during John's absence. She wrote, "I never Wanted to see any Person more in my life than yourself," but she doubted having the opportunity unless she "could prevail On you to come down with your son if please god he returns. . . ."[40]

Despite his wife's and mother-in-law's fears and the pleas that he might delay or abandon the trip, John set out for Kentucky as planned. Relatives sent letters after him almost immediately. And Polly, still finding it hard to forgive him for going, may have overplayed his children's illnesses during his absence. On 12 April 1789, she wrote to John in Kentucky:

My D[r.] Husband

Being informed by Mr. Allen that he sits out for Kentucky tomorrow I think it my duty to let you here from your Family. In a few days after you left me[,] added to my other Distress—which I thought Insuportable of it self—I had the misfortune to see our D[r.] Little Babes at the very point of death. Letticia Was out of senses 2 or 3 days, Mama and myself set up with Them several nights. I thought you could niver more lain your Eyes on eithere of them in this world, but I thank the Lord they Have both recovered—at least there fevers have left them[.] And I think they have mended very much in the cource of a Week, I was in hopes to of had the pleasure of receiving a letter From you before this time, It would give me more satisfaction To here from you than anything in this world[,] except your Return[,] and I know that is a happiness I cannot promise my Self at least for sometime. I am in hopes my D[r.] Husbund this will Find you safe in Kentucky and hope the god that carried You safe there will bring you back to Your little Family Who laments your absence more than you can conceive, I herd the Other day that Poor L. nevils was kild by the Indians pray my Dear Mr. Breckinridge be very caucious in comeing home[,] especially in Comeing through the Wilderness, As my whole happiness or Misery As to this life depends on your return[.] I would wish you to have a large Company, tell Mr. Meredith I herd from Winton [the Meredith home] a few days Ago[;] his family and his Fathers was well . . . the family joins me in love to you And your Daughter bids me tell D[r.] Papa howda. . . .[41]

John's father-in-law also wrote a short letter because, he explained, he had "Just time by Mr. John Allin to Informe" John that his family, especially his wife and children, were well. Also John's family "at home" was well, he wrote, according to "Jack who is now at my House, Excepting George who got byt by a Doge . . . and has a bad Leg." Cabell wrote, "We all Long for y[r.] Returne" and asked John to inquire about his Kentucky lands and greet James Hopkins and all his friends there.[42]

John's mother-in-law also wrote and recounted the family's health and other news. She did not fail to note, "[Y]our poor little Wife seems much distresst at times on account of the dainger She conceives you will be exposed to. . . ." Mrs. Cabell, who shared Polly's fears, seems to have believed "on the western waters" had literal meaning:

> i cant say But i have bin much a larmed on account of High winds we have had for if they ware as high When you ware on the water i am confident nothing But the mercies of that greate god whoes hand Ever Presides over us could have kept you from the bottom. Pray my dear Son be causious how you venter yourself Throw that Savage cuntry. . . .[43]

No letter came from John for weeks. During his absence, his family and relatives could read in newspapers about the Spanish controversy, which seemed to grow more heated in Kentucky as the spring progressed. On 19 March, a week before John set off for Kentucky, the Virginia newspaper reported glowing accounts of westerners' growing relationship with Spain. An extract of a letter "from a gentleman, in St. Augustine, East Florida, to his friend, in Alexandria" [Virginia], dated 12 January 1789, was very likely from a Kentuckian on a trip to East Florida. His interests clearly were in the West as he recounted the cordiality of Spaniards and the success of Alexander M'Gillivray in negotiating navigation rights to part of the Gulf of Mexico, and pointedly criticized the ineptitude of Congress in gaining such rights to the Mississippi River for Kentuckians:

> Our vessels are received with the greatest cordiality by the Spaniards. Governour Zespodez, pays the greatest Attention to every American, who comes properly recommended; and the friendly treatment our countrymen receive from the officers of the Irish brigade, stationed in this town, must lay every American under the greatest obligations, to those hospitable sons of Hibernia. Flour and all kinds of provisions from the United States find a good market here. The commerce in the above articles being entirely free. This indulgence we owe to the uncultivated state of this province, for St. Augustine, the garrisons on St. John's and St. Mary's, are the only inhabited parts of East Florida, and these are occupied by men of the military professions, who raise nothing except money, the whole of which is laid out in American produce. Since my arrival here I had the satisfaction of conversing with the famous Alexander M'Gillivray, whose name you have so often seen in our public prints—this interview has fully convinced me, that he really is the man, our papers sometimes represent him to be, and that his neighbours the Georgians, have much to fear from his penetrating genius and great address. The attention paid him by the Spaniards, seems to have something more than

common politeness in view—they tell me he holds a general's commission under the crown of Spain; this I have reason to believe, and I have seen him in the Spanish uniform at the Governour's table, and receive the military honours of the garrison. This is a policy for which they are not to blame, as M'Gillivray's connections, from his infancy up to this day, with the different Indian nations in the southern part of America, has established him the Supreme Legislator over their countries, The Spaniards but indifferently established in this quarter, and sensible of his power, dread his consequence. A new treaty has lately been established between them and M'Gillivray, as King of the Creek nation, by which it is stipulated, that the navigation of that part of the Gulf of Mexico, on which St. Mark (an old abandoned fort) is situated, shall be free for the vessels belonging to the said nation. Agreeable to this article, M'Gillivray in connection with some of the most respectable merchants, on the Island of Providence, has actually established ware-houses, at St. Mark, in West-Florida; from whence he carries on an extensive and most profitable trade with the Indians and even our white settlements on the western waters. Thus you see! An individual with no other than savage connections, has concluded a treaty of navigation, which the exertion and wisdom of Congress never yet could obtain.[44]

The writer's last sentence seems pointed: if an individual could make treaties for navigation, so could Kentuckians somehow obtain rights to use the Mississippi River.

Some Kentuckians, perhaps alarmed at the growing talk of secession, tried to tone down the likelihood of such a move—while still emphasizing their seriousness about the West's needs. A letter extract from Kentucky, dated 9 March 1789, appeared in Virginia newspapers several days after John Breckinridge set off on his journey west. The writer complained that a letter he had read from "some person in this country" must have been written by "a disappointed man" and should not be accepted as true:

He grossly misrepresented facts, and illiberally reflected on characters much more worthy than himself . . . for no such violent measures as he urges, were publicly avowed; what may be the future conduct of our people on the late act of separation, I know not, but I see a number who are willing to separate on constitutional terms, much displeased.

The writer added that "The Spaniards at the mouth of the Mississippi continue . . . friendly, and I really believe would like to detach us from the Union." He continued that Kentuckians always had ready sale of all tobacco and provisions (at New Orleans?), that about three hundred hogsheads of tobacco plus provisions had recently been sent to New Orleans, and much more would soon be ready to send. Further, a thirty-ton vessel, after passing through ice with much difficulty, had recently arrived safely at Louisville from New Orleans, "loaded with dry goods, grocery, and ironmongery." Although more moderate in tone than the letter from East Florida (above), the writer seized the opportunity to indirectly criticize Congress, noting, "thus you can see we have a sufficient outlet, if not obstructed by some wretched political system." Nor did he let slip the opportunity to directly criticize Virginia. Many Kentuckians, he wrote, believed the statehood question had "been unreasonably procrastinated by the state of Virginia, it being now upwards of four years since their first application, and that there are also some stipulations in the late act more rigorous than the first."[45]

While John traveled in the Kentucky country, the controversy was highly charged. One Virginia newspaper item reflected near gloating by Kentuckians about "uninterrupted" trade with Spain. The item, an excerpt of a Kentucky letter dated 2 March that appeared on 21 May, reported that several boats loaded with "a very considerable amount" of goods arrived from New Orleans and took away "large quantities of tobacco, beef, corn, &c." The writer predicted that trade would continue and grow, "which cannot fail proving of the most infinite mutual advantage."[46]

Still another Kentuckian worried about the impact of such news. Writing from Danville on 2 June 1789, while John still sojourned in Kentucky, he decried some accounts in newspapers, calling them calumnies leading people to believe Kentuckians in a state of anarchy and confusion. He assured readers that "nothing but an attempt to abridge us of the common rights of mankind would force us into measures as inimical to the Union" as joining Spain or England, or creating an independent government. But, he added, the last Virginia Act of Separation probably would be rejected by the July 1789 statehood convention because some thought it "too servile, and others [thought it] too vague."[47]

Mercifully for Polly Breckinridge, the Virginia newspapers published only one item about Indian hostilities during John's trip to Kentucky. On 2 April, one week after he departed, the newspaper reported an extract of a 9 March letter from Danville, Kentucky, that told of Indian raids despite the recent treaty concluded by Congress with the northern tribes:

> You are doubtless informed of a treaty having taken place between the Commissioners from Congress and several Northern tribes. . . . Notwithstanding we have experienced no good effects from it; they have made several incursions on our frontiers since the treaty, and stole a number of

horses; a few days past a party was followed by Col. Johnson, after a pursuit of above forty miles, overtook them, and killed one of the Indians, wounded several, and regained near thirty horses; by the dress, &c. they appeared to be some of those who were in friendship with the late settlers on the northeast side of the Ohio.

The Indians have committed several murders at the settlement on Cumberland lately, and the inhabitants there seem fearful of the hostile intention of the southern nations.

The same item reported election of John Brown as Kentucky district representative in Congress.[48]

John Breckinridge arrived safely in Kentucky on 15 April, twenty-one days after leaving his mother's Botetourt home. Six weeks after leaving his wife in Albemarle, he wrote to his mother on 7 May that his "Company got safely out the 15th of last Month, without finding any danger or much difficulty." He had been "in motion" since his arrival, he wrote, "feasting" on "the View of the north Side of Kentucky." He would not spend time giving his opinions, he said, since he had seen little of the country. But he had seen enough to know that "it fully comes up to . . . expectations." Good land would be hard to find, he explained, because—although it was cheap—money was scarce, he wrote. He reassured his mother that wherever he chose to buy property, his purchase would include two "situations," allowing one for her. He, "Mr. Preston" and "Mr. Meredith" were going to the Falls, he wrote, and would stay a fortnight before starting home. He had heard that a company would start for Virginia on 10 June, and he planned to join it. He enclosed a letter to Polly, saying he had not written earlier, as he had promised her, because he had no certain way of getting the letter to her; he hoped that either Preston or his mother would see that this letter reached her:

> I fear it will not get to her, till her patience is worn out. She comforted herself much on a promise I made her, that as soon as I got to Kentucky, I would enclose her a letter to you; and get the Favour of Preston to carry it down to her. I mentioned it to Preston, but as I got no positive answer, I expected it was inconvenient; and did not insist. Perhaps Preston may have some little desire to see his Sister and Col. Cabells Family, and would not think the Trouble great. If so, he would think the Journey agreeable, and would also lay me under particular obligations to him. You will mention it to him if you please, and if he cannot find it convenient to ride down, you will be pleased to give it a passage if you can. . . .[49]

No other letter was found from John to his family during his sojourn in Kentucky. Letters from Kentuckians to him while there show that he conducted much business during the trip.[50] A rumor circulated in Virginia that he had been killed by Indians, but he returned safely to Albemarle County in June, just after his daughter's third birthday.[51] Many friends and relatives soon wrote to him, expressing relief at his safe return, and some eagerly solicited his opinions of Kentucky.

While in Kentucky, John Breckinridge had ample opportunity to witness the commercial and social growth firsthand, and he could also have read the many advertisements in *The Kentucky Gazette*, which, from its first issue, revealed rapid growth. Although that newspaper did not begin publishing until after what some historians have termed the end of the frontier era in Kentucky (ca. 1784), study of it from its inception reveals a developing society. Numbers during the last half of 1787 suggest a transition stage from a crude face-to-face society to a larger, impersonal society. A published notice by Harry Innes and Horatio Turpin in 1787 reveals Kentuckians' economic struggles during the mid-1780s. Having been "authorized by General Washington" to buy Kentucky produce for shipment to foreign markets, these men warned that merchandise must be good and neat to make foreign merchants want more western products.[52] Such a move may have been designed to placate Kentuckians' dissatisfaction with federal inattention to their needs and to encourage continued settlement in the area.

Advertisements by commercial enterprises, trades, and professions were sparse in 1787 but show much growth in 1788 and 1789. If one uses the number of advertisements as a measure, the year John visited Kentucky (1789) represented an early peak in commercial expansion.

The 1787 advertisements almost exclusively concern Lexington, where the newspaper was published. It would take some time to attract advertisers from other parts of the Kentucky country.[53] The 1787 (August–December) advertisements fall into two categories: merchants announcing wares and tradespeople telling of their skills and businesses.

During the last half of 1787, seven businesses offered hardware, groceries, dry goods, and medicines; all were in Lexington, except for one in Danville. For example, a merchant announced on 8 September, "A FRESH CARGO Just opening for Sale in Lexington . . . a Compleat Assortment of DRY GOODS," and advertised coffee, tea, loaf sugar, raisins, Jamaica spirits, wine, and lime juice, "to dispose of very cheap for CASH." Two weeks later, another "assortment of linen and stuff" was opened. In addition to the above competitor's items, this merchant offered chocolate, muscovado sugar, pepper, allspice, nutmeg, ginger, indigo, coperas, rosin, rice, china and queens ware, glass tumblers, West India rum, writing paper, cotton cards, eight-penny nails, and a collection of unnamed goods. Robert Barr advertised the usual dry goods in the 15 December newspaper, plus a recent shipment of "Grocery and Dye Stuffs with . . . medicines." He listed twenty medicines and indicated more in stock.[54]

In addition to the six dry goods stores in Lexington and one in Danville, the 1787 advertisements showed several trades and at least two professions. Jacob Myers announced that he was building a paper mill, and Joseph Robinson had built a tanning yard "near Mr. Ruddels mill" at Bourbon.[55] One advertisement mentioned a Major Johnston's mill on Elkhorn, and another referred to John Litle as a wheelwright.[56] John Allison advertised as building spinning wheels, and Samuel Blair, who offered stills, copper, and tinware for sale, announced he also made and sold all kinds of men's and women's saddles.[57] Among professsions, names of three lawyers appeared in newspaper notices, and William Scott, a school teacher, asked debtors to pay him.[58] Mentions of "Bray's Tavern" in Lexington appeared, and, of course, there was a printer.[59]

Wagon loads of goods arrived in the Kentucky country twice a year—in summer and autumn—and advertisements clustered in the newspaper at those times. Many merchants announced either appointment of a Kentucky agent or store closings during their trips to Pittsburgh or Baltimore, to bring fresh cargoes. Some travelers or migrants also brought large quantities of goods to sell for equipment, livestock, or other necessities—or for sheer profit. For example, Baker Ewing announced in August 1787 the sale of "a Valuable assortment of merchandise"; Richard Woolfolk auctioned "A Large Quantity of Salt" in Danville in October; and P. Tardiveau announced in December the sale of a "large quantity of dry goods" in Danville in exchange for horned cattle, good horses, some stills (of between sixty- and eighty-gallon capacities), or black servants.[60]

Beginning in 1788, non-Lexingtonian advertisers appeared, as did appeals for especially skilled people and for professions. In addition to reflecting commercial growth, the advertisements show availability and dependability of supplies. By 1788 the number of dry goods merchants had expanded from seven to thirteen, eight of which had not advertised in 1787.[61] One advertised from Danville, twelve, from Lexington; and the usual one-time auctions or sales appeared. Anne Christian, widow of William Christian, offered "a large quantity of salt" for sale in Lincoln [County?], and Moses Moore and John Warren offered dry goods at public sale in Lexington and on Hickman [Creek?], respectively.[62]

Trades and professions also expanded, according to 1788 advertisements, and the many notices calling for skilled labor indicated a new

turn in growth. One called for a hatting apprentice; someone asked
for a person who knew how to run a sawmill; John Clark and Hugh
M'Ilvain asked for packhorses, teams, and wagons to bring salt from
Bullitt's Lick; Samuel McDowell sought an overseer [for his farm?];
and James Wilkinson sought a slave with blacksmith skills.[63] Another
kind of growth was also reflected in advertisements by professionals
and people offering businesses for sale or rent. In May and October,
two teachers advertised their skills and sought jobs. In March Henry
Marshall advertised a tavern opened in Lexington, and Rawleigh
Chinn announced in August a private entertainment house opened
near Lexington. Also in August, Benjamin Frye sought to sell salt
works in Nelson County, and John Caldwell announced a saw and
grist mill to rent. In September James Everet offered two stills for
sale, and in December Jessee Peak announced that he was giving up
his Lexington tavern business.[64]

The year that John Breckinridge visited Kentucky brought added
merchants, trades and professions, and he must have taken note of
the array, which might alleviate his wife's fears of moving to the
wilderness. Fifteen merchants advertised dry goods during 1789 (ten
in Lexington, two in Danville, and two on Hickman Creek; and one
had stores in both Lexington and Danville).[65] Of the fifteen, seven
had not advertised before 1789. In 1789, for the first time, a merchant
emphasized books for sale.[66] Further, more competition appeared in
trades and professions. The newspaper mentioned at least two dance
teachers, four taverns,[67] two clock and watch makers,[68] and two
private entertainment houses.[69] Previously unmentioned trades included a coppersmith, tailor, baker, hat maker, and post rider; and
John Nancarrow advertised his beer brewery at Scott's Landing on the
Kentucky River.[70] Among skilled laborers sought were a blacksmith's
apprentice, a tanner, a currying apprentice, boatmen (to accompany
cargoes to New Orleans), builders, distillers, a miller, and an overseer.[71] Others advertised equipment for sale—masonry tools, a still,
and ironmongery.[72]

Newspaper content also reflected an increasingly diversified, more
complex society. The 1787 issues gave much attention to statehood,
and extant 1788 issues carry nineteen lengthy items about separation
and convention proceedings. After 1788 the statehood issue received
relatively less attention as columns carried more news from abroad,
information about the Virginia Assembly and United States Congress,
and other newspapers' items. In addition, poetry, anecdotes, and
essays on numerous topics appeared frequently; and the newspaper
advertised horse races and horses for stud purposes.[73] Extant issues

for 1789 show only five items about statehood convention proceedings.

Observing the commercial development, John must have considered the kind of life his children might have if transplanted over the mountains. Social institutions were expanding sufficiently to provide for childrens' education and religious instruction. A subscription library had begun in Lexington in 1785,[74] and Transylvania Seminary had been incorporated in 1780.[75] Kentucky newspaper items John might have seen in 1789 concerned education, religious establishments, town bodies, county divisions, and plans for new settlements. There were also announcements of committees, boards of trustees, and letting of contracts for public buildings such as jails and meeting houses; and there was a reference to the *new* court house in Lexington.[76] Committees devised town ordinances, planned for a factory, and took actions on other issues. A dancing assembly was also announced.[77]

John could also observe communications facilities in Kentucky. The newspaper was expanded in 1789, and the editor established a post rider to deliver the newspaper and mail in Kentucky.[78] Newspaper items also referred to roads and ferries and indicated that some people were bringing vehicles other than boats and wagons into the Kentucky country.[79] An important road for eastward travel, besides the wilderness road, had been developed before 1787,[80] and other frequently mentioned Kentucky roads included those from Lexington to Bardstown, Curd's Ferry, and Danville. Lexington by 1790 was the converging point for nine roads, all of which were probably there for John to see in 1789;[81] one advertiser in 1789, announcing a ferry on the Kentucky River, said that roads led from there to Harrodsburg, Bardstown, and Louisville.[82]

John Breckinridge probably hoped what he had observed would allay Polly's fears about venturing into the wilderness. The future state afforded opportunities for young children to grow up with basic needs met. Merchants, tradespeople, and professionals offered almost everything one would need to feel "comfortably fixed" in the Kentucky country. In any event, John had much to think about on the long road home in the summer of 1789.

6
Preparing to Move over the Mountains

Although John Breckinridge had not decided on a moving date, he purchased land while in Kentucky and hired an overseer to look after it. After he returned home, his brother-in-law, Samuel Meredith, Jr., who had accompanied him on the trip, prepared to move to Kentucky and to assist in looking after the family's interest there until John could move. While in Kentucky, he probably learned much about the statehood and Mississippi-navigation issues as well as Indian hostilities, factors that still had bearing on living in the Kentucky country despite the advancing commercial and social development. John's brother Robert was significantly involved in Kentucky politics and probably filled him in on all sides of the controversies dividing Kentuckians. Virtually nothing in the family papers, however, indicates his own attitudes or positions on the issues. Surely, he supported statehood and must have believed the navigation issue and Indian problems would be resolved. Perhaps John decided to delay moving until those issues were more settled, or perhaps he needed considerable time to put his Virginia affairs in order. In any event, plans set in motion while in Kentucky notwithstanding, there seemed to be no urgency to his intentions when he returned home in June 1789.

Indian hostilities continued to be important news from Kentucky. The only new angle to such news reflected a better-organized opposition by western settlers and federal troops (after westerners secured federal military help). After the army began a concerted drive against the Indians in 1791, news of military expeditions and battles dominated the newspapers during 1791 and 1792.

The eighth statehood convention, meeting in Danville in July 1789 after John had returned home, went about its business calmly. The members resolved to ask the Virginia assembly to make the third Act of Separation conform with previous ones. Delegates were charged with establishing precincts and preparing censuses in their respective counties. These actions completed, the members adjourned to await arrival of the amended Act of Separation from Richmond.[1]

While they waited, new conflicts, compounded by increased Indian hostilities, erupted between Kentuckians and Spaniards. Newspapers did not report the source of the new Spanish controversy, but a near-cryptic item published on 8 October 1789 said that Kentuckians had "associated, that they will not after the first of February next, make use of any Foreign luxuries, unless in . . . sickness."[2]

Beginning in July 1789, shortly after John's return home, newspapers reported Indian murders of travelers on the wilderness road and the Ohio River. The first item appeared on 9 July, and another, a week later, told of the murder of two boys who had gone fishing. "They were killed by the savages," the report asserted. "One was shot through the heart, the other slightly wounded in the arm—both were tomahawked in the most shocking manner, scalped, and striped naked." An August newspaper contained two such items. One, based on a letter from Louisville, told of Indian hostilities dominating conversations there. A "very respectable woman" had been murdered "and mangled in the most barbarous manner; and a negro girl and two white children taken prisoners." The report also noted that "Judge Simm's settlement is in the greatest apprehension," that six soldiers guarding the settlement had been wounded, and another soldier and two surveyors had been killed. The other item reported that two men and three boys had been attacked while fishing; the men were killed and the boys taken prisoners. The same item reported other murders and thefts of horses by Indians.[3]

A federal soldier stationed at Louisville wrote to Philadelphia friends in September 1789 that the situation was gloomy. He and fifty-five men had just returned from "Post Vincennes, on the Wabash," he wrote, adding, "believe me Sir, it is almost next to an accident, that the whole of my party was not cut off, the river was lined with Indians." He continued, "The Indians are daily committing depredations in Kentuckey, and from the Miamis we learn, that the troops there would be unsafe to go 200 yards from their post."[4]

Similar items during the remainder of 1789 told of murders by small bands of Indian raiders. These instances of Indian hostilities were not so ominous as news in earlier years when full-scale war often seemed imminent, but the news alarmed John Breckinridge, and he advised his brother-in-law to postpone his move to Kentucky for a year.

By January 1790, some letters indicate Samuel Meredith's intentions to migrate in the spring, while other letters reveal John's efforts to detain him. After a visit to the Merediths, John reported in a letter to his mother on 5 January 1790 that "Sam & Betsy were willing to postpone their January to Kentucky for one Year longer; and the old lady [Samuel's mother?] cordially joined them." But, John wrote, "Col. Meredith [Samuel's father] seemed desirous they should set out in the Spring."[5]

Betsy, who was not happy about moving so soon, wrote to her mother a few days later about their plans. Samuel was determined to go that spring, and her father-in-law and husband had firm plans, she wrote, although she hoped something would prevent such an early departure. Seeming to pout about the proposed move and to take her frustrations out on her mother and siblings, Betsy wrote that she might as well move since her family never visited her in Virginia, anyway:

> My Dear Mother
> Yours I received by my Brother John, and was very sorry to here you are so uneasy about my going to Kentuckey next spring, Mr. Meredith is at present determin'd to go in the spring but I am in hopes something will happin to prevent our going so soon[.] Mrs. Meredith is very unwilling we should go in the spring, I hope when Mr. Meredith considers that our going to Kentucky would be the menes of makeing you and Mrs. Meredith so unhappy that he will put it of [sic] a little while longer.
> I am very much disapoin'ed that you did not come down in the spring[;] if I do not go to Kentucky when you return to Botetourt[,] I will go up with you[.] My Brother James Stay here has been so short that I would rather he had not Call'd to see me[.] I don't Know what should make me so desers [desirous] to stay in this country when my relations come so seldom to see me and stay so short a time when they do come. . . . I have four pounds of pick'd cotton for you that I intend to send you by George[,] but he can't carry it all so will send it up by the first opportunity. . . .
> P.S. I would be glad you would have my beds ready for feare we should go to Kentuckey[.] I would be obliged to you for as much flax as will make a little webb if you can spare it.[6]

On the same occasion, Betsy's father-in-law wrote to Mrs. Breckinridge with great enthusiasm about Samuel's planned move. The older Meredith clearly wanted to prevent any near-departure meeting between mother and daughter. Knowing Betsy's unhappiness about the move, he may have feared her mother could dissuade her from going. Or perhaps he simply wanted to spare both the pain of farewells at departure time. "Our Children set out early in the spring for Kentucky, & as they are to take water at redstone it will not be convenient for them to come through Botetourt," he wrote, and asked Mrs. Breckinrdige to plan to visit them "a Month or two before the young people leave us." Meredith also asked Mrs. Breckinridge to send "Any Necessary that you think proper to furnish towards setting the young folks to house keeping" to "the care of Capt. King at Linchburg from whence they can be easily got here."[7]

Plans for the move continued apace, and six weeks later, Betsy, still unhappy, wrote her mother that the move seemed certain:

> When I wrote to you last I was in hopes that something would happin to prevent our going to Kentucky[,] but it is now reduced to a certainty that We shall go[.] Whe are to set out from this place the first of April. Mrs. Meredith was very averse to our going till very lately[,] but now she is very willing whe should go. Col. Meredith also is very desirous whe should go this spring. I have not the smallest hopes whe shall stay longer than the first of April, every person seems anxious for us to go that I have not the least desire to stay[,] only on your account[;] living [*sic*] you is my greatest objection to going to Kentucky. . . . I want very much to goe up to Botetourt before whe set off[,] but I cant get any person to go with me. Mr. Meredith is so busy preparing for the Jurney that it is out of his power to go with me . . . I must trouble you to fix up my beds as well as you can and pack up what little thing[s] I have in my two hair trunks[.] I would be glad you would put my glass in one of the trunks[;] any Little thing you can spare me towards hous keeping will be very acceptable.
>
> I would be glad when you get my things fix'd you would send them to lynches ferry by the middle of March. . . .[8]

Presumably unaffected by Meredith's earlier letter discouraging a meeting between her and Betsy, Mrs. Breckinridge seems to have resolved to prevent or delay the move. James Breckinridge, in a letter to John dated 20 February 1790, wrote, "My Mother is well torn uneasy about Betsey's moving to Kentucky this April." And in an 18 March letter to John, James wrote, "My mother starts in a few moments for Amhurst to endeavour to detain her daughter a little longer in this country—she will be much hurried & I expect will not have time to go the Length of your house."[9] As determined as she was, Mrs. Brekinridge was unsuccessful in overcoming the will of the Meredith men.

The Meredith men's interest in moving so soon may have been heightened by a turn in Kentucky statehood events. The Virginia Assembly acted on the eighth statehood convention's memorial in December 1789—in accordance with Kentuckians' wishes. A ninth convention would meet in Danville in July 1790 to determine the expediency of separation. Congress was to give consent no later than 1 November 1791, and the separation was to be set after that time. Furthermore, a Kentucky constitutional convention was to meet prior to the actual separation.[10] With statehood more certain in the very near future, the Breckinridge family's concerns must have eased considerably.

Although letters don't clarify why, Mrs. Breckinridge became re-signed to the Merediths' move and probably sent the trunk and other items that Betsy requested. But she remained concerned about her son-in-law's prospects in Kentucky and wrote to John on 2 April 1790, asking him to provide for Samuel's independence in Kentucky by "impowering" him to an equal share of the 4,453 acres Alexander was to locate for her:

> Dear Johnny
> I and Col. Meredith have concluded that it will be best for to place young Mr. Meredith in independent circumstances as soon as possable, therefore I wish you will impower Mr. Meredith to an equal divident of 4453 acres of land[,] it being a Treasury Warr^t· Which Alex. Breckinridge was to locate for me & to be equally divided between Betsey Meredith & her Brother Preston, If the whole of the land is not yet obtained[,] let young Mr. Meredith . . . have such a title given him as will intitle him to an equal part with Preston Breckinridge so that it may be in his Power to make what use he may think proper with his part.[11]

John argued persuasively for a postponement of the move—as indicated in a letter from Samuel on 13 April (quoted below)—and the couple did not depart on the date planned. A week later, the Merediths still had not departed. Letters at the time do not indicate what caused the delay, but it was probably because Betsy was pregnant. A November 1790 letter reported the birth of her child,[12] and, if a normal term, Betsy was two months into the pregnancy by mid-April. Mrs. Breckinridge may have learned this on her March visit to the Merediths and then visited John to implore him to convince Samuel to delay the trip and, failing that, to find a doctor to travel with the couple. According to James's earlier letter to John, Mrs. Breckinridge did not expect to see John on the way to the Merediths, but she saw him sometime between 18 March and mid-April. Samuel's 13 April letter mentions a letter from John that Mrs. Breckinridge delivered and also mentions Dr. "Root," whose arrival Samuel was awaiting (a February 1791 letter from "Dr. [Philip] Rootes" refers to fifty acres John gave him "last March";[13] this very likely was payment for attending Betsy during the trip). The delayed departure probably occurred because Mrs. Breckinridge insisted that Betsy not travel without a doctor, and finding one willing to migrate took time. Although Samuel makes no reference to the pregnancy or Betsy's health, his chagrin at delaying the trip is clear:

I thank you, for your kind Letter by Mrs. Breckinridge & your reasons there assign[d.] for postponing the journey to Kentucky, for sometime [I have] very considerable wait with me—although a Number of reasons concur to induce me to go (my situation is very disagreeable) without a Home[,] a good deal in debt[,] & no prospects of raising any Money, until I can get a place of my own. If I am to judge from what has taken place since I was marri[d.] I feel myself rather in [a] dependant [*sic*] state—My Wife being averse to going Makes me feel very sensible—If you have any Letters for Kentucky or any business that I can do for you in that Country be pleased to inform me by Doc[tr.] Root and it shall be attended to chearfully. I expect to set out the [twenty-] fifth of this month. . . .[14]

The Merediths set off finally on the appointed date. Samuel's father's machinations to prevent a departure meeting between Betsy and her mother failed entirely. Up to this time, there is no evidence that Mrs. Breckinridge had seriously considered migrating. But perhaps deciding to move had been the only way she could reconcile herself to Betsy's moving. As she bade the young couple a tearful farewell, according to a letter from Betsy to John, she promised to join Betsy in Kentucky the following spring:

I have Just parted with my poor Dear Mother in great dell of distress about my going to Kentucky[;] indeed I have never met with any thing in my life that give me so much uneaseness as parting with my Mother, her laste request to me wase to wright to you not to sell the land you bought from Col. Meredith till she saw you, as She intend to get it of you if you would part with and go to Kentucky next spring. I am very sorry I shant have the pleasur of seeing you before I go to Kentuckey[,] but I hope it wonte be longe before I shall see you in Kentuckey, it is the only thing that reconcils going to that Country to me is the prospect of haveing you and my Mother for neighbors. I suppose there never wase a person whent to that Country with more reluctance than [*sic*] I shall do[;] god only knows how whe shall get thare though[;] I am afraid very badly from the manner whe seem to be fixt.[15]

Betsy's preoccupation with how they were "fixed" for travel and settling in Kentucky probably reflects pain at leaving an aging mother and insecurity about the long, tedious, uncertain trip to the "western woods"—from which she had always heard tragic reports. But her pregnancy also must have caused concern about travel comfort. Neither the expected child nor Betsy's daughter, Jane, who was approximately two and a half, is mentioned in letters about the trip. Betsy's youngest brother, Preston, accompanied the Merediths to Kentucky, possibly to assist them until the child's birth.[16]

Another unstated concern probably was fear of encountering hostile

Indians during passage. Perhaps this was viewed as so much a part of life that no one saw need to write of it, although everyone surely discussed it. It is unlikely that anyone took the risks for granted when news reports brought constant reminders of them. A letter fragment in *The Kentucky Gazette* just before the Merediths' departure epitomizes the pathos of tragedies that were all too common. A youth captured on the Ohio River by Indians, who chained him to a tree before plundering his boat, managed to write a letter to his sweetheart and toss it into a boat to be found later. John Boyd of Limestone sent the letter to printer John Bradford with a note saying, "it was found on Tuesday last in an evacuated boat, and by accident fell into my hands." The letter's beginning and end were "so much defaced," he wrote, "that I could not read it." But he wanted to insure that "him, to whom it is addressed, through the channel of your paper may be apprized of the unhappy situation of his friend. . . ." The legible parts of the letter said, in part:

> to be thus cruelly treated—thus detained from the arms of my dear Fanny, is too much for my slender philosophy to support. The Indians are now packing up a part of their plunder, in order I suppose, to send to their towns, or their camps up the Scioto. —Around the saplin to which I am chained (they used some chains which I had on board, & ingeniously, and effectively confine me with the help of two pad-locks, without binding my hands) a part of my merchandize is scattered, and a small bundle of pencils presenting themselves to my view gave me the hint of writing to you—I have determined to conceal it, and when the Indians release me (which I think they will do, when they finish packing) I intend to throw it on board one of the boats and cut her adrift; some person may find it who will forward it to you. In the hope and expectation that you will receive it, and that an expedition will be carried forward against these daring pirates, I shall offer my advice.

The writer added suggestions on how to pursue the Indians. "They have a train of spies on each bank of the river," he wrote, "which extend as far down as Limestone, so that it is impossible to steal a march on them, by following the meanders of the Ohio."[17]

The letter writer and his fate are unknown—nor is it known whether his beloved Fanny received the message he so ingeniously left. But the letter must have been sobering to those who read it. Since it was not published in Virginia newspapers, Betsy Meredith probably did not see it. But her brothers in Kentucky probably did and thought about their sister if they knew the Merediths were en route.

John Breckinridge knew the Indian threat during the Merediths' trip must be taken seriously. A letter from Robert at the time suggests that John regarded his brothers' proximity to the Indians as foolhardy. Even as the Merediths traveled, Robert wrote from Beargrass on 6 June of serious losses to Indians. "I suppose you will laugh at me again," he wrote to John, "if I tell you they [Indians] have Scalped within 4 or 5 miles of this place, & I think myself safe & out of danger while here." He continued, "It is a fact that they attack'd Isaac Hite's Ploughmen in the Corn field the other day, killed a white man & wounded one of his Negroes mortally who is since dead, & took off three of his Horses." He explained, however, that Congress planned to send an expedition against the Indians in the fall.[18]

News of the intended fall expedition was small comfort to John while his sister traveled that spring. But Robert's letter and others during the same period brought many other matters to occupy him while he awaited news of the Merediths' trip. In addition, there is reference to John having been exhausted, and he may have suffered an illness during this period. His duties on the court circuit meant long and frequent absences from home, and he apparently always stopped for a visit with his mother when the circuit took him anywhere near her home. His absences, however, tried his wife's patience, as a January 1790 letter from Polly to her mother-in-law indicates:

My Dr Madam

    Mr. Breckinridge got home safe after a very disagreeable ride on fryday last where he found his little family in grat distress on his account[.] when he left me he Sayed he should return in 9 days[,] but he was gone 3 weeks[.] my Dr Madam, a very happy knew year and a great many of them and that each one may be happier than the last. I was very much disappointed at not seeing you with your Son[.] I flaterd my self with the pleasing hopes that it was your Coming that detaind him[;] as to the thread[,] it macks know odds for james[.] Says he gets his stocking wove, I am very much oblidge to you for your kind and many presents[.] James tels me he intens down In June—.] I hope[,] if you cant come down before[,] you will come down with him. . . .[19]

Despite any indisposition John may have suffered, legal and family matters—in addition to his own work load and concern for getting his Kentucky land ready for occupancy—put excessive demands on him during early 1790. On 8 April 1790, some two weeks before the Merediths departed for Kentucky, John wrote to his Kentucky overseer, William Russell, giving directions regarding his land.

After explaining that at the end of March, while he was in Goochland, he had an opportunity to send Russell a letter informing him of purchasing "600 acres of Col. Meredith's Land" and "Payne's Land," he said he now had another opportunity to send a letter by "Mr. Carrington." Most of his letter concerned the Payne purchase, particularly the possibility for a redivision of it. John explained that after his conversations with Russell about the Payne land in Kentucky and again in Washington, he had asked "Parson Todd" about a division of it. But Todd wanted to keep the "North End" and told him "the land was legally divided by his nephews Robert & Levi Todd, and Jno. Floyd." John asked Russell to ascertain from the Todd nephews if this were true, how the division was made, and "whether they considered the Land as divided by *Quantity* or *Quality*." He instructed Russell to look at the land and tell him whether a redivision would be to his advantage. He also asked Russell to "fix several Tenants at two or three places" on it and, if Russell thought the "South End equally valuable," to put "two or three Tenants" at "judiciously chosen" places so that a "Division Line" could "not possibly affect them." John added that he would gratefully pay for surveys or anything else required to accomplish this. He still wanted a settlement made on land he bought from "Col. Meredith"—particularly at a spot he had shown Russell, he wrote, and said he had "ment^d. that Subject fully" in his previous letter. He wanted tenants on both tracts by "this Fall at farthest."

John assured Russell that his "stay in this Country will be much shortened" if he could "soon get his lands improved . . . & made to look a little less like a Wilderness." He said he could not yet fix a moving date but had it "daily in Contemplation, and adapt my Plans accordingly." John concluded the letter, "I hope you are, or will be elected for Fayette and that I shall have the pleasure of seeing you in that Country," adding, "We have no news;—I cannot even rake up a newspaper at this Place."[20]

In addition to trying to direct this Kentucky overseer from Virginia, John was occupied with a flurry of legal matters during early 1790. Caleb Worley wrote from Fayette County, Kentucky, on 30 April, complaining of not having heard from John since he left Kentucky the previous summer and laying out serious problems with which he wished legal help. Stressing his own financial distress and how much he missed John since his father's death, Worley wrote:

> My D^r. Friend[,]
> I never felt the affects of it so sensable but my Fathers Death—I wrote you a letter by Mr. Green informing you to pay him 60 lbs.—but he went no further than Col. Skillun where he was informed there was no Money

come to hand—was likewise informed there was but 200 lbs. coming which must be altogether a mistake.

Giving an account of payments made, he added, "The Estate is much in Debt and without a relief shortly from Wilson[,] we shall be much distressed—My Dr. friend I hope you will do every thing that layes in your power towards forwarding the money as our all depends on it. . . ." Concerning certain land surveys on behalf of John, he wrote, "Have been out twice to Survey the Entry you put in my hands & [illegible] appointed it lyes near Col. Garrards some settlements [illegible] on it[,] but your claim is Pryor to any of them. Shall survey it shortly[;] the People I find is much disatisfyed—it is fine land."[21]

At the same time Caleb Wallace, of Woodford County, Kentucky, also wrote to John about the Worley estate, asking that he inform the family as soon as possible when the money might be available. Estate debts, he added, would "greatly distress the Family unless the money due from Wilson can be recovered" that year. Wallace pleaded for information about John's moving plans, asking whether his "affections for Kentucky are increasing with time or decaying by absence."[22]

About the time John received these letters, his brother Robert also wrote of legal land matters in Kentucky:

> Some time last spring on Execution, Jno. Breckinridge vs. Isaac Robinson, came inclosed in a letter to me from Archibald Woods, who informed me Robinson had left that part of the Country & was destined for this— He has not arrived here, but from the information received, which I have been particular in making, is at the mouth of the Great Kenaway & proposes being in this Country soon.—I think the Execution in its present form will answer your expectations—it is dated the 15th of Oct[r.] 1789 returnable on the Second Tuesday, in January following[.] You are fully acquainted with the impracticability of making a return from this Country in so short a time—Can't you procure one with the return day blank— blank County &c? Whatever you may adjudge necessary to be done in that business, direct me & I will endeavour to have it put in Execution.

> I think you asked me when here to ascertain in what situation your 2000 acre Survey on the waters of Floyds fork stood as to interfering Claims— the business is not compleated yet—A survey of 7000 acres in the name of Nath[l.] Saunders runs off about one half of yours, which I have laid down precisely, but think it unnecessary to send that alone, particularly as I have not examined the foundation of Saunders Claim, I mean with respect to its being Surveyed in its proper place—Before a clear judgment can be formed of your prospects in that quarter all the interfering Claims should be laid down together with those on which they depend & accompanied

with Copies of their Locations—For these reasons I have declined sending you what I have done—As far as I have been able to form an opinion of Saunders Claim[,] it is improperly Surveyed, but the entry is of an earlier date than yours. I intended to have compleated the business last Spring but the Indians incurtions [*sic*] prevented me.[23]

Before receiving Robert's letter, John probably received Patrick Henry's letter (quoted below), dated a week later, raising other legal matters involving Kentucky land. John had recently argued a case in court against Henry—an event that caused considerable comment. In a letter to John, dated 20 February 1790, James offered his help and chided him for refusing to take a fee for a case argued against Henry, hinting that this might prove embarrassing:

> Hearing that you were to be employed against a criminal who is to be tried for murder at an ensuing district Court, I have thought proper to enclose a copy of the disposition taken at the examining court. It will enable you to prepare for the trial. You will be opposed by Mr. Henry— But it has been reported that you refused to take a fee against him; if that be the case[,] the old Gen. may laugh at any opposition he will meet with from a mountain pettyfogger; and unless you will be so good as to take a glance over the paper, and furnish me with a little assistance[,] it is a doubt . . . whither I will make my appearance on that day.[24]

Others found John's position as adversary to Patrick Henry remarkable and teased about it. Archibald Stuart, in a letter four months later, wrote, "I heard you have acquired immortal Honor in Green Brier & that even Henry was eclipsed"; and J. Preston wrote on 4 July 1790 that John was being perceived as the only match for Henry in court. Preston, who wrote of a legal matter, said he feared that "Henry may be brought in by opponents,"—and requested John—if he should hear that was to be the case—to serve as the opposing attorney.[25]

Henry's June letter to John, however, did not refer to their celebrated adversarial encounter in court. Rather, Henry sought John's help in settling his sister's estate. Upon his return from the trial, Henry had received news that his sister Anne, whose husband, William Christian, was killed in Kentucky in 1786, had died and that John was a witness to her will. From Prince Edward County on 13 June 1790, Henry wrote, entreating John to appear for proving the will at the next court session:

> Dear Sir
>   The News of my dear Sisters Death met me when I got home from Green Bryar. And I am really sorry to find myself obliged to make a Request to you which I know you can't comply with, but at the Expence

of ye ease[?] of which you must stand in great need— You are a Witness to her Will. The Situation of her Children, her Servants & other Estate is such as makes it indispensably necessary to prove her Will next Prince Edward Court. I do earnestly beg therefore that you will be so good as attend there & then to prove it.

Was it possible for me to have this necessary business done without troubling you, believe me it would give me pleasure—For after all the Fatigue you've suffered to take such a Ride, I know it is tiresome. I trust to y^r. good Nature to execute this Trouble, & that the Necessity under which her Family at present lays will plead with you for your attendance. [26]

Among still other legal matters pressing upon John, a 19 June 1790 note from merchant Gordon Croeces in "Warmister" said, "shall procure Answers to the Injunctions against next Buckg^m. Court."[27] And another letter from Caleb Worley, dated 21 June 1790, called another urgent legal matter to John's attention. Worley in Fayette County, Kentucky, again complained of never having received "one line from you Since you left Kentucky [a year ago]" and said he was "veary antious My D^r. friend to hear from you—as we will Shortly be much distressed by two Suits in the Supreme Court to the Amt. of 100 lbs." He wrote that a judge would be "obtained this present Court—& Mr D^r. friend do everything that lays in your power in giting the Money as quick as possable as we are left Fatherless and in much distress." Worley said he would go to Virginia as soon as John had got the money and begged him to write "by every opportunity." John could send letters to the printing office in Lexington, he added.[28]

While legal matters demanded attention, John also had immediate preoccupations. His oldest child turned four, his second child turned two during the summer of 1790, and he and Polly were expecting a third child.[29] Further, later letters indicate that John was much concerned about James, who, apparently having left the College of William and Mary, was engaged in what both brothers viewed as a dead-end job with the court system. In addition, John was concerned about his sister's safe travel to Kentucky and anxiously waited to hear from Betsy and Samuel. By mid-June, the Merediths had not arrived in Kentucky, although they had been en route for two months. According to a later letter from Samuel (quoted below), they completed the first part of the trip by 20 June, at which point Betsy wrote home to give news of their travel, but that letter is not among the family papers.

On 29 June 1790, John's Kentucky overseer, Russell, replied to John's April letter that he was happy to find John still planned to move to Kentucky and added, "I have settled on your five-hundred tract (purchased of Meredith) Seven familye's which hath agree'd to clear out One hundred acres. . . ." He had also placed two or three other families toward the center of the tract, which he planned "as a seat" for John. Writing that he had no "politicks at present worthy your particular observation," Russell confined himself to "what I think the most pleasing to you, when concluding you wish to become a Citizen of Kentucky." He sent the letter with "Mr. J. Russell" as far as Staunton, Virginia, and the letter was forwarded from there to John by Peter Hershell[30] (John responded on 8 October 1790—hence the complete exchange of communication from John to Russell, back to John, and again to Russell took six months).[31]

At last, on 6 July 1790, Samuel and Betsy Meredith arrived at Elkhorn, Kentucky; a week later, they wrote to assure Virginia relatives of their safety. Samuel referred to their passage as "speedy," although it took more than two months. On 15 July 1790, from his new home "about 7 miles from Lexington on N. Elkhorn," Samuel wrote to Mrs. Breckinridge:

Dear Madam
    I have the satisfaction to inform you by Mr. Hambelton of our safe arrival; in this Country which is the first opportunity that has offer'd. since we got home—I will now give you a short detail; of our Journey.
    Betsey wrote you from Kelleys by Mr. Watkins giving an acct. of our Journey at that place which I am in hopes came safe to hand— We got to Kelleys on the twentieth in the evening and Left it finally on the twenty-first with a favourable flood and reach'd. point pleasant (a most delightful situation) early on the twenty-eighth[,] remain'd. there the Latter part of that day[,] the twenty-ninth in the morning discover'd. a boat coming down the River[.] [T]hey were from redstone & confirm'd. the report of the scarcity of provisions in that quarter— We found the Ohio River very full & set out in Company with the Redstone Boat about [mss. torn] reach'd. Limestone the thirtieth [torn] nine oc. at Night[,] and arriv'd. at this fertile place on the sixth Instant[.] Certainly[,] no travellers were ever blessed with so speedy and Lucky a Journey from the best accts. that can be collect'd. from rational people together with my own experience. The fall is the most favourable season for people from your parts to remove to our parts on many accts. The roads are in better order[,] provision plentier[,] a Larger Number of people on the way (of course choice of Company Which is a great Matter). The Water Courses are more certain to be [illegible] and destitute of ye storms that frequently happen in the spring and summer months & compell people to go ashore— I flatter myself[,] Dear Madam[,] when you reflect, that I have brought my family to this Country without sustaining any loss or incountering any danger by the way at an unfavorable season of the year & my family uncommonly helpless that you will yet reconcile it to yourself to come out and live with us. If I am not

mistaken[,] you inform^{d.} your Daughter that after she arriv^{d.} at home[,] if she would let you Know that she Lik^{d.} this Western [torn] here & you thought your self able [torn] take the Journey[,] you wou^{d.} come [torn] this fertile Land. —Now if she has inform^{d.} you in her Letter of her Love and fondness for the place and you [torn] a mind & will certainly remove, if I can have previous notice of y^{r.} intention, My Joy unitted with gratitude will compell me to hasten to Botetourt & wait on you hither as I am now acquainted with ye art of travelling both by Land & water makes me conceive I cou^{d.} be an useful Escort. Consider the pleasure it wou^{d.} afford your Daughter[,] your removal to this Country. I am satisfied that if you were near here to see the Corn which is now [illegible] thirteen to sixteen feet in hight and not done growing that you wou^{d.} not be willing to give this tract of Land for farms such as Winton[,] My Father's place. I must refer you to Betsey's letter for information about our Crop and stock as the gentleman who is the Barrer of this Waits—There is an expedition on foot this fall. The greater part of the Militia are order^{d.} to hold themselves in readyness. I expect to go as those who come last in the Country are generally put in the divisions that stand first[?] for service.[32]

While the Merediths settled into their new surroundings—and even before the Virginia relatives received letters about their arrival— the ninth Kentucky statehood convention met at Danville on 26 July. With Judge George Muter as president, the convention members voted as one body to accept Virginia's last Act of Separation and set 1 June 1792 as the beginning of statehood. They set December 1791 court days for election of delegates for the tenth—and final—statehood convention, which they scheduled to meet in April 1792.[33]

Samuel Meredith was probably too busy with his crops to become involved in the convention and statehood matters. Virginia relatives, more concerned about the Merediths than about Kentucky politics at the time, welcomed and passed around news of their safe arrival. James sent the news almost immediately from Botetourt to John on 18 August 1790, adding, "Betsey is much pleased with the country and the neighborhood," and "They have a fine crop . . . 30 acres of corn & 10 of tobacco."

James himself was unhappy. Bogged down and apparently physically drained by work in which he saw no future, he had received advice from John to pursue a different career. And, in connection with that, perhaps John had been trying to persuade him to join in the move to Kentucky. Writing from his mother's home in Botetourt, James sent the letter by William:

Dear Johny
    Your letter by Mr. Preston came safe to hand & I should have answered

it long since but never had an opp[y.] before the one which now presents itself. Your anxiety and concern for my future success in life fills me with gratitude and were it not for certain reasons, I would at once abandon that laborious practice in which I am now employed and betake myself to that system of study and practice which you have so forcibly urged. I well know my own deficiency both in knowledge legal & oratorical and that unless I curtail my practice and allot more time to close study and application, to expect to arrive at any degree of eminence whither at the bar or in the public councils of my country would be the height of folly. You cannot, I am sure, be a stranger to the reasons which induced me to embark on in so laborious a practice. It was not of choice, but of necessity; You know too the difficulties I have been obliged to encounter; that what little knowledge I possess was bought not only with personal drudgery but with the price of my health & constitution. The practice therefore in which I am now engaged is not followed with an expectation of arriving at eminence[,] but to get rid of these difficulties in which I am encircled[,] with the completion of which I am resolved to abandon the most of my courts and closely follow that advice which you have laid down.[34]

John's precise advice is not clear, but it appears he had encouraged James to become a lawyer. James had not talked of moving to Kentucky for some time, although he had earlier vowed to "bury his bones" there. Perhaps his work had anchored him in Virginia; and perhaps news of his sister and brother-in-law's good fortune in Kentucky only compounded his unhappiness about his own difficulties. James's pessimism about his future contrasted sharply with Samuel Meredith's optimism about his.

While the Meredith's plowed, planted, and harvested during 1790, they may have had little opportunity to explore their new surroundings. Kentuckians had rapidly developed businesses, roads, professions, schools, churches, towns, and new settlements, although *The Kentucky Gazette* advertisements suggest that growth may have slowed somewhat in 1790. During the year, four merchants advertised for the first time, and another, who had never advertised, reported a burglary of his store.[35]

Nine tradespeople also advertised for the first time. Samuel Ayers was a silversmith and jeweller; Thomas Simpson was a gunsmith; and Edward West, Jr., asked for an apprentice to the "Gun and Silver Smith's business."[36] "Craig and Logan" advertised their fulling business; John Hamilton advertised as a rope maker; and Jacob Todhunter advertised plans to build a tan yard "near Mr. John Parker's mill about 6 miles from Lexington."[37] John Smith and Andrew Steiger were butchers, and Philip Rootes (the doctor who accompanied the Merediths to Kentucky and had opened his practice soon after arrival) announced that he practiced "physic."[38] On 14 June 1790, a page-two item mentioned "Kiser's Tavern," and in December Thomas Young announced that he would keep the *Pennsylvania Packet* on file for people to read at his tavern.[39]

Five items during 1790 concerned education, one person advertised subscriptions for the *Encyclopaedia Britannica,* and there were references to the "new" road—an alternative to the wilderness route.[40] As the country increasingly assumed the character of a settled state and prepared for statehood, the first census was conducted in 1790.[41]

Although Kentuckians had settled on their future as part of the union, the Spanish issue had not disappeared. News accounts during the fall of 1790 reveal a belligerence by westerners regarding use of the Mississippi River. In part, the hostility may have developed because Spaniards, seeing Kentucky join the union, turned surly over prospects of trade. A 29 September newspaper item about attempts of English ships to enter a New Orleans port suggests a hardened Spanish attitude:

From the North Carolina Chronicle of the 30th ult. Extract of a letter from a gentleman in Nashville, dated July 28.

A company arrived here a few days ago, by land, from the Natchez, who gave the following account: That an English frigate came up the Mississippi, opposite to New-Orleans, and sent her boat ashore for permission to land, which was refused by the Spanish Commandant; upon which the frigate dropt down two leagues, and cast anchor at a point, fired three[?] guns, and hung out her colours: The troops in the garrison were kept all that night under arms; next morning the frigate fired several guns, at equal spaces of time between each, like signals, keeping her colours flying. Before two o'clock the same day, another armed frigate of 40 guns, came up with the other, cast anchor, hoisted English colours, and fired their guns. A general confusion prevailed through the whole country, all the works were ordered to be manned as soon as possible, the militia called in, and every thing announced, the expectation of an attack on the capital of Louisiana. In the evening the two frigates dropt down and next day disappeared—when this company left the Natchez no communications had transpired from the court of Madrid, except a report prevailing, that a high military commission had arrived at New-Orleans, from Madrid, for General Wilkinson, of Kentucky.[42]

The meaning of the commission for General Wilkinson—or whether, in fact, the commission existed—is not clear. In any event, no easing of relations with Spain was apparent. A 6 October news item reported Kentuckians' determination to use the Mississippi River by force, if necessary. The item, an excerpt from a Kentuckian's letter to a Philadelphia friend (dated 4 August 1790), reported:

> The Gentlemen I mentioned to you in my last, are now forming themselves into a Company, for the purpose of building Three Vessels of Force, mounting from 24 to 40 Twenty-four Pounders, completely manned and equipped; they propose to load the same with Tobacco, Flour, &c. and proceed to Sea by the Gulph of Mexico, with a full Determination to punish, severely, every Insult which in Violation of Treaties, may be offered to the American Flag, sailed down the Mississippi. It is generally supposed they will embark between 12 and 2500 men, in order to assert America's undoubted Right to the Navigation of the Mississippi.[43]

Just a month later, a Virginia newspaper item, suggesting Spaniards disguised as Indians were warring on Kentuckians, reported that an American vessel had been "seized at New Orleans, and her cargo disposed of by the Spaniards." The account related, "Also, that the troops which went out against the Indians had, not far from the banks of the Ohio, fallen in with about 40 of them, whom they made prisoners of after a slight resistance. And that, having washed them, 13 turned out to be white men."[44]

While the navigation issue continued, Kentuckians' attention became increasingly diverted by the Indian wars, which dominated news for the next two years. The first such item, on 1 December 1790, came from a Kentuckian's letter written over a three-day period in early November 1790 to a member of the Virginia Assembly:

> I have waited with expectations of giving you some certain account of our troops, but nothing certain—many improbable conjectures fill the minds of people. —A hand-bill just come to bourbon, contains an extract of a letter from Governor St. Clair, to Gen[l.] Wilkinson, which informs, that our army met with little or no opposition. The Miami villages were abandoned; from thence a detachment was sent up the St. Joseph's river, which fell in with a party of Indians, and had a severe engagement. Gen[l.] Harmar made a shew of retreating, and marched about eight miles, from which he detached a strong party to the field of action, in hopes of finding the Indians on the ground—as they expected, so they found them, and an action commenced, the 22d of October— The action was obstinate, and many fell on both sides. . . . The army is now at Licking, and is expected home hourly. Major Jones may, before he leaves the district (who will give you this letter) collect the whole truth f the matter.[45]

During the late summer and fall of 1790, the Virginia Breckinridges could have read of supreme court actions in Kentucky; could have observed as well the notice of a petition for establishing a warehouse, inspection, and ferry on Green River, advertisements for maps, and Richard Terrell's announcement that he would "undertake business as Attorney in . . . Kentucky." Terrell added that letters could be sent to him "after the rising of the Assembly, through Col. John Overton, Louisa; Col. Charles Dabney, Hanover; Hardin Burnley, Esq., Orange; John Minor, Esq., Fredericksburg; or Mr. Nathaniel Anderson, Richmond."[46]

John Breckinridge had reason to be preoccupied with more personal events during the fall, however. In October or November, his third child, Mary Hopkins, was born,[47] and, according to a letter from his mother, John had a siege of illness during the fall. Mrs. Breckinridge wrote on 6 December, "I am very happy to heare that you eare so fare Recoverd as to tack a Journey to Richmond[,] but I am afraid you have ventered out too soon and will relapse again." She continued:

> I cannot find words to Express the Uneasy situation My mind was in when I hard that you ware Staying very Sick at Amherst Court House, and was not abell to Leve that Place for some Days[.] I would have gon down at that time but theare was not One Hors on the Place that I could rid but Pady and he Was so poor. that I could not think of riding him Such a Long Journey Least he would have given out.

Writing that she had received news from John by "Jammey Preston," she lamented that she was all alone and deplored the distances among her family members. Her loneliness increased her determination to move to Kentucky, for perhaps the family could be closer there, she wrote:

> It is a very Great misfortune to me that I am at such a distance frome you and your Deare family and my Deare Betsy['s] Littell family is at distances for us bouth that we never can be neare each other Except we move to Kentuckey. . . .
> I promise myself the Pleasure of Paying you a Visit sometime this winter or spring, if I get any Persons that will keep the House for me untill I return for I am Really [illegible] Living so Lonsom as I doe at present but hope it will not allways be the Casse without one of my Children with me. . . .

Mrs. Breckinridge wrote with even more resolve about moving, noting that if her "D$^{r.}$ Preston Return Safe home and Likes the Country[,] I am very willing to move as Soon as we Can sell and fix for the Journey." She hoped John and his family would move with her because she said she could not "think of Leeving you in this Country. . . ."[48]

Preston Breckinridge began his trip home from Kentucky in December and brought news to Mrs. Breckinridge of Betsy and a new granddaughter and namesake. Taking advantage of Preston's return to send letters to Virginia, Samuel Meredith wrote to John Breckinridge on 30 November 1790, "We are furnished with another fine girl which we intend calling Letitia after her grandmother." The child's exact birth date is not given, but Meredith reported that "Mr. Robert Breckinridge payd us a visit a few weeks past . . ."—possibly a visit to see his new niece. Samuel, noting that he had received John's 8 October letter, reported general news and promised to assist Russell with John's Kentucky affairs.[49]

James Breckinridge, in the meantime, was preparing for marriage. Although no prior mention of the event occurs in letters, he married Nancy Seldon of Richmond on 1 January 1791, and he talked of moving to Kentucky in the near future.[50] He and others increasingly urged John to move, too. Letter writers from Kentucky hoped he would move in the coming spring, although John had apparently decided to wait until the spring of 1792. Dr. Philip Rootes wrote to John on 22 February 1791, dwelling on his observations of the new homeland and offering his own encouragement:

> I am sincerely glad to be informed of y[r.] final resolution to come to this Hemisphere next year; for want of political News, will substitute a brief detail of domestick matters, we enjoy at present a good state of health, & live in perfect harmony[,] tranquility & felicity, ye Earth is very fertile & female Animals of every sort are very prolifick, its frequent for Ewes to yean 3 Lambs at a time & Women & Cows to have Twins at a time. Yearling Beares weigh 320 Wt. nett; pork from 12 to 18 months old upon a just average weigh from 150 wt. to 240 nett, as I never was raised in a part of ye World famous for Cheese & Butter, it's not in my power to give an Acct; only from report, I have been told that some Families[,] besides making an ample Sufficiency for one year['s] allowance, have disposed of as much of the Superplus as amounted to 20 lbs. Specie, ye Complexion of ye Earth & ye inhabitants will avouch for my Assertions, & y[r.] own ocular demonstration at y[r.] arrival will evince [*sic*] you, & all of y[r.] attendants, that it is a Country replete with all the blessings that this World affords. We have all different Sects of Religion among us[,] ye Baptists are ye most numerous of any— Lexington[,] ye metropolis of this Western Country, is a beautiful inland Town situated in a very healthy place, & far surpasses & excells any of Ye Towns of the same Magnitude upon ye navigable Rivers of Virginia, its Inhabitants are liberal in Sentiments & hospitable to Strangers; a part of them have ye Muses, & some Graces,

each of them flourish as much here, in my Conception & opinion as in Philadelphia or any other Metropolis. . . .[51]

Another Kentuckian, Caleb Wallace, wrote to John from "Locust Grove" on the same date, soliciting his early removal and describing living conditions in Kentucky:

I have received your friendly letter of the 16th of December last; and am happy to find that you speak so much in earnest about removing to Kentucky. It is said that those who have entered into the marriage State; however unhappy it has proved to them, are ever Solicitous to induce others to make the experiment. I hope to live to give you and Mrs. Breckinridge a hearty invitation to eat your first Christmas dinner in my cabin; and with a little industry (which you know I am fond of inculcating) I can promise that you will by the Christmas following have plenty of *corn*[,] *pork* and *pumpkins* to enable you to return the compliment. As money is scarce in this quarter, I cannot say with so much certainty how you will fare as an attorney; but I think I can promise you an extensive practice, if you chuse it. In addition to the considerations of friendship, I have also mercinary reasons for being pleased with the prospect of your coming to this country,—I mean patriotic reasons. We expect a new Government, and wish to have your assistance in turning the weels [*sic*]; and besides the pleasures of public utility; I hope you will aspire to the honour of being a Kentucky Statesman or legislator; or when you are weary of standing at the bar; what do you think of a Seat in the judiciary? —Not to take a circuit over the barren hills of old Virginia, but the fruitful plains of this new world. You will no doubt confess that truely these are Splendid objects of ambition. Well[,] come along as soon as you can get ready and give me an opportunity *in censpecter*[?] to rally you further on these topics.[52]

A few weeks later, John received another letter from Samuel Meredith, who again noted receiving John's 8th October letter, to which he said he replied via Preston Breckinridge. He said he had also sent a letter to John by Caleb Callaway in November, but, he added, "As I find my friends['] letters from the Settlement Miscarry[,] I expect mine share the same fate." He had seen John's recent letter to "Col. Ward" and there learned John had "fixd. Certainly fall 92 or Spring 93" as a moving date. Samuel looked forward to John's arrival in Kentucky, he said, because the company "woud. Contribute greatly to reconcile Betsey to the Country." Then, not wishing to alarm John that Betsy was unhappy, he hastily added, "which she is much plead. with and only Lack[s] her friends to make it perfectly agreeable." He wrote that by John's arrival, his tenants would have "opend. a Large quantity of ground," and asked John to tell Polly that "if she coud. but get a Sight of your tract . . . (at the Season that is Just approaching) she wou^d· not content herself in Albemarle afterward." He continued:

the Comparison between y^r· Lands here & those in Albemarle wou^d· be somewhat like one of your old Fields in the Settlement cover^d· with broomsedge compar^d· to the best improv^d· Spot on James River bottom— To borrow Lewis Craig['s] phrase in Comparing the Kingdom of Heaven[,] he says it is a Mere Kentuckey of a place. . . . My wife writes to Mrs. Breckinridge[;] to her Letter I must refer you for the Domestick News of the family.

Shortly after receiving Meredith's letter, John received a letter from William Russell informing him about his Kentucky affairs. Russell had received John's October letter from Mr. Woolfolk, he said, and, at last, a man who had brought "Mr. William Merediths Negroes to this Country" would carry back a letter for him. Russell reported that he had settled enough tenants on John's six-hundred-acre tract to clear seventy or eighty acres, plus three tenants on the site he had chosen for John's home. The tenants would clear thirty acres there and put three in Meadow." Further, he had settled three tenants on "the south End" to clear 30 acres. He wrote, "I have a great deal to say . . . but find my old piece of Paper will run short & cant raise no other bit nearer than Town. . . ." He would write later, by the first opportunity, he promised. Still, he found space to add:

Our country populates very fast . . . we find our County amounts to nearly twenty thousand souls, every part of our frontier settels very fast and a great number have enter^d· into the Spirit of building and other manufactory's, tho' not so much as I would wish for. The range in this neighbrhood seems to decline very fast.[54]

As March 1791 approached, John's sister and brther-in-law in Kentucky had heard no word from Virginia relatives since the previous October. And they hungered for news. On 1 March 1791 Betsy Meredith wrote to her mother, complaining that she had never heard a word since Preston left and didn't even know if he arrived home. She said she had received a letter from James, who said he would move to Kentucky in "two years at fardest." She had expected him to visit Kentucky "this spring" but had heard of his January marriage and expected, "if that is true," it would be a long time before she would see him. She concluded the letter with family news, asked to be remembered to James and Preston, and asked her mother to send her some garden seed. She reported that her children had the "hooping" cough, that Letitia "grows very fast" and was "very big for her age."[55]

The letters among Breckinridge family members during this period seldom referred to Indian hostilities, although the latter was a prominent subject in Virginia and Kentucky newspapers. By the spring of 1791, General St. Clair was pursuing treaty negotiations with the northern Indians, and an April newspaper reported two battles between his army and the Indians. Another April newspaper announced a Congressional act "for raising and adding another REGIMENT to the MILITARY ESTABLISHMENT of the United States, and for making further Provision for the PROTECTION of the FRONTIERS."[56] A 25 May newspaper reported the growing seriousness of the Indian wars. Labeled "Intelligence from the West," the item related that "A Gentleman just from Kentucky informs us, that Gen. Scott was about to march against the Indians," and "We also hear, that an army will march from Pittsburgh and Muskingum about the same time; a considerable part of which has been inlisted in the back counties of this state." The item reported, "The Indians show a greater disposition for hostility this summer, than for several years past."[57]

As summer approached, further news seemed to confirm the writer's prediction. A 8 June newspaper published an excerpt from a Louisville man's letter, dated 13 April 1791:

I wrote to you from Fort Pitt, which place we left the 3d instant, in company with two other boats, and proceeded to Limestone, without meeting or apprehending danger— At that place we were informed of several disasters which had befallen boats going down the river, and one boat going up to a French station, loaded with corn, buter, &c.— The particulars relative to the latter are as follows— The boat was attacked by about 60 or 70 Indians, and the flankers that were on shore as a guard were fired on by them —immediately after firing, they gave the Indian hoop, and, rushing on the Flankers, scalped them every one (about 25[?]) —they then fired at the boat, but did no damage, as it required some time to make their way into the river. After the savages had executed this terrible act of barbarity, they continued to the river watching for other boats. In the course of about six days five or six boats happened down the river—the savages attacked the foremost of them, in which were two young ladies, of the name of Macdonald, a young gentleman, and some others, passengers, and took it; elevated with this only capture, they imagined themselves capable of taking every boat they might fall in with. In a little time a second boat hove in sight, which they attacked with great fury— they were in three canoes, each canoe containing about twenty—they moved towards the boat, as it came down, and commenced firing; after discharging their guns, they retreated, loaded and came on a second time, fired and returned as before—this mode of fighting they repeated nine different times; as often as they came on, there was a brisk firing kept up from the boat, which contained nine fighting men; —during the conflict two were killed, and five wounded; two only remained to protect the boat, and prevent the Indians from boarding it, which every appearance of their conduct plainly indicated—these two brave fellows exerted themselves in a peculiar manner—on a near approach of the enemy, they threw billets of wood at them, and one of them took up an ax, a weapon of defense, should they persist in boarding, which the Indians perceiving, and, as if supposed, their ammunition being expended, they retreated without accomplishing their object. These inhuman monsters, previous to their attacking the last-mentioned boats, placed the two young ladies in the front of their canoes, in which situation they were both killed. A few days after this transaction, they fired at another boat, and killed one young man—in short, every boat that has gone down the river lately, has been fired at except ours; we saw no Indians; the places where the above depredations happened, we passed in the night.

A paragraph appended to this account announced that "Gen. Scott, with 1500 chosen militia had marched for Fort Washington. . . ."[58]

Another item, in a 29 June newspaper, recounted more of the same. Excerpted from a Kentuckian's letter, dated 12 May in Bourbon County, the item reported that Indians had killed "Mr. Wade and Mr. Reynolds near Morgan's station" and "a considerable number along the Ohio." The account continued:

About the first of April[,] 300 of us proceeded up that river [Ohio], ten miles above the Scioto, and expected to find two hundred Indians . . . but . . . discovered they had returned towards their town;—we followed about 20 miles, but . . . returned to our homes. After burying nineteen persons, all men except three, whose flesh was mostly cut off their bones, we also found three Indians, supposed to have been killed in attempting to board a boat, in which there were seven out of nine men killed and wounded—five of the wounded are since dead.

I have since followed another small party, who stole some horses, but was too late— Capt. Keating, from Limestone, discovered where they had crossed the Ohio, way-layed them, and killed five of that party. Two others have been killed near the mouth of Kentucky. The Indians have been generally troublesome this spring, but our frontiers are so extensive that no part is much distressed through fear of them.

I suppose you have heard we are preparing for another tour to their towns—this party is to consist of 750 horse men, under command of Gen. Scott, who carry with them 30 days provisions, and meet at the mouth of Licking on the 15th instant.

We have not yet attempted to form settlements on the military Lands between Cumberland and Green Rivers—the officers having failed in sending Powers of Attorney—which, together with the continual depredations of the savages, are powerful obstacles. . . .[59]

July newspapers reported General Scott's expedition against Indians on the Wabash River; September brought news that General Wilkinson, in his expedition against the Indians, had "taken 32 prisoners, one of whom a boy, the rest squaws; burnt two towns on the Wabash, and destroyed 400 acres of corn"; and December newspapers carried letters from General St. Clair regarding his expedition against Indians on the Miami River.[60]

Other news during 1791 reported that the British refused to give up their western posts until the United States paid debts due English merchants, and that cross-posts (western postal routes) were being established to Staunton, Virginia, and "towards the Seat of the South Western Government." Richmond printer Augustine Davis, who announced the western postal route, noted that "It is presumed that if the undertaker should extend as far as Main Holston, that letters from the Western Government on Cumberland, and from Kentucky would be greatly profitable." The trips would be weekly.[61]

Although letters rarely refer to it, a severe drought during the summer of 1791 forced many people to sell off livestock because grazing lands dried up. A September news item noted that "almost every day, large droves of cattle from the back parts of Virginia and the Carolinas" were "crossing the Potowmack," destined for Philadelphia. The item continued that "there are thousands coming through the Wilderness from Kentucky," and the reason "for this extraordinary number . . . going to market this year is the great drought, which . . . has been general over the continent this season."[62]

Other reports gave Kentucky court news, and William Randolph—about to move to Kentucky—announced the sale of his entire Virginia property, including furniture.[63] The navigation issue also resurfaced, and an 8 June newspaper report forecast war between Spain and America over navigation of the Mississippi River. Reprinted from a 15 March, London, England, newspaper, the account said in part:

> A war between the Americans and Spaniards is not at all impossible, however injurious it must prove to both countries, especially to the infant States.
>
> Late accounts from the Mississippi positively mention the Spaniards having erected a fort at Walnut Hills and garrisoned it with a considerable number of troops, and they are determined to oppose the settlement intended to be made there by Col. Holder, and a number of Kentuckians, under the auspices of the Gorgians.

Because of the erection of the Spanish fort, the report continued, "many Kentuckians were embodying, and intended marching down to dispossess them of so valuable a situation; and, that this being the case, it was the general opinion, that a war must inevitably be the consequence."[64]

Whether the Breckinridges took the Spanish threat seriously, they surely were discouraged by the Indian news that dominated during 1791, most of which they probably received before seeing it in the newspapers. Such news could not but increase Polly Breckinridge's reluctance about the impending move.

7
Moving, at Last, over the Mountains

The spring of 1791 marked two years since John Breckinridge's visit to Kentucky and more than a decade since he first fixed his attention on the West. Until the spring of 1793, he was absorbed first with assisting his mother move in the fall of 1792 and then with his own final preparations. In 1792 in the spring, he sent slaves ahead and decided on his moving route; in the summer, he made a farewell visit to his childhood home and announced the spring of 1793 as the moving date; and by the end of the year, he had sold his Virginia property.

The finality of each such step distressed Polly. Throughout her marriage she had lived with John's interest in Kentucky. Perhaps he had hoped that in time she would accept the idea of moving. But, regardless what he told her of Kentucky, Polly still envisioned a wilderness and seems to have brooded about the move. In May 1791, when the move was still two years away, she wrote to her mother-in-law for comfort:

> I have nothing new or entertaining to rite you Unless I should begin the subjec of Kentucky[;] that is not Knew[,] but I imagine it would be plesing, however[,] as I expect You down with Mr. Breckinridge[,] I shall refer the particulars Until then. In fact I would be willing to put it off to a much longer Period than I fear I Shall, that is the going part, for I have Almost Got out of the Notion of going and, believe I shall, I know I Shall git quit out of the thoughts if you dont come Down soon.[1]

John moved ahead with plans. On 13 August 1791 he wrote to James of plans to visit him "next summer . . . and spend the last summer with you, we shall ever do in our native Country."[2] The Merediths and Robert and Alexander in Kentucky still expected him in the spring of 1792. An October letter from Alexander in Danville asked John for a specific moving date.[3]

In late 1791 Preston Breckinridge again visited Kentucky and took news from home to his sister. Preston may have made this trip to ready his own Kentucky plot to settle on, for he had—quite unexpectedly—married a few months before. Without prior notice, on 13 February 1791, Preston wrote to his mother to say that he had married Betsy Trigg:

> I . . . saw that she was much distressed & as I sincerely loved her I made free to ask her what might be the cause . . . & she let me know that she detested the man whom her relatives were forcing her to marry & as I loved her affectionately I thought it a good time to let her know it, but to come to the point we were married last Thursday.

Noting that he had to have some means of providing for his wife, he asked his mother when they could come to live with her.[4] Possibly, it was the mother's idea that he look to Kentucky for a home. In any event, Betsy was overjoyed to see him and hear news from home. In November she wrote to her mother that Preston told her he planned to move to Kentucky as soon as he could sell the Virginia property his father left him. Betsy wrote she was glad her mother liked Preston's new wife and told news of Mrs. Breckinridge's acquaintances in Kentucky. She assured her mother that the "things you sent me came safe" and said she was sending her mother "some Callico for a short gown and a cap & handkerchief." Preston would fill her in on other news when he returned, Betsy concluded.[5]

By the time Preston returned to Virginia, rumors were circulating that Fort Jefferson (near Louisville) had fallen to the Indians. But a newspaper reported on 4 January 1792, "There is the highest probability that the reports [were] unfounded," continuing: "It is most probable that Gen. Scott, with the Kentucky militia, may repair to the said post, and bring off the wounded left there, and as it appears too far advanced to be supported, the garrison may probably be withdrawn." The item also reported on General St. Clair's expedition against the Indians.[6]

Amid the intensified battles with Indians, George Washington directed that an explanation of their causes be circulated. On 15 February 1792, Virginia newspapers carried a lengthy account, prefaced by Washington's letter [apparently to Secretary of War John Knox] giving reasons for publishing it. Titled "The Causes of the existing Hostilities between the UNITED STATES, and certain TRIBES of INDIANS North west of the Ohio, stated and explained from official and authentic Documents, and published in obedience to the orders of the President of the United States," the report reviewed efforts to secure peace and was clearly intended to demonstrate that the government had had no choice but to war against the Indians.

Knox began by asserting that examination of congressional journals regarding the early stages of the Indian war would persuade the public to preserve peace and not to "engage in a contest in which they were in no wise interested." Partial treaties in 1775 and 1776 had been too weak to overcome "a combination of circumstances," and several Indian nations had armed against the United States, murdered many, and took many others into captivity. Although such activities were unprovoked, the United States, instead of "indulging resentments against the Indian nations" after the Revolution, sought to establish peace with them. A treaty was concluded in 1784 with the Six Nations, and in 1785 with the Wynadots, Delawares, Ottawas, and Chippewas; still others were concluded with the Cherokees, Choctaws, and Chickasaws; and in 1786 a treaty was concluded with the Shawnee. Soon, however, Knox explained, "certain turbulent and malignant characters" among the northern and western tribes complained about the treaties, and in 1787 Congress directed a treaty to hear and satisfy the complaints and settle all issues regarding trade and boundaries between the United States and the Indian nations. In 1788 Congress appropriated funds to pay Indians for claims on land they had already ceded, and treaties that year with the Six Nations—except the Mohawks—effected the purchase of that land.

These treaties, Knox explained, had not been questioned and did not appear to be the cause of the current war. Rather, "banditti, formed of Shawnese & outcast Cherokees" seemed the sole cause, and he thought it important to explain their conduct. The Miami Indians did not attend the treaties in 1784 and 1785, he said; indeed, messengers attempting to deliver invitations to them in 1785, 1787, and 1788 were badly treated. Wyandot and Delaware chiefs, who implored the Miamis to participate in the treaties were insulted and turned away.

In the meantime, frontier settlers suffered from Indian depredations and, finding no relief coming from the government, had taken matters into their own hands. The government, in one more effort to gain peace, sent an emissary to all tribes on the Wabash River and in the Miami village. Some Indians listened, and others did not; some older Indians said they could not control "their young warriors." The Shawnee chiefs promised to send an answer to Post Vincennes within a month, but it never came. In the meantime, while the emissary was at the Miami village, Indians brought two prisoners from the settlements, and seventy warriors went to invade the frontier settlements. Three days after the emissary left the Miami village, a prisoner was burned, and "similar cruelties" occurred at other Indian towns; further, within three months after the emissary's mission, "upwards of one hundred persons were killed, wounded and taken prisoners" on the Ohio and in Kentucky.

Knox pointed out that on orders of the president, Kentuckians postponed an expedition against hostile Indians until results of the emissary's efforts might be known. Further, the Wyandots and Delawares, after many efforts to persuade the Miami and Wabash Indians, had concluded that only force could gain peace.

The depredations against Kentucky and Virginia counties were not caused by boundary disputes, Knox argued, because the Indians had no claim to these areas. From 1783 until October 1790, he continued, when the United States began offensives, the Indians "killed, wounded and took prisoners" about fifteen hundred, besides carrying off upwards of two thousand horses, and other property to the amount of fifty thousand dollars"; the barbarities against prisoners were "of too shocking a nature to be presented to the public," he wrote, but "the tomahawk and scalping knife" had been the "mildest instruments of death." Noting attacks on troops, he described an assault in which eleven of sixteen soldiers on a friendly mission to an Indian village were "killed and wounded."

Because all peace overtures had failed, force became necessary. Still, after General Harmar's expedition in October of 1790, peace overtures were sent to the Miami Indians; and in early 1791, the Seneca chief, Cornplanter, and other Indians were "engaged" to try to persuade the hostile Indians to make peace. Again, the emissaries were badly treated. Nevertheless, the United States extended peace overtures yet again, followed by a treaty with part of the Six Nations in 1791. An Oneida Indian, sent as a delegate to try again to persuade the hostile Indians to make peace, was frustrated in his efforts.

All the evidence, Knox explained, should show that the government, "uninfluenced by the resentment, or any false principles which might arise from a consciousness of superiority," had used every option to achieve peace through peaceful means. The current war, he explained, was a "remnant of the late general war, continued by a number of separate banditti, who . . . seem to have formed inveterate and incurable habits of enmity against the frontier inhabitants." Frontiers, where citizens had as strong claims to government protection as any citizens, were especially vulnerable, he stressed, and the government was as obligated to protect them as any area within the United States.

Knox concluded that a review of events showed the government had no choice but to apply force and to persist in it to show the "refractory Indians" that "they cannot continue their enormous outrages with impunity" and that "nothing is so much desired by the United States as to be at liberty to treat them with kindness and beneficence."[7]

The navigation issue continued to plague Kentuckians until 1795, when a treaty secured rights to navigate the Mississippi River,[8] but it was news of the Indian wars that dominated newspapers in early 1792. H. H. Brackenridge, of Pittsburgh, contributed a lengthy essay, "Thoughts on the Present Indian War." Another exultant report, published in a 29 February 1792 newspaper, related success of General Scott's campaign. The general brought in "near 700 scalps," the report said, under the heading, "GOOD NEWS—IF TRUE." An item, signed "A Kentuckian," published in 7 March newspapers suggested organized defense against the Indians, while other news in the same issue told of other Indian hostilities. An item also in the 7 March newspaper reported one man's fears of Indian wars, especially in view of the fate of two successive campaigns, and because no considerable army could be raised and sent out before the coming fall. Yet another report two weeks later told of an act for "further and more effectual provision for the protection of the frontiers of the United States." A letter excerpt published on 11 April praised General Wilkinson and gave an account of his expedition. The same item argued that General St. Clair should resign and that Wilkinson should replace him. A postscript noted that several men had been killed at Fort Jefferson, and that General Wilkinson would march there with 250 men to determine what should be done and act accordingly. May newspapers contained more letter excerpts praising Wilkinson and telling of more Indian attacks against Kentuckians and travelers on the Ohio River, plus a report that General St. Clair had, in fact, resigned as commander of the army.[9]

While Indian wars surrounded them, Kentuckians' tenth statehood convention, meeting in Danville in April, produced the new constitution.[10] Although news of the battles must have been unsettling to those planning to move west, no one seemed to doubt that the new state would be safe. Some moving plans were perhaps affected only by delays to assure a safer time for travel and settlement.

In any event, the Virginia Breckinridges continued plans for migrating, although Preston seemed to equivocate about it and James's new wife apparently refused to move. James wrote to John on 19 February 1792 from his mother's Botetourt home, lamenting that Preston had returned from Kentucky without "making any preparations for settling there." Again emphasizing his mother's interest in moving and that her plans would depend on John, James wrote, "The Poor old Lady is incessantly entreating me to go along," adding that he would, if his consent were "all that was necessary." Saying nothing more of his own plans, James asked for John's moving date. A month later John responded that he would move the following spring and was certain he would sell his land before he again saw James. Lamenting Preston's indecision, John wrote that he could not go wrong in migrating, but, although he wanted James near in Kentucky, he conceded that moving might not be to James's advantage. Yet, because of the opportunities migrating offered, John subtly suggested that James might plan for his children's future in Kentucky.[11]

Robert, in Kentucky, seemed impatient with John's delayed arrival. "Do you intend to become a resident of our Western hemisphere, & how soon?" he wrote from Beargrass, Kentucky, on 2 March. In this letter, Robert hinted of political dissension in Kentucky—particularly involving James Wilkinson, with whom John had entrusted some business to Robert:

> Your favour of the 24th of Dec[r.] last reached me about the 8th day of February following at a time when gen[l.] Wilkinson (now Lt. Col. Commdr. of the Second Federal Reg[t.]) was employed in military operations No. Wt. of the River Ohio— Immediately on his arrival at Frankfort I waited on him & presented your Bill of Exchange, the fate of which you will see explained in the back thereof in his own hand writing.
>
> Had I been a few hours later, should have missed seeing him—he was just embarking for Fort-Washington with his family & effects; where it is thought, he will stay pretty close, because of his embarrassed circumstances—The form of the protest is the best I could procure, because no Official officers were present, & his being on the Wing obliged me to acquiesce in whatever he pleased to do.
>
> Your letter dated in Phila. has not yet come to hand, but from that now before me, I conclude there is a probability of an Office opening for the Vacant Lands No. West of the River Ohio under the Auspices of the Congress. —It would be satisfactory to me to have early intelligence of the measures taken by the Congress—it may be used to advantage.[12]

The date of John Breckinridge's trip to Philadelphia—referred to in Robert's letter—is not clear. In February 1792 John was elected to Congress, although he had not sought the seat. Too intent on his moving plans to serve his term, he went to Philadelphia in late 1791 or early 1792, seeking large grants in the Northwest Territory.[13]

At least one of his friends believed John was making a mistake, arguing that he should choose federal office over a move to Kentucky. In a 25 February 1792 letter, Archibald Stuart warned John that the chaotic Kentucky politics might ruin him, should he become involved:

It seems my friend you are bent upon Kentucky & agriculture[.] I beg of you accept no office Under their State government[;] ye society is rent to pieces by faction & I wish rather to see you riding securely on ye shoulders of both than engaged in either—Should you be called on to ye foederal [*sic*] councils[,] well enough[;] there you may acquire honor & be of real service whereas contracted illiberal measures might draw forth a mens [immense?] opposition to ye ruin[?] of dispopularity.[14]

By the time Stuart wrote this letter, however, a letter from "J. Thompson" reveals that John had engaged him to take nineteen slaves to Kentucky:

When I opened the paper you gave Me to day found inclosed twenty pounds two shillings & five pence. Which I believe will Be more than Sufficient to bear the Expence to your Nineteen Negroes, etc. I shall use it Sparingly, at the Same time your people Shall have a plenty. I['ll take particular acct. of all the Expence Which you Shall See When Ever we Meet in Kentucky, Which day I Long to See Come. by the 25th of this month I hope weather will be such that I Can Move off therefore. Y[r.] people had better be Down by 25 or 26 at any rate. I think one Shot gun will be no disadvantage for them to take along. [R]emember linen for a Tent.[15]

Another letter of the same date to John requested that his "people" drive some sheep "as far as Balingers Creek" on their way to Kentucky.[16]

Antislavery agitation had begun early in the Kentucky country, and as Thompson's departure approached, John wrote to his mother of concern about the future of slavery there. He was sending "20 of my negroes immediately to Kentucky," he wrote. "They go this day week with Col. Thompson," he said, but added, "I am somewhat afraid of the Kentucky politicians with respect to negroes; and moreover, without the fear, I shall find it very convenient to have them there one year—before me." He informed her he would, "with great ease[,] make ready for my removal this time twelve months." He fretted that Preston still seemed to make no firm plans. John had pondered the sad prospect of a final departure from his childhood home in Botetourt. He would visit his mother there the first of June, he wrote, "& take our leave of it forever." Concluding the letter, he said the "Rout to Kentucky will be by red stone" and that his wife would write family news.[17]

The Breckinridge slaves did not depart as planned, however. Thompson delayed because of bad roads, he explained in a letter to John on 22 March. But he had learned that "one hundred & fifty

Soldiers" would leave from "fort Pitt . . . down the River Ohio" on 20
April and he intended to travel with them. Therefore, he added, the
slaves should be at his house, ready for the journey no later than 1
April.[18]

While the slaves traveled to Kentucky, Robert Breckinridge, who
had finally received John's letter written at Philadelphia, wrote a
thorough response to John's queries about northwestern territory
lands; giving assessments of quality and costs, he discouraged invest-
ment. Also giving news of Kentucky politics, Robert explained that
the new constitution had been formed and the first state assembly
would meet on 4 June. The issues for discussion would be "land and
Negroes," he wrote, adding:

> Adequate means for the adjustment of titles to lands in this State is of
> great moment to the prosperity and happiness of its inhabitants. As I
> expect, and hope, you intend to become a resident of this State[,] en-
> closed is an Extract from the Constitution respecting the Judiciary in order
> that you may judge of the principals of the Court established for the tryal
> of Land disputes—great advantages are expected from this Court by our
> sanguine petitions— Time will only prove the propriety of the establish-
> ment. I have been frequently interogated as to the time you intend to
> become an inhabitant of this Country— Many important land disputes
> remain to be tried; and I am asked to inform you of one now depending
> [sic] in our Court for about 30,000 Acres, that on your coming to this
> country if you will pay some attention to the business and make yourself
> acquainted with the nature of the dispute, a very liberal fee will be
> given—It is Wilson vs. Mason. . . .[19]

A lengthy letter from James Monroe at Philadelphia on 6 April 1792
also advised John about northwest lands and other issues under consideration in Congress. He wrote that "no attempt has been made to
open an office for the sale of Lands, nor will there be this session,"
and continued:

> The congress have passed a bill for raising the military establishment to
> above 5000 exclusive of a corps of 700 horse—The whole to be regular
> troops & for the war. Whether they will be raised in time to take the field
> this campaign or not is uncertain. The President has power to substitute in
> line of a favr[?] as many volunteer horsemen as he shall think fit from
> Kentucky, to serve for a term not exceeding 9 months.[20]

About the time John received Monroe's letter in mid-May, his
slaves arrived in Kentucky. Samuel Meredith wrote that they had
arrived safely and in good spirits, adding, "[T]he only loss they

suffer^d. on the road was Their Cart which Col. Thompson informs They were oblige[d] to leave in the Mountains before they reach^d. redstone." Meredith promised to assist Russell in hiring the slaves out until John arrived. Relating other news, he said all was quiet with Indians, and politics dominated the day. "Col. I Shelby," he wrote, "was the other day Elect^d. governor of Kentucky by a large majority." Meredith would go next day to Lexington with "old Mr. Patrick Campbell who is the bearer of this Letter," get a copy of the new constitution, if it had been printed, and send it to John.[21]

Two days later, William Russell also wrote about the slaves' arrival, other business, and political news. Lexington had been chosen as the seat of the Kentucky legislature, he wrote, and enclosed a list of the eleven senators. Lamenting "the loss" of John's presence "by this period," he wrote that he had hoped John would be in Kentucky to assist in the new government.[22]

Approximately a month later, on 14 June, Thompson wrote about the trip to Kentucky, telling of bad weather and weary, heartsick slaves, whom he plied with whiskey to keep them going. The letter, dated at "Shawanse Springs," also informed John that Robert was "Speaker of the House of Delegates" in the new legislature:

> This is the first chance that I have had to send you a few lines[,] which I hope will come to your hands & will find you and yours well. On the 3rd day of April I left Fluvianna & from that day till the 2 of May, I was on the road making my way to Red Stone. We had Snow or Rain Every day Except two. [T]he high waters[,] great Rains & snow were Enough to make us lose our patience. Our Negroes Every day out of heart & Sick. Bacon[,] Bread & Molasses they had a plenty, but all this would not have done & Never till then did I know the worth of whiskey. When the Negroes were wet & almost ready to give out. [sic] then I came forward with my good friend whiskey & Once in Every hour[,] unless they were a Sleep[,] I was Oblige[d] to give them whiskey. My Dear Friend[,] wet or dry[,] I kept my Spirits up & therefore went on. Your horses did very well till we got to the Allejany [sic] Mountains & then they faild [sic] & By the time we got to one Jesse Tomlinson's Station I was oblige[d] to leave your Cart as by this time your horses Could not have Carr^d. the Cart Empty. [I]n the Care of Mr. Tomlinson[,] I left the Cart for I Could Not Sell it for any thing. [H]e put it in a house till you or My Self gave further Orders. Tomlinson['s] is a place as well Known as any in the mountains. You Must devise some way What to do abt. the Cart. Well[,] my friend after this Bad Nuse. [sic] let me Say on the 17th May, I Delivered your 18 negroes to Col. Wm. Russell all well fat & hearty & Every one Much pleased with this Country. [A]lso delivered yr. two horses & Every thing you Sent Expect [sic] the Cart. On Sunday 20th May. [sic] I got home. Whear I am now in good health as also all my family. I am better pleased than Ever

with this Beautiful Country. And I wish you & family were here. The assembly in this Country is now sitting. Yr. Bro. Robert is the Speaker of the house of Delegates[.] Col. Bullet is Speaker to the Senate. They meet the 4th of this Month in Lexington. . . . [A]s for the Nuse in gen¹· I shall not Enter on till the next time I write you[.] [I]n October I expect to come in[,] When I hope I shall find you almost ready & Mrs. Breckinridge hurrying you to move to this almost paradise. Col. Rusel [*sic*] told me the day before yesterday that all your Negroes were hired out in his Neighborhood Except Jack[;] him he Keeps. The Constitution of this country you may see by applying to my Bro. John Thompson. I do assure you my Dear Friend I am so engaged abt. my plantation & building that I can not at this time write as much . . . as I wish I had more time— Since I came here have planted upwards of fifty acres of land in Corn[.] My people which I sent last fall had so much fences to do that they only planted abt. 12 Acres. [A]s late as I come[,] Still I hope to Make Seven or Eight hundred Barrels of Corn. I have plenty of Apples & Peaches. [G]ive my compts. to Mrs. Breckinridge & family.²³

Letters from Kentuckians to John continued to urge his early move and praise the opportunities awaiting him. Letters from non-Kentuckians asked him to handle legal matters in Kentucky.²⁴ Those who knew of Polly Breckinridge's reluctance to move wrote with sympathy and encouragement for her. In a letter to John on 22 July 1792, Mary Howard dwelt on Polly's feelings. Mary's letter, rambling and shifting between near incoherence and piercing insight, suggests that she had undergone prolonged psychological distress. She refers obliquely to difficulties before and during the trip to Kentucky, but does not mention her husband. One wonders if there had been a separation, or whether he had simply disappeared, died, or met some tragic fate. Mary pleaded that John not bring Polly against her will, but she was certain he would be a future governor and assured him that Polly's feelings would change once she saw Kentucky. She wrote of riding to the spot she imagined John would build his house and there fantasizing conversations with him and Polly:

My Dearest friend
　　Almost two years has Elapsed since I received your sensible and friendly letter which gave me the most sincere pleasure to be informed of the welfare of your dear little famaly and the agreeable addition of your fine black Eyed Daughter[.] [S]ince I came to kentucky I have made frequent attempts to write to you and my Dr. good Smithfield relations whom I can never think on but with heartfelt gratitude[.] [B]ut the extream Distress and mortification I encountered before I left Botetourt, the horrors and danger I underwent in bringing my famaly in the dead season of the year to this Country all operated so powerfully on my

feelings and stupified every faculty of my soul to such a degree that intensely unfited me to Corespond with my Dr. young friends[.] [A]s this is one of my first letters[,] However incorrect or incoherent it me [*sic*] be[,] I hope you will not be offended at the Contents as the [*sic*] are effects of the most real and disinterested friendship[.] [W]as I to Consult that mean principal selfishness I should advise you warmly to bring your Dr. wife and famaly to kentucky as I am well asured [*sic*] it would be a real akquisition [*sic*] to the Country as well as one of the greatest Comforts to your sister and My self and famaly[.] [B]ut when I reflect on the distress that it would involve my most dear and antient friends Col. Cabbell and his most worthy Lady in[,] I find myself Disolved in tears[.] You my Dear Johnny is now no stranger to aparent [a parent's] feelings and am Convinced you are two [*sic*] tender and human and sets a greater Value on your domestick happiness than to bring my dear polly to this Country without her and her parents['] full consent. I perceive by her letters to Mrs. Meredith that she has a Great conflict in her breast between conjugal affection and filial duty to her dear and best of parents[;] if there is a possibility of reconciling the separation to them or of persuading them to purchase Vaughns or Bucklys military rights[,] how happy and Conveniently Could they settle all their Children on as good land as perhaps is in the World[.] [B]ut I have the utmost Confidence in your prudence and good sense that you will do nothing to wound the feelings of either party[.] [I]t gives me most sincere pleasure every time I visit Cousin Betsy to see your Noble Seat which is vastly preferable to any I ever saw on James river. I ride up to an eminence on which I expect you'll build. I there alight and has many a pleasing interview with you and my dear Polly[;] indeed, I cannot leave the solitary spot without shedding a tear and wishing it real. I can assure you with the most solemn truth that I have found Kentucky to answer my most sanquin [*sic*] expectation[,] both in regard to land and society[.] [I]t has certainly more internal resources then almost any other country[.] [W]e live in our Cabbins in the midst of plenty with half the labor we had in the old Country[.] Want[,] that Meager skelleton[,] has not found the way to our dear delightful Country[.] Would to god the Indians was as great strangers to it[.] [W]e would be the happiest of people[.] [B]ut as I intend to adhere strictly to truth I must Confess the Constant depredations the Indians has been Commiting on our frontiers on the river[,] joined to horred Efusion of human blood last fall over the river[,] has embitered my life as my son is almost half his time after indians and exposed and I am in Constant dread of his falling by there hands[.] I hope the present Company will be more successful and give a different turn to our affairs[.] [I]n your letter you were kind Enough to mention a proposal made by Anderson of five negro girls if Benj. and myself would relinquish our rights to the fishpond land[.] At that time Benny was not of age to join in any relinquishment and I was perfectly [word illegible] to the base principals of the man[.] I expect if I ever Made an offer he would have sum trifling Evasion as he did when I was in great need[,] and indeed to be plain I never want a negro more than we have as I am almost assured Emancipation will by sum means or other be brought about in this state[;] and if that should not be the Case there is nothing to be made by negroes here till there is trade down the river.

Mary wrote of a legal matter she wished John to handle and added that she was glad his slaves arrived safely, that she didn't know about his land improvements because her family never interacted with John's overseer. She wrote, finally, "I believe you are as much longed and wished for as any person that ever intended coming to this Country." She promised that Polly would be a governor's lady in a very short time and be very fond of the Country, but she pleaded that John try hard to bring Polly's father and his family.[25]

Benjamin Howard enclosed a letter with his mother's, offering to help John move and reporting Indian news. Also, in a few short phrases, he revealed his opinions of the new Kentucky government as one of bumbling incompetence and of John as a great asset to the new state's political system:

> I am happy to find you are determined to come out in the Spring at farthest as I can assure twill not only be to your own Interest but will be an acquisition to our political Body[,] for there is the greatest Dearth of abilities here I ever saw for the number of people when put to the Test. There never was a better opp^y· for a man to show his abilities than at this particular Crises when this new Country does undertake to act for itself and a Set of Novices at the Helm that have got entangled with politics and knows not how to extricate themselves without the assistance of our atty. general and if he should refuse or die[,] we would undoubtedly fall to the ground under the pressure of government.

Benjamin asked for a specific moving date, then added a postscript: "I have just heard for certain that both our flags ware killed[,] Major Truman and Col. Hardin[.] [T]he accts. are brought in by two prisoners escaping[.] [T]hey say the Indians are determined for war and will not receive any offers or even a Message from the United States."[26]

In the meantime, Mrs. Lettice Breckinridge was settling her Virginia affairs in preparation for her move. But it was no easy process. She was reluctant to sell property where she had lived independently for nearly twenty years. Additionally, she and Preston had some dispute, the nature of which is not clear but which no doubt concerned disposition of the estate. These facts and her uncertainties about how to prepare to live in Kentucky are revealed in a letter to her from John in August. Apparently, John had assisted her with legal matters when he and his family made that promised trip earlier in the summer to "take leave of" Botetourt forever. Two copies of a will and another legal document, dated 30 July 1792, show Mrs. Breckinridge's preparations for the transition she was about to make. In her will, she designated various grandchildren as beneficiaries and required especially that one slave be freed and others be well cared for. Other papers show she had offered the property for sale and secured a signed promise from Preston that he would care for her the rest of her life. Further, Preston deeded to her 150 acres on Elkhorn River in Kentucky.[27]

After the summer visit with her, John probably pondered his mother's situation and prospects as his family traveled the hot, dusty road from Botetourt to visit his parents-in-law in Albemarle. After returning to the Glebe, he wrote to his mother on 19 August 1792, offering much advice about how to ensure that she would live financially secure. Worried perhaps that Preston might take advantage of her, John especially urged her to guard her independence, reminding her that she was more capable than anyone else of running her own affairs. Asking that Preston write him just before they departed for Kentucky, John fretted about overcoming his family's and friends' opposition to his move and vowed that nothing "terrestial" would keep him in Virginia:

> We all got safely Home, notwithstanding the hotness of the weather and badness of the roads. We went by way of Col. Cabels.
>
> I am in hopes by this time, that you & Preston have made considerable preparations for your Journey, and that Mr. Watts has taken up my order, by whch Means you will not be so cramped in fixing yourself well, for your departure. It is surely within your power to procure every thing that can tend to make the Journey as comfortable as it will admit of. I was sorry to see you so tenacious of your property, as to express reluctance to dispose of it, when your ease & conveniency seem to require it. You have had my opinion fully on the impropriety of undertaking in Kentucky the perplexity of a Plantation. Your Negroes I would endeavour to keep; but as to every thing else, it will answer no other purpose but to give you trouble & disquiet. Should you reach Kentucky in Safety, the hire of your Negroes & rent of your land, will far exceed any annual income you ever enjoyed, & be amply sufficient to support you genteely & independently. Your land & Negroes let no person upon this earth, persuade you to give up, or even part of them as long as you exist; no not even to manage them for you.
>
> You are as able to hire your Negroes, & rent your Land as any person whatever. Should you find at the end of every year, you have any thing to give, it will then be time enough; but never diminish your capital. A dependence on any person is uncomfortable & humiliating; to one of your disposition, it would be intolerable. The disagreement of opinion between Preston & yourself lately, about some little pecuniary matters, must strike you sensibly with the force of this observation. —as your Negroes or

plantation cannot produce any profit until a year after you reach Kentucky, you will probably choose to make your Home with one or other of your children for that time. But should you incline to take a House in Lexington before that time, let me know it some short time before hand. I have funds more, sufficient for that purpose which shall be at your disposal.

You may all rest assured that nothing terrestial will divert me from my proposed Journey. I have numberless difficulties to encounter. I know them & am prepared for them. Reconciling my Family and my Friends are dreadful impediments. The other difficulties generally attendant on such a removal, would have been enough for me; but they are difficulties I would conquer with pleasure, was not every attempt resisted by the influence of my friends.

Pray desire Preston to write fully to me just before he sets out. I shall be anxious to hear, what your prospects for Company are—Perhaps I may have it in my power to write you once more. I will if I can. If not may every blessing attend you.[28]

While preoccupied with his mother's needs, John received a letter from the overseer of his Kentucky land. In a letter dated "Mount Bulliant, August ye 29th, 1792," Russell wrote that he had an opportunity to send a letter with "the Rev[d.] James Blythe, who will be in Prince Edward, and will probably leave this at the court house for you should he not see you." He told John of "the greatest drouth in this Country" he had ever seen and said crops were "not as good as usual," but he believed "we shall have enough to supply all new comers." He continued:

Your Negroes as I observed before to you are hired out in different places in this neighbourhood, and are all at this time well pleased. I was pestered a little to find a place for old Grotty and Tomsey; tho they seem well satisfied at this time.

Jack remains with me. I have agreed with the people who have them to pay in cash or Cattle. The Cattle to be at the cash selling price, I expect the hires will probably all be discharged in cattle.

A note in the margin adds, "The people are very much pleased with the expectation of your coming out next spring. I hope you will not disappoint them." The letter continues:

John and Grotty was hired for five pounds & ten shillings each until the first of December[;] all the young women without encumbrances hired for three pounds, for the same time. Fanny and her children was hired for fifty shillings, Betsy and her children for the same. Ilsey[?] and her children Col. Thompson desired me to hire for a spot[?] for her self as he had taken one from her and applied it to the use of the others. Bill and Stephen is hired at three shillings per month. They are all to be cloathed in the bargain, their cloathing to consist of two strong shirts, a warm strong coat and Britches, also a good pare of shoes and stockens; These Cloaths to be delivered at the expiration of their times unless I should direct them sooner.

Your tennants['] times will not expire untill Christmas come twelve months[,] though I believe the whole of them would sell out immediately. I wrote you in a small Billet about three weeks back and advised you to purchase all Todd's claim on your side Elkhorn, as I understood he wanted to sell same. It would suit you very well to own to the Creek. Lands have risen here latterly, and will rise should the seat of government continue in Lexington.

He continued, "The Indians appear to be disposed for mischief," and it was pretty certain they had "killed Harden & Truman (our flaggs)." The governor had "called the Militia officers for the strength of their militia," he wrote, and added, "'tis generally supposed there will be a draft here this fall, for an Expedition against some Town. . . ." After writing, "I must stop," he added a long postscript:

I have appointed the last day of Sepr with Oto[?] Tolbert to send for six sows and a bore for you. [H]e has promised to pick his stock for you and to put them up in a pen[.] [S]o that I shall not be disappointed[,] I hope you will write me soon how your people are to be disposed of this winter. They will hire better this fall than they did last spring, owing to the season being too far advanced before they got here. I think it will suit you best to hire or purchase one of your tenants out[,] set them to work there, though their not having a crop to begin on will make the latter more inconvenient. Mr. Meredith was here yesterday Even and were all well.[29]

As Mrs. Breckinridge's departure date approached, it was William and not Preston who wrote to John. Mrs. Breckinridge's later letter to John indicates that she and Preston were still having differences, and perhaps Preston refused to write the letter. In any event, William was delighted to inform John that their mother would be able to travel with troops who were to be stationed in Kentucky during the winter.

My Mother will set out in about two weeks fer kentucky and I am happy to inform you that she will have the Company of Capt. Boyles[?] troop of Horse who will set out for the Western Country about the time when she will be ready to go and they are ordered to go with all [word illegible] to the Brink[?] of the Big Kennanyhaw from which place it is more than probable then some of the Troops may Continue on down the River as I understand they are to be Quartered in Kentucky this winter. My Mother has a Sale on saturday then of such things as she can't take with her. . . .[30]

A few days later, Mrs. Breckinridge wrote to John that she was on the way to Kentucky. But she was not happy, particularly because of Preston's behavior, and she lacked confidence in their wagon drivers. She worried about a slave left behind—because he had no friends— and about William, who apparently had never settled on a productive pursuit:

My dear Johnny,

I am thus fare on my way to Kentucky[.] [G]od only knows whether I shall evere be able to Mack out the Jurney for I have had a very Despeart Time since I sawe you fixing for the Journey—and think that we eare verey poorly fixed[.] After all the [word illegible] I have had for Preston as he will not mind his business and I have been much affeared that Anthony and Petter will not Mack out well for neither of them understands Driving the wagonig[.] Jack has left us in a very bad time[.] I hope you will try to bring him out in the Spring for I am Determined not to Sell him.

Johnny Preston has not come in and I have got nothing Done with my accts. and has Left them [in] the hands of your Brother James. I beg you will Try and Settle in the Best manners you can.

Your order on mr. Watts has been of very great servis to me[.] [I]t has been a meenes of Cleringe me out of this Place for there came Debts I did not Expect but I have payd Every Person[.] I have enclosed my will to you to keep and I depend uppon your Good ness that you will [illegible] care of your Poor Brother Billy and I request you will have a Tender[?] eye overe him and not let him want the Common neserys [necessaries] as fare as the [illegible] of the Negroe Joe[,] he says he will come to Kentucky this winter. I wish he wod. as he has no friends.

I hop[e] in the Lord I will see you and your Dr. family in the spring in kentucky. I refer you to Jamy who will enform you in what manner Preston conducted his business in this place. I am Determined to tack your advise [sic] concerning my affairs if the Lord spares me.

I am in Hast and must conclude. [R]emember me to Dear Polly and Tell her I will Doe every thing in my Powers to Mack her happy [when] she Comes to Kentucky. Give my Love [to] My Dr. Children.

I beg you will writ by every oppertunity. I am very much distressed to leve Jamey and his family behind and my other relasins[,] but I hope Jamey will move to kentucky in the cours of toow [sic] or 3 years for this Place will be Setled with Dutch so that I hope he will not stay here. May Lord bless you and your Dr. family is [the] Prayer of [your] affe. mother.[31]

In a letter John wrote in July, Betsy and Samuel Meredith learned of Mrs. Breckinridge's journey about the time she set out. Samuel responded to John on 19 September:

Your Letter of the 14th July favd. by Mr. Flemming, was handd. me by Col. Thompson Seventh of Augt. [I]t afforded me much pleasure to be informed that Mrs. Breckinridge had sold her Lands & intend^d. to Kentucky this fall.

I came here yesterday expecting Col. Thompson was to have set out for yr. Country tomorrow but has postponed it for some weeks. —[M]ust request you to inform Col. Russell & myself whether you wd. wish yr. negroes continued hired after the expiration of the time for which they are hired expires or whether you wd. prefer them to be settl^d. on one of the [illegible] improvements which may be procur^d. if you advise (their time is up in December for which they were hir^d.) you may have an opportunity of writing before then. Yr. Slaves are all well & at good places[.] Col. Russel wrote to you some time ago by Mr. Blyth[,] our minister who wd. leave the letter at Prince Edward court House. There is great quarreling about the seat of government. Much party spirit prevailing in our country at present. We want yr. aid very much. —We have experienced a most uncommon drouth in our Country. Indians are all quiet at present. Col. Thompson is the barrier [sic] of this Letter. Must refer you to him for news of Kentucky. . . . My wife writes Mrs. Breckinridge the News of our Neighborhood. We shall expect you in the Spring without fail.[32]

Five weeks after the date of this letter, Meredith received news that Mrs. Breckinridge had arrived at Limestone, Kentucky. Uncertain if the news was true, he nevertheless sent horses, two slaves, and some provisions for the remainder of her journey to his home. He wrote to her at Limestone on 26 October 1792:

Dear Madam,
Late last evening, I receiv'd the agreeable News of your safe arrival at Limestone, which afford^d. myself & Betsey infinite pleasure. —The information comes to us at second hand which makes us rather fearful of its not being certain. Also no letter accompanied the News. Are likewise inform^d. the Rivers is very low. We are told you are in want of [MS torn] Horses in Consequences of which I have dispatch^d. two Negroe men & four Horses by light this morning with some provisions. I sh^d. undoubtedly have come with them [remainder of MS missing].[33]

Indeed, Mrs. Breckinridge arrived safely and was reunited with her daughter in Kentucky two and one-half years after Betsy moved from Virginia.

Meantime, friends in Virginia wrote to John and Polly of sadness at their impending departure, and some wrote of plans to accompany them or of matters concerning their moving preparations. Others asked John to take over legal matters for them in Kentucky. In December 1792 James Hopkins wrote of hearing that John had sold his house and vowed he would try to detain him in Virginia if he thought it would do any good; a few days later, he sent two horses to

John, writing that he had "procured two Nags conditionally, which are these I send you by Jack." He continued:

> I am told they can eat corn very well, and are very thrifty, & work in a Cart very well, & probably may work well in a waggon behind, but it is thought they are too fiery to work before, especially when fat. I am told they have been well kept till now. If they will (or either of them) work well in a waggon & you can get them in good order enough, you are perfectly welcome to either or both of them for waggon Horses to Kentucky, & you can let me ride your mare or sorrel Horse, or some other Horse.[34]

W. Warfield, who planned to travel with John's family, wrote on 11 February 1793 that he might have to postpone the trip because of his wife's pregnancy. She was in the fifth month and avoided exertion because of "repeated disasters . . . when in a similar situation," he wrote. "Capt. Sorrell," whose wife was also pregnant, had been at Warfield's house for two days, very anxious to move with John and "determined to go," despite his wife's condition. Warfield fretted that losing the chance to accompany John would be very "prejudicial to my circumstances, and I shall despair of getting a good company."[35]

James sent two servants to help John move—although one went very unwillingly. James wrote on 19 March that Mrs. John Owen Smith "will set out for your house on Monday next . . . to accompany you to Kentucky," and he was sending with her "a great deal of [Kentucky] business" for John's attention. Lamenting his inability to see John before the moving date, James sent his best wishes to Polly.[36]

One friend, whose signature is illegible, wrote to John on 23 March of deep sadness about the departure and offered food and anything else John and Polly might need for their journey:

> I sit down to take my Final Leave of my best Friend and neighbor, and must tell you when you and your Lady take leave of our Family, it will be the heaviest day they have felt since the loss of my poor daughter Patty. A thought just struck me to fill your case with some June Peach brandy or a keg of 5 or 10 gallons for your Journey; should the corn not hold out send for more. I am so poor I can't think of any thing that I have worth your acceptance besides, but should there be any thing my Dear Friend you & your Lady may stand in need of or that we have[,] do ask for it. May every day be productive of some nice Scene to perpetuate the happiness of you and your Spouse &c. is the Sincear Wish of your friend.[37]

In anticipation of the family's arrival, Russell and Meredith rented property adjoining Lexington, Kentucky's most populous town, which in 1790 had 834 people, 250 houses, three churches, a court house, and a jail—in addition to the numerous businesses already mentioned.[38] Lexington's leading dry-goods company had advertised the property in *The Kentucky Gazette* on 2 March 1793. According to a document dated 9 April 1793, the house was rented from Peter January & Son for a year for sixty-eight pounds.[39]

By the spring of 1793, John Breckinridge had long made careful moving plans, and most family members had migrated. But nothing made the thought of moving more tolerable to Polly, whose pain at leaving her own parents probably overwhelmed any immediate comfort she might have felt in knowledge that her mother-in-law would be close by in Kentucky. And the winter of 1792–93 brought still another event to bear on the move—the birth of her fourth child, Robert.[40] Embarking on such a long journey with four young children, including an infant-in-arms, surely intensified Polly's reluctance about moving.

8
A Pleasant Journey and Arrival in Kentucky

By the spring of 1793, the progression begun by John Breckinridge's decision five years earlier to move to Kentucky had nearly run its course. The major hurdle of accomplishing the actual move remained; then would follow the tasks of notifying relatives and friends in Virginia of arrival and establishing his family in their new home. During those five years, he had acted on information carefully gathered and studied, and this may have distinguished his migration from that of most. His overriding interest in Kentucky may have been a primary force conducting other family members ahead of him, but he seems to have timed his move to coincide with the beginning of statehood, decreasing threats of Indian hostilities, and established residence of other family members—especially his mother—in the new state.

In late March 1793, the Breckinridges set out for their new home. The departure was surely an occasion of mixed emotions. John must have eagerly anticipated finally realizing a goal so long in the planning while harboring sadness about leaving Virginia. Polly's dread of the move had not abated. The children were too young to realize the import of the trip, but six-year-old Letitia and four-year-old Joseph Cabell, in all likelihood, were excited about setting out on what must have seemed an adventure. Mary, who was two, and Robert, an infant, probably caused their mother concern as she contemplated the weeks of hard travel ahead. One of John's final acts of preparation was securing an arm chair, perhaps as travel comfort for Polly and the baby on the flatboat and on the occasions she could ride in the wagon.[1]

Some sense of the depth of sadness at departure is felt in an anecdote Polly's brother related in a letter to her later. Writing about an incident as the Breckinridges departed, young Joseph Cabell seemed to struggle to be humorous:

> altho' I was as much distressed as possible at parting with you I could not refrain laughing at a circumstance which happened a few minutes after we

184

took leave[;] you went of [*sic*] crying one way. Joe C. Migginson, Bob Harrison & myself another; before we got to the yard Gate, Bob Harrison discovered Peter with his Saddle Bags, prancing his Mare, & scarcely able to keep the Saddle, at which sight he bestowed a thousand curses on drunken Peter & declared he would not have been prevented taking leave of my Sister for five hundred pounds, his Expression as sad as possible, & his mouth extended from Ear to Ear, as he boarded Peter, which sat [*sic*] all present laughing with tears in their Eyes.

Young Joseph wrote that he would try to visit Polly in Kentucky and added that his father also talked of visiting but implied that was unlikely:

> our Father talks of visiting you then, whether able or not to go through the fatigue of so Tedious a journey I am confident he will attempt it[;] should we like the Country, & there can be no doubt in that instance, seriously we shall be your neighbors; Our Father is still very infirm mostly owing to your departure, & had a fit or two lately something like the apoplectic, has refrained from drinks, which induced me to hope he will recover to bless you. . . . [H]e has heard Mr. Breckinridge declare he would not stay here longer than could move, in consequence of his saying Mr. Breckinridge was in combination with Col. Meredith against him, which sometimes renders him uneasy, though generally treats it as it deserves[—] with disbelief. . . .[2]

The "Mr. Breckinridge" Joseph referred to presumably was James. And Colonel Meredith, Betsy's father-in-law, also remained in Virginia, although he had invested in Kentucky land. Colonel Cabell's fear of the loss of companionship of these individuals who were close through family ties may have been real—or it may indicate senility or infirmity of mind due to illness. Or sadness at the loss of his daughter may have been too much for him to cope with rationally. At the least, he must have been frustrated that his age and health might prevent a future reunion with his daughter and grandchildren. Women and children seldom made return trips through the wilderness—although men, of course, frequently did so to conduct business. If Colonel Cabell drank, had "apoplectic fits," and imagined people conspiring against him, who could fault him? He was facing weeks of anxious waiting to learn whether his daughter and grandchildren were safe, and then he could look forward to continued anxiety about their safety in a land where he knew many had not survived the dangers.

In addition to the sadness at parting from friends and relatives, some sense of desolation about their own lives in those left behind must have lurked below the surface in every such farewell. Having heard glowing reports of opportunities over the mountain, they must have considered—but very likely never mentioned—the contrast between their own futures and the prosperity they imagined awaited those departing. They would write, look for letters in return, and seek news from travelers. In time, pain of separations would heal with acceptance of what could not be changed.

Breckinridge relatives and others in Kentucky viewed John's journey from a very different perspective. Not only did they anticipate a warm reunion with a loved relative and friend; they were confident that John would bring enlightened leadership to an infant state government. Exultant, they prepared a reception and eagerly awaited the family's arrival. William Russell received news from John en route indicating he and his family were well on the way. Russell responded in a letter dated at "Mount Bulliant," Kentucky, 1 May 1793, which he dispatched via "Mr. Lindsay," with whom he also entrusted some business needing John's attention:

> This will be handed you by Mr. Lindsay who waits on you, on business of importance. I am happy to hear you are so far safe on your journey to Kentucky.
>
> I expect you will come past my house on your way to Lexington. Mr. Lindsay will return by me, which will furnish you with an opportunity of sending me word which road will be your rout.
>
> I shall send word in the morning to Mrs. Breckinridge of your coming & expect we shall be able to meet you with a caravan of horse as an escort.

Russell explained that he had rented "comfortable" dwellings for John. Noting that many people had appealed to him to speak to John about undertaking business for them, he added, "I flatter myself Kentucky will be equal [MS torn] to your wishes. . . ."[3]

While the Breckinridges approached their new home, Virginia relatives anxiously awaited word of their safe arrival. They imagined all kinds of eventualities during the trip and worried that Polly's unhappiness about the move would endanger her marriage. Letters John and Polly sent from Redstone, Pennsylvania, may have revealed her persisting despair. Harrison reports that after nearly a month en route, John confided to a traveler that Polly had not smiled once during the trip.[4] Possibly, young Joseph Cabell's letter (cited above) was, in part, a response to such news, for he seemed to strain to cheer her. Reminding her subtly of all she had to enjoy and treasure, he warmly defended John's decision to move:

> Having neither heard or received any certain account from you since our separation at Scotts, our family have formed divers conjectures some good

some bad about your Journey; & all wait with anxiety to hear of your safe arrival at your destined home, for my part I hope for the best & think you have had time to get there by this should no difficulties have befallen you, which may god omnipotent prevent for Jesus' sake.

I ardently hope my dear Sister however distressing a separation of Parents & near Relations must be you will be happy under the banners of a prudent sensible Husband with the innocent pledges of your love about you, under a well regulated government where the brightness of Breckinridge must be exalted, a country fertile as Eden of old, & in the blessing of a good neighborhood[;] these are blessings few can boast, & few deserve.

Had I the prospects Mr. Breckinridge had I certainly would have regulated my conduct sooner or later in the like manner[;] this fall, next spring, or the fall after, you may expect to see me under your roof, whether any of my relations accompany me or not . . . our other friends are well & expect Sister Harrison has increased her family before this.

William Warwick shut Col. Meredith out of his Election to the utter disgrace of the freeholders in Amherst, & Col. Sam. talks of purging the pole, being fully possessed he is yet a member to Congress on a minute investigation. . . .

I shall be happy to render you any service here in my power to perform, & have to request you will make choice of the handsomest thirty pound Horse in Kentucky, & have him well gated [*sic*] against my arrival, which in some measure will be regulated by the health of my Father, that is, as to the time mentioned.

Being hurried by Mr. Patterson who has taken charge of our letters, & having no news to communicate.[5] . . .

At last, in early May 1793, thirteen years after William Breckinridge first visited the Kentucky country, John and his family arrived to settle in Lexington. John was thirty-two years old, and Polly was twenty-four. Although less enthusiastic than John about their new home, Polly was surely happy to see her sister-in-law and nieces and nephews when the young family reunited on 3 May with Samuel and Betsy Meredith.

After a week of checking on business affairs and waiting for the family's rented house to become available, John wrote from the Meredith's home to his parents-in-law about the trip and prospects in Kentucky:

I hope our letters written from Red Stone by Mr. Burten came safe to hand. In those we give you an acct. of our Journey to this place. From that place to Limestone we had as pleasant a journey as it was possible. When any danger was apprehended we were comfortably fixed in boats & provided with every necessary for the voyage. We were 8 days on water including the one Spent at the Mouth of the Kentucky. We saw no Indians & little sign of any. We did not dread them for the party was very strong.

We landed at Limestone the last day of April & reached Mr. Meredith's this the third day after[,] where we now are.

Col. Russell has rented a very convenient House & lot for us in Lexington. We get possession of it to-morrow & shall leave this place.

I have been employed principally since I came here on my plantation in Settling my Nergoes &c, so that I cannot yet say what is to be expected from the practice of law. There is a large Dockett & a large number of Lawyers. When I get home & a little settled you shall soon hear from us. Polly has written—I think she looks greatly better than when she left Albemarle, and I am sure my little children were never so fat & healthy. Be pleased to remember me to Mrs. Cabell, Miss Betsy &c.[6]

The Breckinridge family settled into Kentucky life and politics. Married just eight years and the mother of four—of whom the oldest was nearly seven—Polly would live the rest of her life in Kentucky. Whether she ever was as happy as before the move, only she knew. From the beginning, her life in Kentucky brought experiences unlike any she had known before and which thrust upon her the primary responsibility of conducting and shaping the family legacy.

The winter after arriving in Kentucky, the two youngest children, Mary and Robert, died of smallpox—and Polly almost died.[7] Although other children came—Mary Ann in 1795, John in 1797, Robert in 1800, William Lewis in 1803, and James Monroe in 1806,[8] Polly lost significant components of her support system in 1797 when her mother-in-law died in Kentucky and in 1798 when her father died in Virginia.[9] She saw even less of her husband than she did in Virginia. John plunged immediately into state politics and moved on to national politics. In 1800, he began service in Washington, D.C., and that kept him away from home much of the next six years. Polly was left with the responsibilities of raising the children and overseeing the farm and John's other business interests in Kentucky.[10]

In the winter of 1806, the worst blow of all for Polly was the loss of her husband. After a short and brilliant career as Kentucky state attorney general, state representative, United States senator, and United States attorney general, John died at forty-six in 1806.[11] Married twenty-two years, Polly, then thirty-eight, was left with five children still at home, ranging in ages from five months to eleven years. The oldest, Letitia, twenty, had married in 1804, and Joseph Cabell, eighteen, was studying at Princeton University.[12]

Polly lived as a widow fifty-two more years—nearly two thirds of her life. Having already buried her husband and two children by 1807, she lived to bury five more children, Mary Ann died as a young bride in 1816; her youngest, James Monroe, died at age thirteen in 1819; especially difficult was the death in 1823 of her oldest son, Joseph Cabell, who had inherited his father's political talent and at thirty-five was a star in state politics; Letitia died in 1831 at forty-five; John, a Presbyterian minister and chaplain of the U.S. House of Representatives, died in 1841 at age forty-four. [13]

Polly doted on her grandson, John C. Breckinridge, who was an infant when his father Joseph Cabell died. She watched him gain Henry Clay's former seat in Congress in 1852 and become vice president of the United States in 1856—the youngest in American history. But she did not live to see him become a candidate for the presidency in 1860. [14] Only two of Polly's nine children, Robert Jefferson and William Lewis, lived beyond her death at age eighty-nine in 1858. [15] Breckinridges have been leaders in Kentucky and the nation since the beginning of both, and, due in large measure to Polly's nurturing strengths, the name remains one of the most distinguished in Kentucky.

The communication framework structuring people's lives during the years the Breckinridges prepared for migrating and moved across the Appalachian Mountains may seem to have changed little from a twentieth-century perspective. However, to those affected, each change was significant. Travel facilities improved in that better stages, carriages, and boats were built; and comforts such as fireplaces, covered bedrooms, and even full roofs were added to flatboats. Experimentation had begun on steamboats, but none existed for migrants through 1793. [16]

Circulation of information depended on the exigencies of travel. As travel increased, so did information circulation. Although a postal system conducted mail north to south along the colonial and new-nation coastline, mail to the interior depended entirely on who traveled where and when throughout the years under study. Travel from the Kentucky frontier increased, especially after 1780, and organized companies leaving there every other Monday from 1788—and probably earlier—meant a fairly steady circulation of news by letter, word-of-mouth, and newspapers between West and East. A published history of Kentucky in 1784, including Daniel Boone's account of exploring, building a road across the mountains, and settling there, spread information about a bountiful West throughout the new nation. [17] By 1788, newspapers in Pittsburgh and Lexington sent western news east and brought eastern news to the West. Daily newspapers had begun in Philadelphia, but it would be years before dailies appeared in Kentucky or Pittsburgh, [18] primary sources of news about the West.

Primary, or interpersonal, information networks varied according to individuals' reference groups. John Breckinridge's primary information sources conducted his interest in the West from an early age. His earliest information about the West came from his uncle William Preston, the first surveyor for territory encompassing Kentucky, and then from surveyors who brought back reports to Preston's Fincastle office, where John worked during the years Kentucky settlements were established. During the same years, newspapers increasingly carried reports about the Kentucky country, as did representatives from the new district on regular trips to the Virginia Assembly from 1776. During the American Revolution, John's brother William, who seems to have served in 1780 as a soldier in Kentucky, could give John his own firsthand accounts of the land—as could Kentucky representatives to the Assembly, to which John was elected in 1780. The end of the war brought a surge in westward migration, joined by John's brothers and relatives, who kept him informed as continuously thereafter as news could physically circulate to and from the tramontane region.

The communications infrastructure put great demands on people. One is struck by the amount of attention given in letters to efforts and conditions generated by communication facilities. Psychological demands may have been greatest, the extent of which may be beyond the understanding of people in the twentieth century. Physical distances between family members, relatives, and friends caused homesickness, worry, loneliness, frustration, anger, and even serious illnesses as time stretched on without news. Often, people accepted that someone away an unduly long time was dead—perhaps to reconcile themselves to an unexplained absence and get on with their lives. Stresses on families and individuals are apparent in most letters. A dominant demand was on people's patience. Sprague's description of John Brown's 1788 trip to Kentucky from Philadelphia via the Ohio River epitomizes the trials of patience: "The stage's horses slogged through deep mud as 'excessive rain' turned dusty roads into quagmires" and Brown "was a captive of the stage with his servant as his sole companion" for thirteen days. Arriving at Pittsburgh, he could find no water transportation and traveled to Wheeling by land, hoping to get a boat there. He finally arrived too late for the beginning of the September court in Danville, complaining that he was sick of the "continuous scene of fatigues and embarrassments" and longing "to converse one hour with any" of his old friends in Williamsburg.[19]

Another demand, of course, was on physical health. Travel facilities exposed travelers to the elements, a factor perhaps responsible for the cough that nagged John Breckinridge and hastened his death.[20]

Horseback trips on the court circuit in Virginia gave way to longer horseback rides from Kentucky to Washington, D.C., extending duration of exposure and travel fatigue as his political fortunes rose.[21]

The greatest demand of all was time, and people tempered expectations and conducted affairs accordingly. The word "appointment" (as in keeping an appointment) was not part of the language; one could not rely on being at a given place at a given time. For trips over a few miles, arrival times could be estimated only in a given week or month. During illnesses, one knew that the day or so required to fetch a doctor might be too long. Sending letters required time to locate a traveler and get mail written and to the carrier; and then one knew travel exigencies could cause the letters to go astray. One also had to plan what one wrote because of the public nature of letter delivery. Acquiring necessities, taking a trip, or moving one's residence required even more careful planning and time, as the Breckinridge family papers show.

The sum effect created a pattern of life, replete with values, that has gradually receded from American culture. The migration across the Appalachian Mountains, specifically of the John Breckinridge family, illustrates cultural patterns and behavior conditioned by the communications infrastructure over a period of twenty-three years. Polly Breckinridge lived to be part of a later stage of communication development in America, and hence to experience the passing of patterns promulgated in an earlier stage. She lived to rely on the poastal service for timely letter delivery; and perhaps before her death she knew that the telegraph conducted messages through space apart from human travel and a cable soon would carry information between America and Europe.[22] She may not have traveled on trains and steamboats, but she must have known of them.[23] She lived during a period when the number of news periodicals grew from thirty-five along the East coast at the end of the American Revolution to nearly four thousand, including proliferating dailies, across the nation by 1858.[24] And she may have learned before her death of the new invention, photography, that could capture one's likeness for loved ones to keep close while apart.[25] She must have marveled if she knew of the second great wave of migration that surged toward California in the mid-nineteenth century, a wave shaped by a communication infrastructure both akin to and differing from that which conducted her to Kentucky in the late eighteenth century.

Notes

Introduction: The Westward Migration as Communication History

1. Rev. John Brown to William Preston, [n.d.] May 1775, William Preston Papers, Lyman C. Draper Manuscripts (hereafter referred to as Draper Mss), State Historical Society of Wisconsin, Madison, 4 QQ 15. All material used from the Draper Manuscripts is from the 1949 microfilm edition. All quoted excerpts are presented as in the originals. In some instances, to aid reader comprehension, [*sic*] and punctuation, signified with [ ], have been added.

2. Thomas D. Clark, *A History of Kentucky* (New York: Prentice-Hall, 1937), 130–31; Lewis Collins, *Historical Sketches of Kentucky* (Maysville, Ky.: L. Collins, 1847), xiv, 19–29; Samuel W. Wilson, "West Fincastle—Now Kentucky," *Filson Club History Quarterly* 9 (April 1935): 65–94. See also F. B. Kegley, *Kegley's Virginia Frontier* (Roanoke: Southwest Virginia Historical Society, 1938), 377–400, and William Broaddus Cridlin, *A History of Colonial Virginia* (Richmond, Va.: Williams Printing Co., 1923), 153–76.

3. Charles B. Heinemann, *First Census of Kentucky* (Washington, D.C.: G. M. Brumbaugh, 1940), 3; Albert H. Redford, *The History of Methodism in Kentucky* (Nashville: Southern Methodist Publishing House, 1868), 1:21–22; Howard Elmo Short, "Some Early Kentucky Church Experiences," *The Register of the Kentucky Historical Society* 49 (October 1951), 269–79. Heinemann gives Kentucky's 1790 population as 73,677. According to Redford, "When Lewis Craig left Spottsylvania County, Va. [for Kentucky], most of his large church left with him. They were constituted when they set out and an organized church on the road. Wherever they stopped they would transact church business." The group settled at Craig's Station on Gilbert's Creek, a few miles east of present Lancaster, Kentucky. Short (pp. 271 and 276) says that Craig's "Travelling Church to Kentucky" included the whole Spottsylvania County congregation, and that in 1785 sixty families of St. Mary's County, Maryland, formed a league to migrate to Kentucky and settled on Pottinger's Creek, Nelson County. See also Robert Davidson, *History of the Presbyterian Church in the State of Kentucky* (New York: R. Carter, 1847); John H. Spencer, *A History of Kentucky Baptists from 1769–1885* (Cincinnati: J. R. Baumes, 1886).

4. John C. Rainbolt, "The Absence of Towns in Seventeenth-Century Virginia," *Journal of Southern History* 35 (August 1969): 343–60.

5. Gaye Tuchman, "Women's Depiction by the Mass Media," *Signs: Journal of Women in Culture and Society* 4 (Spring 1979): 528–42; Kathryn Weibel, *Mirror, Mirror: Images of Women Reflected in Popular Culture* (New York: Doubleday, 1977); Bernard Rubin, ed., *Small Voices and Great Trumpets: Minorities and the Media* (New York: Praeger Publishers, 1980).

6. Linda Kerber, *Women of the Republic: Intellect and Ideology in Revolutionary America* (Chapel Hill: The University of North Carolina Press, 1980), 290–91, com-

ments on periodical coverage of women. See also Karen List, "Magazine Portrayals of Women's Role in the New Republic," *Journalism History* 13 (Summer 1986): 64–70; sources on lives of women during this era include Lee Virginia Chambers-Schiller, *Liberty, A Better Husband: Single Women in America: The Generations of 1780–1840* (New Haven: Yale University Press, 1984), and Joan M. Jensen, *Loosening the Bonds: Mid-Atlantic Farm Women, 1750–1850* (New Haven: Yale University Press, 1983). For a late eighteenth-century essay on women's subjection to men, see *The Kentucke Gazette*, Library of Congress, 17 November 1787, 1, 2 (the spelling changed to Kentucky on 14 March 1789).

7. Leland D. Baldwin, *The Keelboat Age on Western Waters* (Pittsburgh, Pa.: University of Pittsburgh Press, 1941), 2–3.

8. Quinn Hartwell Lockhart, "Colonel Arthur Campbell, 1743–1811: A Biography" (Ph.D. diss., University of Georgia, 1972), 20.

9. Harriette Simpson Arnow, *Seedtime on the Cumberland* (New York: Macmillan, 1960; Lexington: The University Press of Kentucky, 1983), 96–97.

10. Ibid., 106–7. Keith Ryan Nyland, "Doctor Thomas Walker (1715–1794) Explorer, Physician, Statesman, Surveyor and Planter of Virginia and Kentucky" (Ph.D. diss., Ohio State University, 1971), 15–16.

11. Nyland, "Doctor Thomas Walker," 30–31. Various names, derived from Indian usage, referred to Kentucky. The Cherokee called the area "the dark and bloody ground" because, according to Chief Attakullakulla, when they went to the area, it "ran with blood." The Delaware and Shawnee tribes called it *Kuttaawa*, meaning "great wilderness." The state name seems to have come from the Iroquois word *Kentake*, meaning "place of the meadows," "place of fields," or "hunting grounds."

12. Paul A. W. Wallace, *Pennsylvania: Seed of a Nation* (New York: Harper & Row, 1962), 86–87.

13. Baldwin, *The Keelboat Age*, 6–7

14. Wallace, *Pennsylvania*, 87; Nicholas Wainwright, *George Croghan: Wilderness Diplomat* (Chapel Hill: The University of North Carolina Press, 1959), 57–80; Ray Allen Billington, *Westward Expansion* (New York: Macmillan, 1960), 124–25.

15. Lockhart, "Colonel Arthur Campbell," 1–14; Archer Butler Hulbert, *Historic Highways*, vol. 4, *Braddock's Road* (Cleveland, Ohio: Arthur H. Clark Company, 1903), 133.

16. Lockhart, "Colonel Arthur Campbell," 20; Otis K. Rice, *The Allegheny Frontier: West Virginia Beginnings, 1730–1830* (Lexington: University Press of Kentucky, 1970), 20; Robert S. Cotterill, *History of Pioneer Kentucky* (Cincinnati, Ohio: Johnson and Hardin, 1917), 82–83. For a good general discussion of this period, see D. W. Meinig, *The Shaping of America: A Geographical Perspective of 500 Years of History*, vol. 1, *Atlantic America, 1492–1800* (New Haven: Yale University Press, 1986), 284–95.

17. Dale Van Every, *Forth to the Wilderness: The First American Frontier, 1754–1774* (New York: William Morrow, 1961; New York: Quill, n.d.), 295.

18. Lockhart, "Colonel Arthur Campbell," 29–36.

19. Draper's Life of Boone, Draper Mss., 2 B 168ff; Lucien Beckner, "Eskippakithiki: The Last Indian Town in Kentucky," *Filson Club History Quarterly* 6 (October 1932): 355–82; John A. Caruso, *The Appalachian Frontier* (Indianapolis,. Ind.: Bobbs-Merrill Co., 1959), 166–67; Billington, *Westward Expansion*, 160.

20. Draper's Life of Boone, Draper Mss., 2 B 194ff.; John Filson, "The Adventures of Col. Daniel Boon," in *The Discovery and Settlement of Kentucke* (Wilmington: James Adams, 1784; reprint, Ann Arbor, Mich.: University Microfilms, 1966), 53–57; Michael A. Lofaro, *The Life and Adventures of Daniel Boone* (1978; reprint, Lexington: The University Press of Kentucky, 1986), 23–35; Clark, *A History of Kentucky*, 45–47.

21. Lofaro, *The Life and Adventures of Daniel Boone*, 37–38; James W. Hagy, "The Frontier at Castle's Woods, Virginia," *Virginia Magazine of History and Biography* 75 (October 1967), 410–28; James W. Hagy, "The First Attempt to Settle Kentucky: Boone in Virginia," *Filson Club History Quarterly* 44 (July 1970): 227–34; Robert L. Kincaid, *The Wilderness Road* (Indianapolis, Ind.: Bobbs-Merrill Co., 1947), 78; Ruby Addison Henry, *The First West* (Nashville, Tenn.: Aurora Publishers, 1972), 10ff.

22. William Preston to ———, n.d., 1774, William Preston Papers, Draper Mss., 3 QQ 46; Lofaro, *The Life and Adventures of Daniel Boone*, 40–41; Thomas Speed, *The Wilderness Road* (New York: Burt Franklin, 1886), 25.

23. "Extracts of a Journal kept on the River Ohio in the year 1774 by Thomas Hanson," Reuben T. Durrett Collection (hereafter referred to as Durrett), Department of Special Collections, University of Chicago Library, Chicago, Codex 87; Kathryn Harrod Mason, *James Harrod of Kentucky* (Baton Rouge: Louisiana State University Press, 1951), 50–52, 58–62; Lucien Beckner, "Captain James Harrod's Company," *The Register of the Kentucky Historical Society* 20 (September 1922): 280–82; Neal O. Hammon, "Captain Harrod's Company, 1774: A Reappraisal," *The Register of the Kentucky Historical Society* 72 (July 1974): 224–42; Willard R. Jillson, "Old Fort Harrod," *The Register of the Kentucky Historical Society* 27 (September 1929), 563–68; Willard R. Jillson, "Harrod's Old Fort," *The Register of the Kentucky Historical Society* 28 (January 1930), 104–14; Willard R. Jillson, "The Founding of Harrodsburg," *The Register of the Kentucky Historical Society* 27 (September 1929), 559–62; Kathryn Harrod Mason, "Harrod's Men—1774," *Filson Club History Quarterly* 24 (July 1950), 230–33; W. H. Perrin, J. H. Battle, and G. C. Kniffin, *Kentucky: A History of the State* (Louisville, Ky.: F. A. Battey and Company, 1887; Easley, S.C.: Southern Historical Press, 1979), 118–19.

24. Lofaro, *The Life and Adventures of Daniel Boone*, 43; Archibald Henderson, "The Creative Forces in Westward Expansion: Henderson and Boone," *American Historical Review* 20 (October 1914): 86–107.

25. Lofaro, *The Life and Adventures of Daniel Boone*, 44–47; Clark, *A History of Kentucky*, 59–61; John Bakeless, *Daniel Boone* (New York: William Morrow, 1939), 47ff.; Caruso, *The Appalachian Frontier*, 78, 143–46; Kincaid, *The Wilderness Road*, 93–111; Thomas L. Connelly, "Gateway to Kentucky: The Wilderness Road, 1748–1792," *The Register of the Kentucky Historical Society* 59 (April 1961): 109–32; Archibald Henderson, "Richard Henderson and the Occupation of Kentucky," *Mississippi Valley Historical Review* 1 (December 1914): 341–63; Henderson, "Henderson and Boone," 86–107; Collins, *Historical Sketches of Kentucky*, 18–19; Cotterill, *History of Pioneer Kentucky*, 90–99.

26. Reuben Gold Thwaites and Louise Phelps Kellogg, *Frontier Defense of the Upper Ohio, 1777–78* (Madison: State Historical Society of Wisconsin, 1912), 7–9, 234–35 n. 98; 281–83; "Col. William Fleming's Journal in Kentucky from Nov. 10, 1779, to May 27th, 1780," in *Travels in the American Colonies*, ed. Newton D. Mereness (New York: Macmillan, 1916), 619–55.

27. "John Cowan's Journal, 1777," Durrett Codex 51; "Diary of Major Eskuries Beatty, Paymaster of the Western Army, 1786–1787," Durrett Codex 11; Durrett Personal Papers, Box 1, "Notes," 51; "Forts and Stations," Durrett, Maps, Sketches, and Pictures, Box 1; "Col. William Fleming's Journal," 619–55; Charles G. Talbert, *Benjamin Logan: Kentucky Frontiersman* (Lexington: University of Kentucky Press, 1962), 36, 70, 82, 91–93. Beatty recorded that "in the latter end of . . . 1779 this whole extent of country only contained 170 Souls." Durrett noted that by 20 April 1779, only eighty persons lived at Louisville, the fourth settlement in the Kentucky country; Lexington emerged as a new settlement in April 1778, but on a 1786 trip,

Beatty noted only twelve houses there. John Cowan's journal gives Harrodsburg population as 198 on 7 May 1777. Talbert gives Kentucky's total population as 280 at the same time.

28. Clark, *A History of Kentucky*, 94; 105–7; Cotterill, *History of Pioneer Kentucky*, 150–76.

29. Clark, *A History of Kentucky*, 112–31. *The Virginia Gazette, or, the American Advertiser*, printed by James Hayes in Richmond, 4 June 1785, reports the first convention. See also James Rood Robertson, *Petitions of the Early Inhabitants of Kentucky to the General Assembly of Virginia* (Louisville, Ky.: J. P. Morton and Company, 1914; reprint, New York: Arno Press, 1971), 79–82, 121–22, 140–41.

30. Lillian Schlissel, *Women's Diaries of the Westward Journey* (New York: Schocken Books, 1982).

31. Joanna L. Stratton, *Pioneer Women: Voices from the Kansas Frontier* (New York: Simon and Schuster, 1981; reprint, first Touchstone edition, 1982).

32. Nicholas Perkins Hardeman, *Wilderness Calling: The Hardeman Family in the American Westward Movement, 1750–1900* (Knoxville: University of Tennessee Press, 1977).

33. Ibid., 30. According to the census, Tennessee had 70,000 free inhabitants by 1795. *The Kentucky Gazette*, 28 May 1791, 2, gives the population of white women as 28,922 and white men as 32,211 (15,154 of whom were over sixteen); no breakdown by age for white women and none by sex or age for the 12,544 blacks is given.

34. Schlissel, *Women's Diaries*, 10, notes that more than a quarter million moved west between 1840 and 1870.

35. Daniel Drake, *Pioneer Life in Kentucky, 1785–1800* (New York: Henry Schuman, 1948), 9 n.7.

36. Schlissel, *Women's Diaries*, 27.

37. Ibid., 20, 23, 38.

38. Caruso, *The Appalachian Frontier*, 21; Kincaid, *The Wilderness Road*, 36; Richard L. Morton, *Colonial Virginia* (Chapel Hill: University of North Carolina Press, 1960), 2:448.

39. John P. Hale, *Trans-Allegheny Pioneers: Historical Sketches of the First White Settlements West of the Alleghenies, 1748 and After* (Cincinnati, Ohio: Samuel C. Cox and Co., 1886), 18–19.

40. Lloyd A. Brown, *Early Maps of the Ohio Valley* (Pittsburgh, Pa.: University of Pittsburgh Press, 1959).

41. *The Virginia Gazette*, printed by Alexander Purdie and John Dixon in Williamsburg, 8 September 1774.

42. Draper's Life of Boone, Draper Mss., 1 B 151, 3 B 34; folder marked "August 22, 1674," Durrett, Miscellaneous Papers, Box 1; S. P. Hildreth, *Pioneer History* (Cincinnati, Ohio: H. W. Derby Co., 1848), 68ff.; Wainwright, *George Crogan: Wilderness Diplomat*, 3ff.; Caruso, *The Appalachian Frontier*, 65–68. See also Willard R. Jillson, *Tales of the Dark and Bloody Ground* (Louisville, Ky.: C. T. Dearing Printing Co., 1930); Howard H. Peckham, ed., *George Croghan's Journal* (Ann Arbor: The University of Michigan Press, 1939). The Durrett collection contains an account, copied from the British Public Records Office, of Englishman Gabriel Arthur, who crossed Kentucky while in Indian captivity in the 1670s. Jillson describes this trip. In late 1744 George Croghan, who spent his life promoting western lands, established a base on the Cuyahoga River (site of present Cleveland, Ohio), and from there traveled often down the Ohio River and occasionally to Virginia. In the summer of 1746, he was in Philadelphia, built a trading post at present Pittsburgh, returned to Cuyahoga, went back to Pittsburgh, went again to Philadelphia, and then went down the Ohio River.

43. Kentucky Papers, Draper Mss., 5 CC 12; Draper's Life of Boone, Draper Mss., 1 B 151–54; Nyland, "Doctor Thomas Walker," 16–30; Arnow, *Seedtime on the Cumberland*, 107–71; Caruso, *The Appalachian Frontier*, 64–66; "Christopher Gist's Journal," in Hildreth, *Pioneer History*, 26ff.; Hale, *Trans-Allegheny Pioneers*, 15; Lucien Beckner, "John Findley: The First Pathfinder to Kentucky," *Filson Club History Quarterly* 43 (July 1969): 206–15; Brent Altsheler, "The Long Hunters and John Knox, Their Leader," *Filson Club History Quarterly* 5 (October 1931): 167–185; Billington, *Westward Expansion*, 160ff.; Kenneth P. Bailey, *Christopher Gist: Colonial Frontiersman, Explorer, and Indian Agent* (Hamden, Conn.: Archon Books, 1976), 32–47. See also J. Stoddard Johnston, ed., *Colonel Christopher Gist's Journal of a Tour through Ohio and Kentucky* (Louisville, Ky.: J. P. Morton and Company, 1898); Thomas Walker, *Journal of an Exploration in the Spring of the Year 1750* (Boston: Little, Brown and Co., 1888). Walker and Gist conducted the first known serious explorations in Kentucky in 1750 and 1751. Walker, employed by the Loyal Land Company of London, trekked over a small mountainous portion of southeastern Kentucky; Gist, employed by the Ohio Land Company to explore locations for settlements, descended the Ohio River toward present Louisville before growing fearful of Indians; he then hurried homeward through northern Kentucky, crossing Walker's route, to the Kanawha River. Several hunters and explorers spent time in Kentucky during the 1760s.

44. Thomas Hanson, "Extract of a Journal Kept on the River Ohio in the Year 1774," Durrett, Codex 87; *The Virginia Gazette*, Purdie and Dixon, 21 December 1769, and 8 September 1774; *The Virginia Gazette*, printed by William Rind in Williamsburg, 31 January 1771; Neal Hammon, "The Fincastle Surveyors in the Bluegrass, 1774," *The Register of the Kentucky Historical Society* 70 (October 1972): 277–94. Neander Montgomery Woods, *The Woods-McAfee Memorial* (Louisville, Ky.: Courier Journal Job Printing Company, 1905), 428–37, contains journals of James and Robert McAfee, who were among the first surveyors in Kentucky.

45. Thomas Kemp Cartmell, *Shenandoah Valley Pioneers and Their Descendants* (Winchester, Va.: The Eddy Press Corporation, 1909), 27ff; Collins, *Historical Sketches of Kentucky*, 19ff.; Kegley, *Kegley's Virginia Frontier*, 374, 394.

46. *The Virginia Gazette*, Purdie and Dixon, 9 April 1772.

47. Cartmell, *Shenandoah Valley Pioneers and Their Descendants*, 27ff.; Collins, *Historical Sketches of Kentucky*, 19ff.; Kegley, *Kegley's Virginia Frontier*, 377, 394.

48. Stratton, *Pioneer Women*, 13; Schlissel, *Women's Diaries*, 47, 11. Arthur M. Schlesinger, Jr., refers to the pioneer Kansas women as stoic in his introduction to Stratton's book.

49. Stratton, *Pioneer Women*, 11.

50. John Donaldson [*sic*], "Journal of a Voyage, intended by God's permission, in the good boat Adventure, from Fort Patrick Henry on Holston River, to the French Salt Springs on Cumberland River," in *The Annals of Tennessee to the End of the Eighteenth Century*, ed. J. G. M. Ramsey (Charleston, S.C.: John Russell, 1853), 198–99. Ramsey spells the name Donaldson.

51. Ibid., 200, 202. Arnow, *Seedtime on the Cumberland*, 236, concluded that Mrs. Peyton in the panic to lighten the boat and escape the Indians, accidentally threw her baby overboard with cargo.

52. Lofaro, *The Life and Adventures of Daniel Boone*, 37–38.

53. Filson, *The Discovery and Settlement of Kentucke*, 57, 76.

54. Lofaro, *The Life and Adventures of Daniel Boone*, 37–40.

55. Speed, *The Wilderness Road*, 20.

56. See, for example, quotations from Daniel Trabue's diary in chap. 1.

57. Schlissel, *Women's Diaries*, 13, 28–31.

58. See, for example, the Breckinridge brothers' letters to John in chap. 4.

59. See discussions of Polly Breckinridge's feelings about moving to Kentucky and then to Washington in James C. Klotter, *The Breckinridges of Kentucky, 1760–1981* (Lexington: The University Press of Kentucky, 1986), 32–35; Helen Congleton Breckinridge, "Cabell's Dale: The Story of a Family, 1760–1876" (Lexington, Ky.: unpublished paper, copyright 1983), 8–9. Lowell H. Harrison, *John Breckinridge: Jeffersonian Republican* (Louisville, Ky.: The Filson Club, 1969), 195, says Breckinridge's only concession to Polly by late 1805 on moving to Washington, D.C., was to postpone the decision until the entire family could vote.

60. See, for example, James's letters to John, dated 29 August 1788 in chap. 5, and 19 Feb. 1792 in chap. 7; Klotter, *The Breckinridges of Kentucky*, xvii. James Breckinridge died in Virginia in 1833, having served as militia officer, representative in the House of Delegates, Federalist candidate for governor, congressman, and member of the Board of Visitors of the University of Virginia.

61. Lofaro, *The Life and Adventures of Daniel Boone*, 21.

62. Arnow, *Seedtime on the Cumberland*, 135.

63. Patricia Watlington, *The Partisan Spirit: Kentucky Politics, 1779–1792* (New York: Atheneum, 1972), 12. See also Willard F. Bliss, "The Rise of Tenancy in Virginia," *Virginia Magazine of History and Biography* 58 (October 1950): 427–41; Henry, *The First West*, 14.

64. Harrison, *John Breckinridge*, 8–18, 22–27; Klotter, *The Breckinridges of Kentucky*, chap. 1; Stephen Hess, *America's Political Dynasties* (Garden City, N.Y.: Doubleday, 1966), 239–71.

65. Harrison, *John Breckinridge*, 1–3: Klotter, *The Breckinridges of Kentucky*, 6.

66. Michael Emery and Edwin Emery, *The Press and America: An Interpretive History of the Mass Media*, 6th ed. (Englewood Cliffs, N.J.: Prentice-Hall, 1988), 65. See also Clarence S. Brigham, *History and Bibliography of American Newspapers, 1690–1820*, 2 vols. (Worcester, Mass.: American Antiquarian Society, 1947); a count, using Brigham, showed a total of seventeen newspapers in the colonies in 1760, the year of John Breckinridge's birth, and thirty-two in 1769.

67. Brigham, *History*, 2:965, 2:1104–685, 1:163. For more about newspapers of the era, see also Isaiah Thomas, *The History of Printing in America*, edited by Marcus A. McCorison from the second edition (New York: Weathervane Books, 1970).

68. Stuart Seely Sprague, "Senator John Brown of Kentucky, 1757–1837: A Political Biography" (Ph.D. diss., New York University, 1972), 129–30.

69. Baldwin, *The Keelboat Age*, 175.

70. Arthur M. Schlesinger, *Prelude to Independence: The Newspaper War on Britain, 1764–1776* (Westport, Conn.: Greenwood Press, 1957), 52–54, 303–4; Thomas, *The History of Printing in America*, 13–21; Clarence S. Brigham, *Journals and Journeymen: A Contribution to the History of Early American Newspapers* (Philadelphia: University of Pennsylvania Press, 1950), 19–21. Early circulation data indicate that John Campbell, printer of the *Boston News-Letter*, complained on 10 August 1719 that he could not "vend 300 at an Impression, tho' some ignorantly concludes he Sells upwards of a Thousand." Thomas attributed an average of six hundred copies per issue to each of the four Boston newspapers in 1754 and said, "It has always been allowed that 600 customers, with a considerable number of advertisements, weekly, will but barely support the publication of a newspaper." Brigham said circulation increased in the 1790s but generally averaged six hundred to seven hundred, with a few exceptions.

71. Arnow, *Seedtime on the Cumberland*, provides one of the most sensitive narratives of Indian-white relationships during this era.

72. Clark, *A History of Kentucky*, 110–37; Patricia Watlington, "Discontent in Frontier Kentucky," *The Register of the Kentucky Historical Society* 65 (April 1967): 77–93; see also Watlington, *The Partisan Spirit*.

73. E. Merton Coulter, "The Efforts of the Democratic Societies of the West to Open the Navigation of the Mississippi River," *Mississippi Valley Historical Review* 11 (December 1924): 376–89; George L. Rives, "Spain and the United States in 1795," *American Historical Review* 4 (October 1898): 62–64; Sprague, "Senator John Brown," 58–223; Elizabeth Warren, "Senator John Brown's Role in the Kentucky Spanish Conspiracy," *Filson Club History Quarterly* 36 (April 1962): 158–76; Patricia Watlington, "John Brown and the Spanish Conspiracy," *Virginia Magazine of History and Biography* 75 (January 1967): 52–68.

74. Lofaro, *The Life and Adventures of Daniel Boone*, 107–8; Bakeless, *Daniel Boone*, 340–416.

75. Watlington, *The Partisan Spirit*, 11–30; Clark, *A History of Kentucky*, 85–94.

Chapter 1. Traveling over the Mountains

1. William Hickman, "A Short account of My life and travels. For more than Fifty years; a Professed servant of Jesus Christ," Durrett, Codex 94.

2. Letter fragment dated Kentucky Wilderness, 16 June 1785, Charles Scott Papers, Division of Special Collections and Archives, University of Kentucky Libraries, Lexington, Ky.

3. Hickman, "A Short account of My life and travels," Durrett, Codex 94.

4. Bayrd Still, "The Westward Migration of a Planter Pioneer in 1796," *William and Mary Quarterly* 2d ser., 21 (October 1941): 320; 329–30; 334; 340–41.

5. Letter fragment, 16 June 1785, Charles Scott Papers, Division of Special Collections and Archives, University of Kentucky Libraries, Lexington, Ky.

6. George P. Garrison, " 'A Memorandum of M. Austin's Journey from the Lead Mines in the County of Wythe in the State of Virginia to the Lead Mines in the Province of Louisiana West of the Mississippi,' 1796–1797," *American Historical Review* 5 (April 1900): 525–26. Quoted material is reprinted with permission of the American Historical Association.

7. Rice, *The Allegheny Frontier*, 3–9.

8. Distances are based on information in: Kentucky Papers, Draper Mss., 14 CC 221; Speed, *The Wilderness Road*, 16–21; Thomas Hutchins, *The Courses of the Ohio River, 1766*, ed. Beverly W. Bond. (Cincinnati: Historical and Philosophical Society of Ohio, 1942), 77, 85; William Allan Pusey, *The Wilderness Road to Kentucky* (New York: George H. Doran Co., 1921), 26–27.

Travel times are based on information primarily from diaries and letters: Durrett Miscellaneous Papers, Box 2, folder marked "March 30, 1778," contains George Rogers Clark's diary, which also appears in James Alton James, *The George Rogers Clark Papers, 1777–1781* (Springfield: Illinois State Historical Library, 1912), 20–28; John L. Blair, "Mrs. Mary Dewees's Journal from Philadelphia to Kentucky," *The Register of the Kentucky Historical Society* 63 (July 1965): 195–217; *The Pittsburgh Gazette*, printed by John Scull, 15 May 1788; Dale Van Every, *Ark of Empire: The American Frontier, 1784–1802* (New York: William Morrow, 1963), 101. The Dewees family travelled 366 miles (from Pittsburgh to the mouth of Scioto Riverd in Ohio) in eight days, averaging nearly forty-six miles daily in low water. A 1788 writer to *The Pittsburgh Gazette* told of traveling even further—from Pittsburgh to Limestone (present Maysville, Kentucky)—in four days.

9. George Rogers Clark's diary of his 1778 trip from Harrodsburgh to Wil-

liamsburg specifies each day's mileage. Van Every notes that the wilderness route trip usually took five weeks.

10. Still, "The Westward Migration," 331.

11. *The Kentucke Gazette,* printed by John Bradford in Lexington, 29 November 1788. Such notices appeared in virtually every issue of the newspaper read from 12 April 1788. Rare notices also advertised trips up the Ohio River. See the issue for 15 January 1791, for example.

12. In the late 1770s, when Kentucky settlers were besieged by Indians, Benjamin Logan may have traveled alone from Crab Orchard, Kentucky, to the Holston River. See Talbert, *Benjamin Logan: Kentucky Frontiersman,* 27, 29.

13. Drake, *Pioneer Life,* 8.

14. Seymour Dunbar, *A History of Travel in America* (Indianapolis, Ind.: Bobbs-Merrill, 1915), 190.

15. "Diary of James Nourse, of Berkeley County, Va., 1775–1780," Durrett, Codex 142 (23, 29 April entries).

16. Dunbar, *A History of Travel in America,* 194.

17. Blair, "Mrs. Mary Dewees's Journal," 204. Quoted material from *The Register of the Kentucky Historical Society* is reprinted with permission of the editor, James C. Klotter.

18. Arnow, *Seedtime on the Cumberland,* 214.

19. Drake, *Pioneer Life,* 11–12; Kentucky Papers, Draper Mss., 13 CC, 202.

19a. "Diary of James Nourse," Durrett, Codex 142.

20. Ibid.

21. Arnow, *Seedtime on the Cumberland,* 215.

22. Dunbar, *A History of Travel in America,* 192. Packhorses averaged ten miles per day bearing averages of two hundred pounds.

23. Blair, "Mrs. Mary Dewees's Journal," 201.

24. Speed, *Wilderness Road,* 34–38.

25. Blair, "Mrs. Mary Dewees's Journal," *The Register of the Kentucky Historical Society,* 204.

26. Speed, *The Wilderness Road,* 34–35.

27. Kentucky Papers, Draper Mss., 13 CC 70–72; Blair, "Mrs. Mary Dewees's Journal," 205–9.

28. Baldwin, *The Keelboat Age,* 410, 47.

29. W. Wallace Carson, "Transportation and Traffic on the Ohio and the Mississippi before the Steamboat," *Mississippi Valley Historical Review* 7 (June 1920): 28; Baldwin, *The Keelboat Age,* 7, 47.

30. Dunbar, *A History of Travel in America,* 190; Arnow, *Seedtime on the Cumberland,* 215.

31. Kentucky Papers, Draper Mss., 13 CC 82.

32. Baldwin, *The Keelboat Age,* 49.

33. Ibid., 42–47.

34. Arnow, *Seedtime on the Cumberland,* 215.

35. Blair, "Mrs. Mary Dewees's Journal," 210. Dewees refers to the children "playing with Daddy on the shore" while the boat stopped sixty-five miles below Pittsburgh.

36. Ibid., 203, 204.

37. Drake, *Pioneer Life,* 10.

38. William Sudduth, "Sketch of the life of W. Sudduth," Durrett, Codex 179.

39. Blair, "Mrs. Mary Dewees's Journal," 205, 206. Dewees wrote that the boat "got fast on the lower ford but by the agility of our men soon got off."

40. Drake, *Pioneer Life,* 10.

41. Baldwin, *The Keelboat Age*, 83.
42. "Diary of Joel Watkins—1789," Durrett, Codex 198 (8, 9 May entries). See also Virginia Smith Herold, ed., "Joel Watkins' Diary of 1789," *The Register of the Kentucky Historical Society* 34 (July 1936): 215–50; Alonzo Barton Hepburn, *A History of Currency in the United States* (New York: Macmillan, 1915), 33. Twelve d. equaled one shilling, and 20 shillings equaled one pound. Generally, after 1776, the exchange rates in shillings per dollar were: Virginia and New England, six; New York and North Carolina, eight; Georgia, five; South Carolina, thirty-two and one-half; remaining states: seven and one-half.
43. Sudduth, "Sketch of the life of W. Sudduth," Durrett, Codex 179.
44. Arnow, *Seedtime on the Cumberland*, chaps. 4 and 7.
45. Samuel and Jean Shannon to Thomas Shannon, 24 November 1784, Shannon Family Papers, Department of Library Special Collections, Manuscripts, Western Kentucky University, Bowling Green, Ky.
46. "Diary of Daniel Trabue," Durrett, Codex 186.
47. Garrison, " 'A Memorandum," 525.
48. William Christian to Col. Gilbert Christian, 13 Aug. 1785, William Preston Papers, Draper Mss., 5 QQ 122.
49. "Diary of Joel Watkins—1789," Durrett, Codex 198.
50. "Rev. James Smith, Three Journals to the Western Country from Powhatten County, Va.—1st Oct. 1785—Dec. 21st," Durrett, Codex 171.
51. Blair, "Mrs. Mary Dewees's Journal," 199.
52. Drake, *Pioneer Life*, 9, n.7
53. Blair, "Mrs. Mary Dewees's Journal," 202.
54. Kentucky Papers, Draper Mss., 13 CC 63.
55. Kincaid, *The Wilderness Road*, 152.
56. Nicholas Meriwether to William Meriwether, 25 February 1784, Nicholas Meriwether Papers, 1749–1828, Manuscript Department, The Filson Club, Louisville, Ky.; copies from Manuscripts Division, Kentucky Historical Society, Frankfort, Ky.
57. W. Warfield to John Breckinridge, 11 February 1793, Breckinridge Family Papers, Manuscripts Division, Library of Congress (hereafter referred to as Breckinridge Family Papers, Library of Congress) (28 January 1793–30 October 1793), 9:1381.
58. Blair, "Mrs. Mary Dewees's Journal, 201–2.
59. Hickman, "A Short account of My life and travels," Durrett, Codex 94.
60. Drake, *Pioneer Life*, 9.
61. *The Kentucky Gazette*, 12 December 1789.
62. Sudduth, "Sketch of the life of W. Sudduth." Durrett, Codex 179.
63. "Diary of James Nourse," Durrett, Codex 142.
64. Blair, "Mrs. Mary Dewees's Journal," 205, 207, 202.
65. Ibid., 206–7, 209. On 7 November, three Frenchmen invited the Deweeses to a ball at Colonel Butler's, "where 30 Ladys & Gentlemen were to Assemble. . . ." Dewees wrote, "It is hardly worthwhile to say we declined . . . as it was out of our power to dress fit at this time, to Attend such an Entertainment. . . ."
66. *The Kentucky Gazette*, 3 December 1791.
67. *The Pittsburgh Gazette*, 15 May 1788.
68. Baldwin, *The Keelboat Age*, 82.
69. Van Every, *Ark of Empire*, 158–59.
70. Harry Innes to John Knox, 7 July 1790, The Papers of Harry Innes, Manuscript Division, Library of Congress, Washington, D.C., 19:40.

71. *The Pittsburgh Gazette,* 15 May 1788.

72. *The Pittsburgh Gazette,* 19 June 1788, 9 July 1788, 15 July 1788; *the Kentucky Gazette,* 12 July 1790.

73. Speed, *Wilderness Road,* 36–37.

74. "Diary of Daniel Trabue," Durrett, Codex 186.

75. Durrett, Miscellaneous Papers, Box 2, folder Marked "March 30, 1778"; James, *The George Rogers Clark Papers,* 20–28. Martin's Station, when established in 1775, was the westernmost settlement east of the Kentucky settlements. Clark's 1778 mileage record from Harrodsburg (Kentucky) shows 150 miles to Martin's Station, 498 to the east side of the Blue Ridge Mountains, and 689 to Williamsburg (including a short detour via his father's home in Caroline County). Thus, by Clark's calculations, the Kentucky settlements were 150 miles from any source of assistance and nearly 700 miles from the government seat in Virginia.

76. Kentucky Papers, Draper Mss., 13 CC 238–39.

77. Dunbar, *A History of Travel in America,* 194.

78. Kentucky Papers, Draper Mss., 13 CC 137–38; 14 CC 7–8.

79. Sarah Wigginton to Mrs. William Calk, 6 September 1783, William Calk Papers, 1753–1784, Division of Special Collections and Archives, University of Kentucky Libraries, Lexington, Ky.

80. Hickman, "A Short account of My life and travels," Durrett, Codex 94.

Chapter 2. Sending Letters over the Mountain

1. Companies traveling to or from the Kentucky country gave letter writers opportunities to send mail. Regular trips probably dated from early 1776 when the Kentucky country representatives began attending the Virginia Assembly.

2. William Preston to Col. ————, n.d., 1774; William Christian to William Preston, n.d., 1774; William Christian to William Preston, 12 July 1774; [Henry Russell] to William Preston, 12 July 1774; Henry Russell to William Preston, 27 August 1774, William Preston Papers, Draper Mss., 3 QQ 46, 60, 63–64, 84.

3. Wesley E. Rich, *History of the United States Post Office to the Year 1820* (Cambridge: Harvard University Press, 1924), 33ff.; Carl Scheele, *A Short History of the Mail Service* (Washington, D.C.: Smithsonian Institution Press, 1970), 45ff.; Fairfax Harrison, "The Colonial Post Office in Virginia," *William and Mary Quarterly* 2d ser., 4 (April 1924): 73–99; Alvin F. Harlow, *Old Post Bags* (New York: D. Appleton and Company, 1928), 255ff.; *The Virginia Gazette,* printed by William Parks in Williamsburg, 22 June 1739.

4. *American Heritage Pictorial Atlas of United States History* (New York: American Heritage Publishing Company, 1966), 80; Rich, *History of the United States Post Office,* 70–71, 64; Scheele, *A Short History of the Mail Service,* 45–70.

5. Rich, *History of the United States Post Office,* 30.

6. James Truslow Adams, *Atlas of American History* (New York: Charles Scribner's Sons, 1943), plate 55.

7. Harlow, *Old Post Bags,* 247ff.

8. Rich, *History of the United States Post Office,* 71ff.

9. Ibid., 35.

10. Harrison, "The Colonial Post Office in Virginia," 85–86; W. Harrison Bayles, "Postal Service in the Thirteen Colonies," *Journal of American History,* no. 3, 5 (1911): 439.

11. *The Virginia Gazette,* printed by William Parks in Williamsburg, 23 April 1738.

12. Rich, *History of the United States Post Office*, 35.

13. Ibid., 34, 39–40.

14. Harlow, *Old Post Bags*, 241, 253–55; Rich, *History of the United States Post Office*, 33, 40, 43, 54–55; William Smith, *The History of the Post Office in British North America, 1639–1870* (Cambridge: Cambridge University Press, 1920), 50–51.

15. Rich, *History of the United States Post Office*, 43; Smith, *History of the Post Office*, 50–51.

16. Harlow, *Old Post Bags*, 241, 253–254.

17. Kentucky Papers, Draper Mss., 14 CC 221, gives distances from Philadelphia via the Great Valley (of Virginia) to the Falls of the Ohio (present Louisville, Kentucky) as 826 miles. Hutchins, *The Courses of the Ohio River (1766)*, 77, gives distances from Fort Pitt (present Pittsburgh) to the Falls of the Ohio as 682 miles; Speed, *Wilderness Road*, 16, gives distances from Philadelphia to Pittsburg as 320 miles. This totals 1,002 miles via the river route from Philadelphia, Pennsylvania, to the site of present Louisville, Kentucky.

18. Bayles, "Postal Service in the Thirteen Colonies," 429; Smith, *History of the Post Office*, 2; Rich, *History of the United States Post Office*, 3–4; Harlow, *Old Post Bags*, 226ff.; Frank Staff, *The Transatlantic Mail* (London: Adlard Coles Ltd., 1956), 19ff.

19. No information was found about exactly when express riders were first used to send special messages in the colonies. Generally, such individuals were hired as the need arose, but the military hired riders to assure someone would be available to deliver urgent messages.

20. Edward Johnson to William Preston, 2 September 1777, 28 October 1779, 10 December 1779, Preston Family Papers-Davie Collection, 1658–1896, Manuscript Department, The Filson Club. Edward Johnson, a Manchester, Virginia, merchant, regularly sent goods to William Preston on the frontier in the 1770s. With each wagon load, he sent a letter and newspapers, and occasionally magazines. On one occasion, he sent eight newspapers plus "the magazines promised," and on another he complained that his wife cut most magazines into dress patterns before he could send them.

Thomas Hart, a Hagerstown, Maryland, merchant who sent goods to families in Kentucky in the 1780s, also sent letters, newspapers, and magazines to friends and relatives there. Thomas Hart to ———, 30 September 1784; Thomas Hart to Isaac Shelby, 5 May 1785, Thomas Hart to ———, 4 November 1789, Thomas Hart Papers, 1767–1790, Samuel Wilson Collection, Division of Special Collections and Archives, University of Kentucky Libraries, Lexington, Ky.

The Kentucky district representatives to the Virginia Assembly made the trip twice yearly. Letter writers (chaps. 3 through 6) often indicated that a "delegate" would carry their letters.

21. Writers of letters reported in chaps. 3 through 8 tell of hastily writing while the "bearer" waited.

22. Mary Howard to John Brown, 15 January 1787, Preston Family Papers-Davie Collection, 1658–1896, Manuscript Department, The Filson Club.

23. *The Kentucky Gazette*, 5 December 1789, 6 February 1790; Dwight Mikkelson, "*Kentucky Gazette*: The 'Herald of a Noisy World'" (Ph.D. diss., University of Kentucky, 1963), 29.

24. John Floyd to William Preston 15 April 1775, William Preston Papers, Draper Mss., 4 C 9. Floyd copied Boone's letter from Kentucky to Henderson in the spring of 1775 and sent it to Preston. Nathaniel Hart to ———, Spring Hill, 27 April 1839, Durrett, Codex 89. Hart included extracts of Floyd's letters.

25. One size, called a "quire," contained twenty-four sheets, each of which made two of approximately the "legal size" of today when cut. Quires of paper are on display in the Colonial Williamsburg, Virginia, post office.

26. David Campbell to Arthur Campbell, 14 August 1787, Arthur Campbell Letters, Manuscript Department, The Filson Club.

27. Rev. John Brown to William Preston, 23 March 1781, William Preston Papers, Draper Mss., 5 QQ 93.

28. William Preston to Lettice Breckinridge, 9 October 1774, Breckinridge Family Papers, Library of Congress (7 April 1752—1 March 1784), 1:42. Preston wrote that "Major Robinson" was "going to open a school again," and advised Mrs. Breckinridge, "by all means," to "send Johnny the sooner the Better."

29. John Breckinridge to Lettice Beckinridge, 18 September 1783, Breckinridge Family Papers, Library of Congress, 1:121. John wrote, "The packett of letters which accompanies this I wrote a month ago to send by Mr. Madison who declined going. . . ."

Chapter 3. Assessing the Kentucky Country

1. William Preston to Major Robert Breckenridge, 16 November 1769, Breckinridge Family Papers, Library of Congress, 1:1. William Bumpass carried the letter. Major Robert Breckenridge spelled his name with three *e*'s; his offspring changed the spelling. Preston wrote, "The Bearer is Just going[,] therefore have not time to write to my Wife," but he begged "you will show her this Letter."

2. William Allen Pusey, *Three Kentucky Pioneers: James, William and Patrick Brown* (Louisville, Ky.: J. P. Morton, 1930), 2; Speed, *Wilderness Road*, 6, notes that Fort Pitt probably had no more residents than Kentucky settlements by 1775.

3. *The Virginia Gazette*, printed by William Rind in Williamsburg, 7 September 1769. The letter was dated 26 July 1769.

4. *The Virginia Gazette*, Purdie and John Dixon, 7 September 1769.

5. Perrin, Battle, and Kniffin, *Kentucky*, 79–80; Billington, *Westward Expansion*, 148–49, 156.

6. *The Virginia Gazette*, Rind, 14 December 1769.

7. *The Virginia Gazette*, Purdie and Dixon, 21 December 1769.

8. Ibid., 3 December 1771.

9. *The Virginia Gazette*, Rind, 31 January 1771.

10. *The Virginia Gazette*, Purdie and Dixon, 29 July 1773.

11. Ibid., 21 May 1772, 18 February 1773.

12. *The Virginia Gazette*, Rind, 15 July 1773, 12 August 1773.

13. Ibid., 3 March 1774.

14. *The Virginia Gazette*, Purdie and Dixon, 24 October 1771.

15. Ibid., 8 October 1772, 10 December 1772, 18 March 1773, 2 September 1773, 10 June 1773, 5 August 1773.

16. *The Virginia Gazette*, Rind, 25 March 1773.

17. *The Virginia Gazette*, Purdie and Dixon, 29 July 1773.

18. *The Virginia Gazette*, Rind, 23 December 1773.

19. *The Virginia Gazette*, Purdie and Dixon, 5 December 1771.

20. Ibid., 17 September 1772, 1 October 1772, 8 October 1772, 12 November 1772; *The Virginia Gazette*, Rind, 10 December 1772.

21. *The Virginia Gazette*, Rind, 14 January 1773.

22. Ibid., 10 March 1774.

23. Ibid., 31 January 1771.

24. *The Virginia Gazette*, Purdie and Dixon, 10 December 1772.

25. *The Virginia Gazette*, Rind, 16 June 1774.

26. Ibid., 7 July 1774.

27. Ibid., 17 March 1774.

28. *The Virginia Gazette*, Purdie and Dixon, 8 September 1774.

29. Breckinridge, "Cabell's Dale," 1; Harrison, *John Breckinridge*, 4; Klotter, *The Breckinridges of Kentucky*, xvi; Robert Breckenridge to William Robinson, 16 November 1772, Breckinridge Family Papers, Library of Congress, 1:21. See also Kegley, *Kegley's Virginia Frontier*, 508–10, 536, 538. Ages are approximate within a year because sources disagree on the year of Major Breckenridge's death. Breckinridge and Klotter give it as 1773, and Harrison gives it as late summer or fall of 1772. Kegley printed Robert Breckenridge's will, dated 17 August 1772, and indicates (p. 536) that on 13 July 1773 Robert Breckenridge was charged "to lay off the tithables to work under him and John May respectively" regarding a road survey; and on 11 August 1773, he was among those charged to "view the way proposed by David May for altering the road." Continuation of the same records (p. 538) in 1776 refers to appointment of James Robinson to serve "in the room of Robert Breckenridge . . . deceased." A note to William Robinson, 16 November 1772, was signed by Robert Breckenridge: "Please to pay the bearer, James Mackiney[?] three pounds eighteen shillings on my account as I could not make up that sum and oblige your friend." This, of course, may have been John's stepbrother Robert.

30. William Preston to Lettice Breckinridge, 9 October 1774, Breckinridge Family Papers, Library of Congress, 1:42; "Miss Joan Buchanan" carried the letter.

31. Clark, *A History of Kentucky*, 59–63; Caruso, *The Appalachian Frontier*, 78, 143–46; Kincaid, *Wilderness Road*, 93–112; Perrin, Battle, and Kniffin, *Kentucky*, 126.

32. *The Virginia Gazette*, printed by Alexander Purdie in Williamsburg, 10 March 1775; *The Virginia Gazette*, printed by John Pinkney in Williamsburg, 23 March 1775.

33. William Preston to Governor Dunmore, n.d., January 1775, and 10 March 1775, William Preston Papers, Draper Mss., 4 QQ 1, 7; William Preston to George Washington, 31 January 1775, and 9 April 1775, William Preston Papers, Samuel Wilson Collection, Division of Special Collections and Archives, University of Kentucky Libraries, Lexington, Ky.

34. Nathaniel Hart to ———, 27 April 1839, Durrett, Codex 89.

35. Cotterill, *History of Pioneer Kentucky*, 169–70; Perrin, Battle, and Kniffin, *Kentucky*, 264.

36. Talbert, *Benjamin Logan: Kentucky Frontiersman*, 36, 56.

37. Durrett, Personal Papers, Box 1, Notes, 51.

38. Ben Cassedy, *The History of Louisville From Its Earliest Settlement to the Year, 1852* (Louisville, Ky.: Hull and Brother, 1852), 52––53; Perrin, Battle, and Kniffin, *Kentucky*, 170.

39. "Col. William Fleming's Journal," 621 (14 November 1779 entry).

40. Ibid., 626–28.

41. Ibid., 630.

42. Ibid., 636.

43. Ibid., 629–30 (22, 24 January 1780; 2, 4, 5, 11, 12, 13 February 1780).

44. *The Kentucke Gazette*, printed by John Bradford, Lexington, 3 January 1789.

45. Biographical Sketch of John Floyd, Draper's Life of Boone, Draper Mss., 5 B, Appendix 6.

46. Cotterill, *History of Pioneer Kentucky*, 161; *The Independent Ledger, and the American Advertiser* (Boston: printed by Edward Draper and John W. Folsom, 20 December 1780), 2; Perrin, Battle, and Kniffin, *Kentucky*, 169, cite the Floyd correspondence. The Boston newspaper contains a letter from "an officer of the government, dated at Fort Jefferson, mouth of Ohio, June 13, 1780," that boasted, "we have already twenty thousand inhabitants," adding, "The emigration to these parts is incredible. . . . The lands are equal to the best in America; and salt, iron and lead mines are

in sufficient plenty." For Clark's efforts against the British, see James, *The George Rogers Clark Papers, 1777–1781.*

47. John Breckinridge to Lettice Breckinridge, 7 June 1781, Breckinridge Family Papers, Library of Congress, 1:93–94. Breckinridge's election at age nineteen to the Virginia Assembly in 1780 was a surprise because he had not sought office. See Harrison, *John Breckinridge,* 6–10.

48. Harrison, *John Breckinridge,* 5.

49. William Breckinridge to William Preston, 1 June 1780, William Preston Papers, Draper Mss., 5 QQ 31.

50. Harrison, *John Breckinridge,* 6–7; Klotter, *The Breckinridges of Kentucky,* 8.

51. *The Virginia Gazette, or, the American Advertiser,* printed by James Hayes in Richmond, 11 May 1781; 8 June 1782, 15 June 1782. In 1780 the Virginia capital moved from Williamsburg to Richmond, where Hayes's newspaper competed with John Dixon's and Thomas Nicolson's *The Virginia Gazette,* which moved from Williamsburg and began publishing in Richmond on 9 May 1780. That newspaper was interrupted on 21 April 1781; only one single-sheet issue was published on 19 May 1781 before publishing was resumed by Thomas Nicolson and William Prentis on 29 December 1781. Hayes began publishing in Richmond on 22 December 1781. See Brigham, *History,* 2:1145–51, 1158–63.

52. John Breckinridge to Lettice Breckinridge, 22, 23 June 1782, Breckinridge Family Papers, Library of Congress, 1:107–8.

53. Biographical Sketch of John Floyd, Draper's Life of Boone, Draper Mss., 5 B, Appendix 6.

54. John Breckinridge to Lettice Breckinridge, 22, 23 June 1782, Breckinridge Family Papers, Library of Congress, 1:107–8.

55. *The Virginia Gazette, or, the American Advertiser,* Hayes, 3 August 1782.

56. Ibid., 17 August 1782.

57. Ibid., 28 September 1782.

58. Ibid., 5 October 1782.

59. Perrin, Battle, and Kniffin, *Kentucky,* 188–90.

60. *The Virginia Gazette, or, the American Advertiser,* Hayes, 6 July 1782, 2 November 1782.

61. Alexander Breckinridge to William Preston, 21 October 1782, William Preston Papers, Draper Mss., 5 QQ 112.

62. Note signed by William Breckinridge, 20 November 1782, Breckinridge Family Papers, Library of Congress, 1:113.

63. Perrin, Battle, and Kniffin, *Kentucky,* 190.

64. Ibid., 225–26, gives migration and population figures. See also Cotterill, *History of Pioneer Kentucky,* 161, 244.

65. John Breckinridge to Lettice Breckinridge, 28 January 1783, Breckinridge Family Papers, Library of Congress, 1:117, "favor'd by Mr. Fulton." John wrote, "Mr. Fulton has been waiting, & I have been in such a hurry that I am afraid you cannot read it—I have sent a Bag full of things with him which you will be pleased to send to town for."

66. James Breckinridge to Lettice Breckinridge, n.d., 1783, Breckinridge Papers, Library of Congress, 1:151, "favoured by Mr. Howard."

67. *The Virginia Gazette, or, the American Advertiser,* Hayes, 3 May 1783, 10 May 1783. The Boone-Hays item was dated in Fayette County on 22 April 1783; the Marshall item was undated.

68. John Breckinridge to Lettice Breckinridge, 28 May 1783, Breckinridge Family Papers, Library of Congress, 1:126–27, sent "To the Care of Mrs. Howard."

69. *The Virginia Gazette,* printed by John Dixon and Thomas Nicolson in Richmond, 1 January 1780.

70. Harrison, *John Breckinridge,* 7.

71. John Breckinridge to William Preston, 26 November 1781, William Preston Papers, Draper Mss., 5 QQ 100.

72. *The Virginia Gazette, or, the American Advertiser,* Hayes, 24 May 1783.

73. Note signed by Alexander Breckinridge and James Warren, 1 June 1783; Alexander Breckinridge to Lettice Breckinridge, 6 September 1783, Breckinridge Family Papers, Library of Congress, 1:130–31, 145. On 6 September 1783, Alexander was in Manchester, Virginia. He wrote to his stepmother via "Mr. Davis": "Mr. Lewises Waggoner has the Charge of the few things I have been able to procure, or at least, what I could get him to carry, as he has already loaded. I have it not in my power to send you any rum this opportunity, but old Mr. Howe I have just spoke to, he informs me he shall leave this on Monday next, at which time I hope to send the rum. . . . I have also sent a loaf of white sugar by the bearer and many other things which will be delivered at Mr. Howards, to wit a large box of Queens China, a large or middle sized Trunk full of other articles, two covered tin Kettles lying in the wagon."

74. *The Virginia Gazette, or, the American Advertiser,* Hayes, 28 June 1783.

75. Ibid., 26 July 1783. See also issues for 23 August 1783, 6, 13, 20, 27 September 1783, 4, 18 October 1783.

76. Ibid., 16 August 1783, 23 August 1783.

77. Ibid., 18 Oct. 1783.

78. Ibid., 1 Nov. 1783; 15 Nov. 1783.

79. William Breckinridge to Lettice Breckinridge, 16 November 1783, Breckinridge Family Papers, Library of Congress, 1:147, carried by John Brown.

80. *The Virginia Gazette, or, the American Advertiser,* Hayes, 6 December 1783, 13 December 1783.

81. Ibid., 20 December 1783, 10 January 1784, 27 December 1783.

82. John Breckinridge to Lettice Breckinridge, 26 December 1783, Breckinridge Family Papers, Library of Congress, 1:149. John wrote, "You shall not complain of my not writing more frequently to you from Williamsburg. I will always have some letter in the hands of Mr. Hunter in Mr. Hays [*sic*] Printing Office, & if any one who shall come from Botetourt will apply to him they will find a letter. . . ."

83. *The Virginia Gazette, or, the American Advertiser,* Hayes, 31 May 1783.

84. Ibid., 14 June 1783, 12 July 1783, 23 August 1783.

85. Ibid., 1 November 1783.

86. Ibid., 10 January 1784, 7 February 1784, February 1784.

87. Ibid., 28 February 1784.

88. Alexander Breckinridge to John Breckinridge, 4 March 1784, Breckinridge Family Papers, Library of Congress (4 March 1784–31 July 1785), 2:165–66, "Hon^d. by Capt. Hunter."

89. Perrin, Battle, and Kniffin, *Kentucky,* 225–26; Cotterill, *History of Pioneer Kentucky,* 244; J. Winston Coleman, *Slavery Times in Kentucky* (Chapel Hill: The University of North Carolina Press, 1940), 14.

90. John Breckinridge to Lettice Breckinridge, 17 March 1784, Breckinridge Family Papers, Library of Congress, 2:169–70. The letter, written "at the Rawleigh, Williamsburg," was sent "To the Care of the Hble. William Christian." John wrote, "I have little expectations of hearing from you, till Mr. Stewart comes to the Genl. Court."

91. A. Stuart to John Breckinridge, 1 April 1784; William Breckinridge to James Breckinridge, 8 August 1784 [chap. 4, n.3], Breckinridge Family Papers, Library of Congress, 2:171–72, 232. Stuart wrote, "perhaps you may be at yr. Brother Jas· wedding with Miss Katey Kenelly. . . ."

92. *The Virginia Gazette, or, the American Advertiser,* Hayes, 20 March 1784, 17 April 1784.

93. J. Preston to John Breckinridge, 3 May 1784, Breckinridge Family Papers, Library of Congress, 2:206–7, "hon'd. by Capt. Barber." Preston wrote, "I shall write you very fully by your worthy colleague Capt. Sayer who goes down & send some business to you & trouble you a little more."

94. James Breckinridge to John Breckinridge, 23 May 1784, Breckinridge Family Papers, Library of Congress, 2:211–12, 215. James, whose letter was "Hond· by Capt. Hancock," received John's letter via "Mr. Stewart."

95. *The Virginia Gazette, or, the American Advertiser,* Hayes, 26 June 1784, 3 July 1784, 10 July 1784, 17 July 1784.

96. Ibid., 26 June 1784.

97. Clark, *A History of Kentucky,* 303–4; Charles R. Staples, *The History of Pioneer Lexington, 1779–1802* (Lexington, Ky.: Transylvania University Press, 1939), 26–30. Dwight Mikkelson, *"Kentucky Gazette,* 'The Herald of a Noisy World'" (Ph.D. diss., University of Kentucky, 1963), 39–40; Cassedy, *History of Louisville,* 83; Cotterill, *History of Pioneer Kentucky,* 213; Huntley Dupre, "The *Kentucky Gazette* Reports the French Revolution," *Mississippi Valley Historical Review* 26 (September 1939): 164; Cassedy says Daniel Brodhead established the first store in Louisville in 1783; Cotterill says James Wilkinson went to Louisville as a merchant in 1784, and Dupre says he established a store in Lexington in the same year.

Virginia newspapers did not carry information about the stores in Kentucky, of course, but letters and diaries refer to some. For example, Alexander Breckinridge to John Breckinridge, 8 August 1784, Breckinridge Family Papers, Library of Congress, 2:228–29; "Diary of Major Eskuries Beatty, paymaster of the Western Army, 1786–1787," Durrett, Codex 11; William Johnston to Doctor Ben Johnston, 12 July 1783, William Johnston Papers, Manuscript Department, The Filson Club. Breckinridge mentions the death of Mr. Knightly, who was a "merchant at the Falls." Johnston wrote from Sullivan's Station in Kentucky to his father in Virginia that he had just escaped from six months of Indian captivity; before that, he ran a boarding school at the falls and planned to continue it. He asked his father to send his brother with books "immediately," and a horse, a cow or two, and a particular breed of hogs. He hoped to get the clerkship and establish a public house—for which he asked that his father send a billiard table. Finally, he asked his father to bring whiskey and flour so he could pay for planned purchases at a forthcoming auction. Sources also indicate that Mr. Lacassagne was a merchant at Louisville in the early 1780s.

98. The Thomas Hart papers reveal such activity [see chap. 2, n. 20]; after *The Kentucke Gazette* began publishing in 1787, advertisements frequently noted auctions by merchants bringing goods from Pittsburgh, Philadelphia, and Baltimore.

99. Clark, *A History of Kentucky,* 303–04; Staples, *The History of Pioneer Lexington,* 26–30; Mikkelson, *"Kentucky Gazette,"* 39–40; Cotterill, *History of Pioneer Kentucky,* 151, 213, 229–40; Redford, *The History of Methodism in Kentucky,* 1:21ff.; Hickman, "A Short Account of my life and travels," Durrett, Codex 94; Short, "Some Early Kentucky Church Experiences," 269–79; Perrin, Battle, and Kniffin, *Kentucky,* 217–19. See also Walter W. Jennings, *Transylvania: Pioneer University of the West* (New York: Pageant Press, 1955); Davidson, *History of the Presbyterian Church;* William Dudley

Nowlin, *Kentucky Baptist History, 1770–1922* (Louisville: Baptist Book Concern, 1922); M. J. Spalding, *Sketches of the Early Catholic Missions in Kentucky* (Louisville: B. J. Webb and Brother, 1844); and Spencer, *A History of Kentucky Baptists.*

Chapter 4. Discussing the Move over the Mountains

1. Alexander Breckinridge to John Breckinridge, 8 August 1784, Breckinridge Family Papers, Library of Congress, 2:228–29. The letter, "honored by Mr. Z. Johnston," reached John on 10 September, and he wrote a reply the same day.
2. William Breckinridge to John Breckinridge, 9 August 1784, Breckinridge Family Papers, Library of Congress, 2:231; carried by "Mr. Johnston" and answered on 10 September 1784.
3. William Breckinridge to James Breckinridge, 9 August 1784, Breckinridge Famiy Papers, Library of Congress, 2:232. "Mr. Johnston" carried the letter.
4. Alexander Breckinridge to John Breckinridge, 14 August 1784, Breckinridge Family Papers, Library of Congress, 2:233–34. The letter was "Honored by Mr. Carney."
5. *The Virginia Gazette, or, the American Advertiser,* Hayes, 21 August 1784.
6. Ibid., 18 September 1784.
7. John Brown to John Breckinridge, 20 September 1784, Breckinridge Family Papers, Library of Congress, 2:239–40, sent by "Mr. Morris" and answered on 25 September. James carried the letters from John Breckinridge to John Brown.
8. William Breckinridge to John Breckinridge, 5 October 1784, Breckinridge Family Papers, Library of Congress, 2:237.
9. William Breckinridge to Lettice Breckinridge, 6 October 1784, Breckinridge Family Papers, Library of Congress, 2:241.
10. William Breckinridge to Lettice Breckinridge, 25 October 1784, Breckinridge Family Papers, Library of Congress, 2:246, written "at Mrs. Floyds," and "Honour[d.] by Mr. James Buchanan."
11. James Breckinridge to John Breckinridge, 25 October 1784, Breckinridge Family Papers, Library of Congress, 2:247.
12. Alexander Breckinridge to John Breckinridge, 6 November 1784, Breckinridge Family Papers, Library of Congress, 2:249–50, "Hono'd by Col. McLanahan."
13. See William Breckinridge letter to Lettice Breckinridge, 22 December 1784 (n. 21 below). Concerning Floyd's death, see Perrin, Battle, and Kniffin, *Kentucky,* 190–91; Biographical Sketch of John Floyd, Draper's Life of Boone, Draper Mss., 5 B, Appendix 6.
14. Klotter, *The Breckinridges of Kentucky,* 8.
15. "Major William Croghan's Diary of a Trip from Louisville to Nashville," William Croghan Papers, Draper Mss., 1 N 1–9. See Alexander Breckinridge to John Breckinridge, 14 August 1784 (n. 4 above) and William Breckinridge to Lettice Breckinridge, n.d., 1784 (n. 20) and 22 December 1784 (n. 21), Breckinridge Family Papers, Library of Congress, 2:233–34, 7:1188, and 2:226. Only the brothers knew the truth, of course, and all had died before relatives divulged the information— Alexander in 1801, Robert in 1833, and William in 1838, all in Kentucky; James died in 1833 in Virginia. See Klotter, *The Breckinridges of Kentucky,* 385, xvi–xvii.
16. James Breckinridge to John Breckinridge, 22 March 1788, Breckinridge Family Papers, Library of Congress, 5:693. Writing from Williamsburg that "Billy has been in town this month almost without my hearing of it," James said he inquired "into the cause of his detention here so long & found he had not money . . . to pay

off his tavern account." Although nothing could have been more inconvenient, James wrote, he "was obliged to assume the payment of [William's] account which amounted to 8 or 9 lbs."

17. James Breckinridge to John Breckinridge, 18 November 1784, Breckinridge Family Papers, Library of Congress, 2:56. Colonel Fleming carried the letter.

18. "Col. William Fleming's Journal in Kentucky from Jan. 4th to April 22nd, 1783," in Mereness, ed., *Travels in the American Colonies*, 661–674.

19. *The Virginia Gazette, or, the American Advertiser*, Hayes, 4 June 1784; Clark, *A History of Kentucky*, 112–14; Cotterill, *History of Pioneer Kentucky*, 211–12; Sprague, "Senator John Brown," 43–45; Perrin, Battle, and Kniffin, *Kentucky*, 263–66.

20. William Breckinridge to Lettice Breckinridge, n.d. [before 22 December] 1784; Samuel ——— to Lettice Breckinridge, 23 November 1784, Breckinridge Family Papers, Library of Congress, 7:1188; 2:257. William's letter appears out of sequence in the family papers. On 23 November Samuel [McDowell?] wrote to Mrs. Breckinridge from Pleasant Vale, Lincoln County, Kentucky: "I arrived safe at home the 23d. of October after a troublesome Journey through the Wilderness, the Road being very Bad. found my family all well. You have no doubt heard that the Indians Routed two companies on the Road, and were followed both times and the Plunder &c. Retaken. Since which they took 30 odd horses from a Company near Cumberland River, also 150 bells[?] [bales] & forty head of Cattle. . . ."

21. William Breckinridge to Lettice Breckinridge, 22 December 1784, Breckinridge Family Papers, Library of Congress, 2:266.

22. Clark, *A History of Kentucky*, 112–14; Cotterill, *History of Pioneer Kentucky*, 209–11; Sprague, "Senator John Brown," 43–47; Perrin, Battle, and Kniffin, *Kentucky*, 263–66. See also Robertson, *Petitions*, although the book includes little of the proceedings of the conventions.

23. *The Virginia Gazette, or, the American Advertiser*, Hayes, 4 June 1785.

24. William Breckinridge to John Breckinridge, 7 February 1785, Breckinridge Family Papers, Library of Congress, 2:291, "Hon'd by Mr. Jonathan Taylor."

25. Harrison, *John Breckinridge*, 22–23.

26. *The Virginia Gazette, or, the American Advertiser*, Hayes, 2 Apr. 1785.

26a. Ibid., 14 May 1785.

27. Ibid., 10 May 1785.

28. Ibid., 14 May 1785.

29. Ibid., 4 June 1785, 9 July 1785.

30. Ibid., 9 April 1785, 2 April 1785.

31. Ibid., 9 July 1785, 23 July 1785.

32. Ibid., 16 August 1785, 27 August 1785.

33. Sprague, "Senator John Brown," 47–49; Cotterill, *History of Pioneer Lexington*, 214–15; Clark, *A History of Kentucky*, 116–18; Perrin, Battle, and Kniffin, *Kentucky*, 268–71.

34. John Breckinridge to Lettice Breckinridge, 12 November 1785, Breckinridge Family Papers, Library of Congress (August 1785–12 March 1787), 3:336, sent "To the particular Care of Mr. Bourne Price—New London." Harrison, *John Breckinridge*, 23, notes the farm was a wedding gift from the Cabells.

35. Perrin, Battle, and Kniffin, *Kentucky*, 270–71, 271n.

36. John Breckinridge to James Breckinridge, 29 January 1786, James Breckinridge Collection, Manuscripts Division, Special Collections Department, University of Virginia Library, Charlottesville, Va.

37. James Breckinridge to John Breckinridge, 8 March 1786, Breckinridge Family

Papers, Library of Congress, 3:359–60, "favor^d. by Mr. May." James received John's 29 January letter on 6 March via John Brown.

38. *The Virginia Gazette, or, the American Advertiser,* Hayes, 8 February 1786.

39. William Breckinridge to John Breckinridge, 19 March 1786, Breckinridge Family Papers, Library of Congress, 3:361, carried by "Col. McClannahans Boy." Writing from Botetourt, William informed John that "the Family are all in tolerable good Health Except Mammy," who had "been very unwell ever since I came from Kentucky."

40. Mary Howard to John Breckinridge, 8 May 1786, Breckinridge Family Papers, Library of Congress, 3:372, "fav^d. by Mr. Jones."

41. William Fleming to William Preston, 28 August 1780; James Brown to William Preston, 3 September 1789, William Preston Papers, Draper Mss., 5 QQ 65, 122. Fleming wrote about Howard's abuse of his wife, Preston's sister; the letter from James Brown in Danville may refer to the same Howard: "Ben ^j. Howard still lives in his little hut without any company but mine, which he has occasionally. he is impatient for the arrival of his family." Information in the Breckinridge Family Papers about the sale of the "Fishpond," the Howard farm in Amherst County, Virginia, includes a writ assuring that Mary Howard acted without threat of her husband in the sale. Breckinridge Family Papers, Library of Congress, 6:720–21.

42. John Breckinridge to Lettice Breckinridge, 23 and 25 March 1786, n.d., June 1786, Breckinridge Family Papers, Library of Congress, 3:364–65. John wrote on 23 March, "I left Polly not very well and am uneasy about her. I sincerely wish you would let Betsy come down with my Brother Billy who wrote to me he would come . . . Polly is extreamly [*sic*] impatient to see her; & does scarcely any thing but talk of her. & I believe I could not have got off to this Court if I had not have promised to have gone up for Betsy." On 25 March he wrote, "I had just time the other Day to insist on Billy by letter to come down immediately. If you can with any Conveniency spare Betsy, I should be very glad she would come with him. . . ." In late June he wrote, "We have kept my Brother Billy & Betsy as long as possible. Betsy has grown so uneasy; she has visited so little, & there has been so little mirth . . . since she came down that I believe she is sick of the visit."

43. Lettice Breckinridge to John Breckinridge, 11 May 1786, Breckinridge Family Papers, Library of Congress, 3:376–77, "Favored by Mr. Craig."

44. *The Virginia Gazette, or, the American Advertiser,* Hayes, 17 May 1786.

45. John Brown to John Breckinridge, 20 May 1786, Breckinridge Family Papers, Library of Congress, vol. 3:381–82.

46. John Breckinridge to Lettice Breckinridge, n.d., June 1786, Breckinridge Family Papers, Library of Congress, 3:387–88; Klotter, *The Breckinridges of Kentucky,* 11. John wrote that he had moved to his parents-in-law's home on June 12 "from the great Anxiety Col. & Mrs. Cabell have to have their Daughter with them, & also Polly's desire to be with her mother. . . . She was on the 14th delivered of a fine Daughter . . . called *Letitia Preston.*"

47. *The Virginia Gazette, or, the American Advertiser,* Hayes, 19 July 1786.

48. Alexander Breckinridge to John Breckinridge, 21 August 1786, Breckinridge Family Papers, Library of Congress, 3:404, "Hon^d. by Mr. Ja^s. Breckinridge."

49. John Breckinridge to Lettice Breckinridge, 21 August 1786, Breckinridge Family Papers, Library of Congress, 3:406, sent "by Mr. Watkins."

50. Lettice Breckinridge to John Breckinridge, 24 August 1786, Breckinridge Family Papers, Library of Congress, 3:409, sent "by Mr. Watkins."

51. Lettice Breckinridge to John Breckinridge, 5 September 1786, Breckinridge Family Papers, Library of Congress, 3:418.

52. Alexander Breckinridge to John Breckinridge, 22 September 1786, Breckinridge Family Papers, Library of Congress, 3:423–24.

53. *The Virginia Gazette, or, the American Advertiser,* Hayes, 11 October 1786.

54. Sprague, "Senator John Brown," 58–63; Clark, *A History of Kentucky,* 118–20; Cotterill, *History of Pioneer Kentucky,* 216–220; Perrin, Battle, and Kniffin, *Kentucky,* 271–73.

55. Perrin, Battle, and Kniffin, *Kentucky,* 225–26; *The Continental Journal, and the Weekly Advertiser,* printed by James D. Griffith in Boston, 16 March 1786.

56. William Breckinridge to Lettice Breckinridge, 2 November 1786, Breckinridge Family Papers, Library of Congress, 3:435. The letter was delivered by "Mr. Wall," who was going to Botetourt "at the request of Mr. Madison & Mr. May . . . to teach their Families the Guittar." William told his mother that Wall "proposes having a school" at her house and asked her to give him William's "little Bay Horse" as payment for teaching him musical instruments. He and James were Wall's students, he wrote.

57. John Breckinridge to Lettice Breckinridge, 8 November 1786, Breckinridge Family Papers, 3:443. John wrote from Colonel Samuel Meredith's, and "Mr. Brooks" carried the letter.

58. See William's letter to his mother, 2 November 1786 (n. 56 above).

59. James Breckinridge to John Breckinridge, 6 November 1786, Breckinridge Family Papers, Library of Congress, 3:438, sent "per Anthony."

60. Mary Cabell Breckinridge to Lettice Breckinridge, 19 November 1786; John Breckinridge to Lettice Breckinridge, 8 November 1786; Samuel Meredith to Lettice Breckinridge, 12 November 1786; Elizabeth Meredith to Lettice Breckinridge, n.d., Breckinridge Family Papers, Library of Congress, 3:451–52, 443, 447–48; 7:1195. Betsy's letter, out of sequence in the family papers, was probably written on 12 November 1786, a date that Samuel Meredith indicated she would write to her mother, and the letter refers to her new in-laws. She wrote, "My Dr. Mother I cant express uneasiness I have felt about you since I heard of the bad state of health you ware in and what you have suffered since I left you."

61. Mary Howard to John Breckinridge, 24 March 1787, Breckinridge Family Papers, Library of Congress (14 March 1787–8 March 1788); 4:527.

62. *The Pittsburgh Gazette,* printed by John Scull and Joseph Hall, 9 September 1786, 4 November 1786.

63. Ibid., 10 February 1787 (opening of an office for buying and selling continental and state certificates), 17 February 1787 (opening of a "dry and wet goods" store), 3 March 1787 (openings of a liquor store and another dry goods store). Through 1787 and 1788, still other "inns for travelers" opened in Pittsburgh. Numerous available issues of the newspaper were illegible, so a full accounting of the advertisements during those years is not possible.

Chapter 5. "I Find Myself Determined [to Move to Kentucky]"

1. *The Kentucky Gazette,* 1 August 1789.

2. *The Virginia Gazertte and Weekly Advertiser,* printed by Thomas Nicolson in Richmond, 12 December 1786.

3. Ibid., 31 January 1787.

4. Ibid., 8 March 1787.
5. Ibid., 5 April 1787.
6. Brigham, *History*, 1:163–64; Mikkelson, *"Kentucky Gazette,"* 1–4; *The Kentucke Gazette*, 18 August 1787. See also G. Glenn Clift, comp., "John Bradford, 'The Caxton of Kentucky': A Bibliography," *American Notes and Queries* 8 (June 1948): 35–41; John Coleman, *John Bradford (1749–1830), Esquire: Pioneer Kentucky Printer and Historian* (Lexington, Ky.: Winburn Press, 1950); Willard R. Jillson, *The First Printing in Kentucky* (Louisville, Ky.: C. T. Dearing Printing Co., 1930).
7. James Beckinridge to John Breckinridge, 13 July 1787, Breckinridge Family Papers, Library of Congress, 4:584–85, sent "To the particular care of Col. Meredith."
8. David G. Smith, *The Convention and the Constitution* (New York: St. Martin's Press, 1965), 1–2, 33, 99; Clark, *A History of Kentucky*, 125; Sprague, "Senator John Brown," 65–69; Perrin, Battle, and Kniffin, *Kentucky*, 275–76; Cotterill, *History of Pioneer Kentucky*, 220; *The Kentucke Gazette*, 17 November 1787, 1, 8, 15, 33, 29 March 1788, 5 April 1788.
9. *The Pittsburgh Gazette*, 9 June 1787, 24 November 1787, Perrin, Battle, and Kniffin, *Kentucky*, 225–26.
10. Roger Thompson to John Breckinridge, 17 January 1788, Breckinridge Family Papers, Library of Congress, 4:677–78, sent by "Mr. Hopkins."
11. *The Virginia Gazette and Weekly Advertiser*, 12 March 1788. John Brown was in New York at the time. See Sprague, "Senator John Brown," 70, 73–75.
12. *The Virginia Gazette and Weekly Advertiser*, 3 April 1788.
13. Clark, *A History of Kentucky*, 125–26; Sprague, "Senator John Brown," 72–93.
14. *The Virginia Gazette and Weekly Advertiser*, 10 July 1788.
15. Sprague, "Senator John Brown," 98–99; Perrin, Battle, and Kniffin, *Kentucky*, 277–78; Clark, *A History of Kentucky*, 126; *The Kentucke Gazette*, 23, 30 August 1788; 6, 13, 27 September 1788; *The Pittsburgh Gazette*, 1 November 1788.
16. *The Virginia Gazette and Weekly Advertiser*, 28 August 1788.
17. Harrison, *John Breckinridge*, 46–59; Sprague, "Senator John Brown," 166–168.
18. Sprague, "Senator John Brown," 72–146; Watlington, "John Brown," 52–68. Sprague and Watlington provide different interpretations of Brown's activities. See also Warren, "Senator John Brown's Role," 158–76.
19. *The Kentucke Gazette*, 15 March 1788. Perrin, Battle, and Kniffin, *Kentucky*, 275–76. Robert Breckinridge served as Jefferson County delegate to the convention. John Brown had corresponded with James Breckinridge more frequently than with John, but letters indicate a closeness that ended after a confrontation over business matters during John Breckinridge's trip to Kentucky in 1789. Breckinridge, whose papers reflect a steady temperament and absence of rancor, left a careful explanation of his disappointment in Brown, declaring, "My confidence he will never regain; For a Century spent in a different habit of thinking, would not in my opinion so regenerate him, as to qualify him for *real friendship*." Statement by John Breckinridge, n.d., December 1790; John Brown to John Breckinridge, 11 October 1787, Breckinridge Family Papers, Library of Congress, 7:1006, 4:616.
20. James Breckinridge to John Breckinridge, 31 October, 14 December 1787; John Breckinridge to James Breckinridge, 25 January 1788, Breckinridge Family Papers, Library of Congress, 4:627, 649–50, 680–81. John also informed James that "sister Betsy has a fine new daughter" [born sometime before 5 December 1787].
21. James Breckinridge to John Breckinridge, 13 June 1788; Breckinridge Family Papers, Library of Congress (22 March 1788–15, December 1789): 5:710.
22. Archibald Stuart to John Breckinridge, 19 June 1788, Breckinridge Family Papers, Library of Congress, 4:712.

23. Harrison, *John Breckinridge,* 28.

24. Sprague, "Senator John Brown," 87–88; Charles G. Talbert, "Kentuckians in the Virginia Convention of 1788," *The Register of the Kentucky Historical Society* 58 (July 1960): 187–93.

25. The *Columbian Magazine,* printed by William Spotswood in Philadelphia, 2 (November 1788): 664; (December 1788): 716; *The Pittsburgh Gazette,* 22 March 1788; 1 November 1788. The March item reported that since the recent opening of the Ohio and Monongahela rivers—closed since the previous December—many boats with twenty to thirty persons each had passed on the way to Kentucky, and the November item said ten thousand had passed down the river "within twelve months past." See also Perrin, Battle, and Kniffin, *Kentucky,* 225–26.

26. Samuel Meredith [Jr.] to John Breckinridge, 4 July 1788; Elizabeth Meredith to John Breckinridge, 4 July 1788, Breckinridge Family Papers, Library of Congress, 5:715, 716, "fav^d. by Genl. Russell."

27. Joseph Cabell [Sr.] to John Breckinridge, 25 July 1788, Breckinridge Family Papers, Library of Congress, 5:723; Harrison, *John Breckinridge,* 23.

28. John Breckinridge to James Breckinridge, 17 August 1788, Breckinridge Family Papers, Library of Congress, 5:715–16, "Favored by Col. J. Nicholas."

29. James Breckinridge to John Breckinridge, 29 August 1788, Breckinridge Family Papers, Library of Congress, 5:748–49, "favored by Col. Nicholas."

30. *The Virginia Gazette and Weekly Advertiser,* 9 October 1788.

31. Ibid., 16 October 1788.

32. Ibid., 4 December 1788.

33. Sprague, "Senator John Brown," 102; Robertson, *Petitions,* 121–22. Convention proceedings were reported in *The Kentucke Gazette,* 30 January 1789 and 7 February 1789.

34. *The Virginia Gazette and Weekly Advertiser,* 11 December 1788.

35. Ibid., 12 February 1789.

36. Anne Christian to John Breckinridge, n.d., February 1789; Samuel Meredith to John Breckinridge, 19 March 1789; M. Irving to John Breckinridge, n.d., March 1789, Breckinridge Family Papers, Library of Congress, 5:786–7, 795, 798.

37. James Breckinridge to John Breckinridge, 6 March 1789, Breckinridge Family Papers, Library of Congress, 5:789, sent "By Mr. Norvile."

38. Robert Breckinridge to John Breckinridge, 6 March 1789, 2 October 1787, 26 November 1788, Breckinridge Family Papers, Library of Congress, 5:790, 753–54, 762; Robert Breckinridge to James Breckinridge, 2 July 1788, Breckinridge-Marshall Papers, Manuscript Department, The Filson Club. Robert may have returned to Kentucky after the ratifying convention and gone back to Virginia in early fall, although his October letter from Richmond indicates that he had been at his stepmother's Botetourt home, where he saw John. He wrote that he had not heard from James since arriving but would write to him. His July letter was written at Richmond to James in Williamsburg. His November letter from Richmond reflects alarm about James's illness.

39. M. Cabell to Lettice Breckinridge, 23 March 1789, Breckinridge Family Papers, Library of Congress, 5:797.

40. Mary Cabell Breckinridge to Lettice Breckinridge, n.d., March 1789, Breckinridge Family Papers, Library of Congress, 5:799–800.

41. Mary Cabell Breckinridge to John Breckinridge, 12 April 1789, Breckinridge Family Papers, Library of Congress, 5:801–2, "Hon^d. by Mr. Allen."

42. Joseph Cabell to John Breckinridge, 13 April 1789, Breckinridge Family Papers, Library of Congress, 5:803, "Fav^rd. by Mr. John Allen."

43. M. Cabell to John Breckinridge, 13 April 1789, Breckinridge Family Papers, Library of Congress, 5:804, "Hon^d. by M. John Allen."

44. *The Virginia Gazette and Weekly Advertiser,* 19 March 1789.

45. Ibid., 9 April 1789.

46. Ibid., 21 May 1789.

47. Ibid., 28 June 1789.

48. Ibid., 2 April 1789.

49. John Breckinridge to Lettice Breckinridge, 7 May 1789, Breckinridge Family Papers, Library of Congress, 5:811. John wrote the letter at William McDowell's in Mercer County, and John Brown carried it.

50. *The Kentucky Gazette,* 1 May, 1789. In addition to business for other clients, John, as an attorney for Samuel Meredith, advertised several tracts on Salt, Elkhorn, Licking, and Ohio rivers, saying purchasers could receive titles while he was in Kentucky.

51. S. Richardson to John Breckinridge, 23 July 1789; Robert Breckinridge to John Breckinridge, 23 June 1789, Breckinridge Family Papers, Library of Congress, 5:830, 818. Richardson wrote that he had heard of John "having fallen a victim to the cruel Savages."

52. *The Kentucke Gazette,* 15 December 1787.

53. No single source enumerates merchants, teachers, innkeepers, and tradespeople and their activities in other parts of the Kentucky country as the newspaper does for Lexington. Other scattered sources refer to some. See chap. 3, nn. 97–99.

54. *The Kentucke Gazette,* 8, 22 September 1787, 15 December 1787.

55. Ibid., 25 August 1787, 6 October 1787. The Myers advertisement was dated at Lincoln [County?], 15 August 1787, and Robinson's was dated at Bourbon, 26 September 1787.

56. *The Kentucke Gazette,* 3 November 1787, 25 August 1787.

57. Ibid., 8 September 1787, 24 November 1787.

58. Ibid., 27 October 1787, 15 December 1787. John Brown announced in the October issue that he was turning over his clients' business to Stephen Ormsby during his absence. Harry Innes announced in the December issued that he would share Brown's business with Ormsby since Brown had been elected to Congress.

59. *The Kentucke Gazette,* 15 September 1787.

60. Ibid., 18 August 1787, 27 October 1787, 15 December 1787.

61. Lack of previous advertisements does not mean these stores were new, of course. Some merchants never advertised, some advertised throughout the five years, and others rarely did.

62. *The Kentucke Gazette,* 12 April 1788, 5 January 1788, 2 August 1788.

63. Ibid., 19 January 1788, 6 December 1788, 6 December 1788, 15 March 1788, 24 May 1788, 30 August 1788.

64. Ibid., 24 May 1788, 11 October 1788, 1 March 1788, 15 August 1788, 21 August 1788, 30 August 1788, 27 September 1788, 20 December 1788.

65. Ibid., 11 July 1789, 18 April 1789, the store was called "Benjamin Beall & Co."

66. Ibid., 3 January 1789. John Duncan advertised "A Collection of Books in Divinity, Law and Physic; several entertaining Histories; —some English and Latin School Books—A Variety of Books for instruction & entertainment of Children; American Magazines & Museums of the latest dates. . . ." Some other merchants advertised books as secondary items, but Duncan's advertisements continually emphasized books.

67. *The Kentucke Gazette,* 2 March 1788, 10 January 1789, 30 January 1789, 7 March 1789. *The Kentucky Gazette,* 23 May 1789, 28 November 1789. Jeremiah Morariaty and

John Davenport taught dancing (23 May and 2 March). Tavern keepers included Captain Thomas Young (10 January), Stephen Collins (30 January), and Henry Marshall (7 March). There was a "River's tavern" (28 November), and "McNair's Tavern" may have also existed as "The Sign of the Buffalo"; see *The Kentucky Gazette*, 16 May 1789 and 7 January 1792. The latter suggests the two names may refer to the same establishment.

68. *The Kentucke Gazette*, 15 August 1788, 16 May 1789. Edward West and David Humphreys were clock and watch makers. West's advertisements appeared in 1788 but not in 1789.

69. *The Kentucky Gazette*, 28 November 1789, *The Kentucke Gazette*, 16 August 1788. Andrew Gatewood opened a private entertainment house for "man and horse on the road from Lexington to Curd's ferry" in 1789 and advertised in November; Rawleigh Chinn had opened a private entertainment house "on the road . . . from Lexington to Bourton Court house" in 1788 but did not advertise in 1789.

70. *The Kentucky Gazette*, 12 December 1789 (Charles White, coppersmith). W. Butler, tailor, advertised 28 November 1789; Nicholas Wood, baker, advertised 26 April 1789; Horatio Hall, hatter, advertised on 7 March 1789. John Bradford announced on 5 December 1789 that "A Post Rider will start from this place on Mon. the 14th inst., to Harrodsburgh, Danville, Lincoln, Madison, Boonesborough and Bourbon, and if sufficiently encouraged, will continue to ride once a week for a year." John Nancarrow's brewery advertisement appeared 12 September 1789.

71. *The Kentucke Gazette*, 30 January 1789; *The Kentucky Gazette*, 18 April 1789, 2 May 1789, 12 September 1789, 8 October 1789, 12 December 1789. Someone asked for a blacksmith's apprentice in January and a similar advertisement asked for an apprentice to the tanning and currying business in May. In April James Wilkinson called for "a number of hands to conduct my boats to . . . New Orleans . . . to whom I will give ten Dollars per Month, and a bounty of twenty Dollars, or thirty-five Dollars for the trip. . . ." Joseph Gale asked in September for "A JOURNEYMAN MASON, BRICK LAYER, or PLASTERER." In October John Allen asked for a "MILLER and DISTILLER"; in December Samuel Lamme asked for a distiller and William M'Dowell sought an overseer.

72. *The Kentucke Gazette*, 30 January 1789; *The Kentucky Gazette*, 27 June 1789, 10 October 1789. The January ad announced a public sale of "Drawing knives, Carpenters and Coopers Adzes, Plastering Trowels, Turning, Mortoise and Socket Chisels, 2 feet Rules, Padlocks, Gimblets assorted. Double plane Irons, Plated shoe and knee buckles. A quantity of Cutlery. . . ." The June ad offered a still, and the October ad offered ironmongery for sale.

73. *The Kentucke Gazette*, 21 February 1789; *The Kentucky Gazette*, 14 March 1789, 28 March 1789, 4, 18 April 1789, 25 April 1789, 13 June 1789, 30 June 1789, 22 August 1789.

74. Dupre, *"The Kentucky Gazette* Reports the French Revolution," 164.

75. Jennings, *Transylvania*, 4–14; Mikkelson, *"Kentucky Gazette,"* 53. For development of schools in Kentucky, see Wenonah Elizabeth Marman, "Some Phases of Pioneer Education on the Kentucky Frontier with Emphasis on Nelson County, 1785–1860" (Master's thesis, University of Louisville, 1943), 4–24.

76. *The Kentucky Gazette*, 21 March 1789, 26 December 1789; 27 June 1789, 23 May 1789, 6 June 1789, 9 May 1789. These ads concern jails in Louisville and Lexington, a meeting house in Danville, two public schools, and the "new" court house, respectively. A Separate Baptist Association was active by the time the newspaper began publishing. See *The Kentucke Gazette*, 15, 22 September 1787; regarding churches and denominations, see Cotterill, *History of Pioneer Kentucky*, 242–43.

77. *The Kentucke Gazette*, 10 January 1789.
78. *The Kentucky Gazette*, 8 August 1789, 4 December 1789.
79. Ibid., 27 June 1789.
80. *The Kentucke Gazette*, 10 November 1787, *The Kentucky Gazette*, 3 January 1789.
81. Cotterill, *History of Pioneer Kentucky*, 236.
82. *The Kentucky Gazette*, 6 December 1789.

Chapter 6. Preparing to Move over the Mountains

1. Perrin, Battle, and Kniffin, *Kentucky*, 284; Clark, *A History of Kentucky*, 129; Sprague, "Senator John Brown," 113–14.
2. *The Virginia Gazette and Weekly Advertiser*, 8 October 1789.
3. Ibid., 9 July 1789, 16 July 1789, 13 August 1789, 13 August 1789.
4. Ibid., 10 September 1789.
5. John Breckinridge to Lettice Breckinridge, 5 January 1790, Breckinridge Family Papers, Library of Congress (28 December 1789–11 November 1790), 6:876.
6. Elizabeth Meredith to Lettice Breckinridge, 9 January 1790, Breckinridge Family Papers, Library of Congress, 6:877–78.
7. Samuel Meredith [Sr.] to Lettice Breckinridge, 9 January 1790, Breckinridge Family Papers, Library of Congress, 6:879, "Hon^d. by Mr. Breckinridge."
8. Elizabeth Meredith to Lettice Breckinridge, 26 February 1790, Breckinridge Family Papers, Library of Congress, 6:890.
9. James Breckinridge to John Breckinridge, 20 February, 18 March 1790, Breckinridge Family Papers, Library of Congress, 6:893, 901. The first letter was sent via "Mr. Green," and the second, by William Breckinridge.
10. Perrin, Battle, and Kniffin, *Kentucky*, 284–85; Clark, *A History of Kentucky*, 129–30.
11. Lettice Breckinridge to John Breckinridge, 2 April 1790, Breckinridge Family Papers, Library of Congress, 6:911, sent to Prince Edward Court.
12. Samuel Meredith [Jr.] to John Breckinridge, 30 November 1790, Breckinridge Family Papers, Library of Congress, (30 November 1790–26 December 1791), 7:1028.
13. Philip Rootes to John Breckinridge, 23 February 1791, Breckinridge Family Papers, Library of Congress, 7:1073. Sources use various spellings for Dr. Rootes's name; the spelling used here is as he signed his letters.
14. Samuel Meredith [Jr.] to John Breckinridge, 13 April 1790, Breckinridge Family Papers, Library of Congress, 6:925–26.
15. Elizabeth Meredith to John Breckinridge, n.d., April 1790, Breckinridge Family Papers, Library of Congress, 6:935, sent by "Col. Meredith."
16. Preston carried Samuel's November 1790 letter home to Botetourt (see n. 49 below); Mrs. Breckinridge's 6 December 1790 letter refers to Preston being in Kentucky (see n. 48 below).
17. *The Kentucky Gazette*, 12 April 1790.
18. Robert Breckinridge to John Breckinridge, 6 June 1790, Breckinridge Family Papers, Library of Congress, 6:947.
19. Mary Cabell Breckinridge to Lettice Breckinridge, n.d., January 1790, Breckinridge Family Papers, Library of Congress, 6:889.
20. John Breckinridge to William Russell, 8 April 1790, Breckinridge Family Papers, Library of Congress, 6:921, "Favored by Clement Carington, Esquire."
21. Caleb Worley to John Breckinridge, 30 April 1790, Breckinridge Family Papers, Library of Congress, 6:934.

22. Caleb Wallace to John Breckinridge, 30 April 1790, Breckinridge Family Papers, Library of Congress, 6:932, "commanded to the care of Col. George Thompson."

23. Robert Breckinridge to John Breckinridge, 6 June 1790, Breckinridge Family Papers, Library of Congress, 6:947, sent by "Mr. Buchanan."

24. James Breckinridge to John Breckinridge, 20 February 1790, Breckinridge Family Papers, Library of Congress, 6:893.

25. A. Stuart to John Breckinridge, 29 June 1790; J. Preston to John Breckinridge, 4 July 1790, Breckinridge Family Papers, Library of Congress, 6:956, 963. "Mr. Jacob Kenny" carried Stuart's letter, and "Mr. Preston" carried Preston's.

26. P. Henry to John Breckinridge, 13 June 1790, Breckinridge Family Papers, Library of Congress, 6:948, sent by "Mr. Venable."

27. Gordon Croeces to John Breckinridge, 19 June 1790, Breckinridge Family Papers, Library of Congress, 6:950. John's servant, George, carried the note with a supply of groceries; Croeces' note further said, "By George have sent you Two Loaves of Sugar & 22 lb. [sic] Coffee[.] I expect a hhd. of Brown Sugar up in about Ten Days; shall reserve as much as you want, I intirely forgot you the last that I had. I wrote to Mr. Gals for a hat agreeable to your Memorandum, but he has not Sent it, I have had none of the kind you wanted—."

28. Caleb Worley to John Breckinridge, 21 June 1790, Breckinridge Family Papers, Library of Congress, 6:953, sent via "Mr. Roundtree."

29. Harrison, *John Breckinridge*, 23.

30. William Russell to John Breckinridge, 29 June 1790, Breckinridge Family Papers, Library of Congress, 6:954.

31. William Russell to John Breckinridge, 13 March 1791, Breckinridge Family Papers, Library of Congress, 6:1095, refers to receiving John's 8 October letter and having no opportunity for "conveyance" of a reply until March.

32. Samuel Meredith [Jr.] to Mrs. Lettice Breckinridge, 15 July 1790, Breckinridge Family Papers, Library of Congress, 6:965, sent via "Hambleton"; *The Kentucky Gazette*, 19 July 1790. Dr. Rootes gives the Meredith home location in advertising his services.

33. Perrin, Battle, and Kniffin, *Kentucky*, 284; Clark, *A History of Kentucky*, 130–31; Sprague, "Senator John Brown," 130.

34. James Breckinridge to John Breckinridge, 18 August 1790, Breckinridge Family Papers, Library of Congress, 6:980.

35. *The Kentucky Gazette*, 19 May 1790. Isaac Orchard reported that his Bourbon store had been broken into.

36. Ibid., 23 January 1790, 26 July 1790, 4 December 1790.

37. Ibid., 23 January 1790, 19 July 1790, 4 December 1790.

38. Ibid., 6 March 1790, 19 July 1790.

39. Ibid., 14 June 1790, 18 December 1790.

40. Ibid., 13 February 1790, 19 April 1790.
The first mention of using the "new road" via Strodes Station appeared on 1 August 1789. On 19 April 1790 an individual advertised plans to go up the Ohio and advised those wishing to accompany him to meet at Limestone. Other references to the road appeared before it had actually been cleared. See *The Kentucke Gazette*, 10 November 1787.

41. Heinemann, *First Census of Kentucky, 1790; The Kentucky Gazette*, 28 May 1791, contains census data.

42. *The Virginia Gazette, and General Advertiser,* printed by Augustine Davis in Richmond, 29 September 1790.

43. Ibid., 6 October 1790.

44. Ibid., 10 November 1790.

45. Ibid., 1 December 1790.

46. Ibid., 25 August 1790, 4 October 1790, 29 September 1790, 29 September 1790.

47. Harrison, *John Breckinridge*, 23.

48. Lettice Breckinridge to John Breckinridge, 6 December 1790, Breckinridge Family Papers, Library of Congress, 7:1031, sent "to the Care of James Wilson."

49. Samuel Meredith [Jr.] to John Breckinridge, 30 November 1790, Breckinridge Family Papers, Library of Congress, 7:1028, sent "to the care of Mr. P. Breckinridge."

50. *The Virginia Gazette, and General Advertiser,* 5 January 1791. See Elizabeth Meredith to Lettice Breckinridge, 1 March 1791, Breckinridge Family Papers, Library of Congress, 7:1100–1 [see n. 55 below].

51. Philip Rootes to John Breckinridge, 22 February 1791, Breckinridge Family Papers, Library of Congress, 7:1069–70.

52. Caleb Wallace to John Breckinridge, 22 February 1791, Breckinridge Family Papers, Library of Congress, 7:1071.

53. Samuel Meredith [Jr.] to John Breckinridge, 2 March 1791, Breckinridge Family Papers, Library of Congress, 7:1086, "favd. by Mr. Woodard."

54. William Russell to John Breckinridge, 13 March 1791, Breckinridge Family Papers, Library of Congress, 7:1095–96, "Favour'd by Mr. I. Woodard."

55. Elizabeth Meredith to Lettice Breckinridge, 1 March 1791, Breckinridge Family Papers, Library of Congress, 7:1100–1, "favd. by Mr. Woodard."

56. *The Virginia Gazette, and General Advertiser,* 6 April 1791, 20 April 1791.

57. Ibid., 25 May 1791.

58. Ibid., 8 June 1791.

59. Ibid., 29 June 1791.

60. Ibid., 20 July 1791, 21 September 1791, 28 December 1791.

61. Ibid., 2 March 1791, 10 August 1791.

62. Ibid., 28 September 1791.

63. Ibid., 27 October 1791, 7 December 1791.

64. Ibid., 8 June 1791.

Chapter 7. Moving, at Last, over the Mountains

1. Mary Cabell Breckinridge to Lettice Breckinridge, 14 May 1791, Breckinridge Family Papers, Library of Congress, 7:1114.

2. John Breckinridge to James Breckinridge, 13 August 1791, Breckinridge Family Papers, Library of Congress, 7:1137.

3. Alexander Breckinridge to John Breckinridge, 30 October 1791, Breckinridge Family Papers, Library of Congress, 7:1165.

4. Preston Breckinridge to Lettice Breckinridge, 13 February 1791, Breckinridge Family Papers, Library of Congress, 7:1064.

5. Elizabeth Meredith to Lettice Breckinridge, 25 November 1791, Breckinridge Family Papers, Library of Congress, 7:1175, "favd. by Mr. Breckinridge."

6. *The Virginia Gazette, and General Advertiser,* 4 January 1792.

7. Ibid., 15 February 1792.

8. Clark, *A History of Kentucky*, 163.

9. *The Virginia Gazette, and General Advertiser,* 22 February 1792, 29 February 1792, 7 March 1792, 21 March 1792, 11 April 1792, 25 May 1792, 2 May 1792.

10. Perrin, Battle, and Kniffin, *Kentucky*, 284–85; Clark, *A History of Kentucky*, 130–37.

11. James Breckinridge to John Breckinridge, 19 February 1792, Breckinridge Family Papers, Library of Congress (7 January 1792–23 January 1793), 8:1223, sent by "Mr. Mickie"; John Breckinridge to James Breckinridge, 18 March 1792, Department of Library Special Collections, Manuscripts, Western Kentucky University, Bowling Green, Ky. I wish to thank Dr. Lowell H. Harrison, owner of John's 18 March letter to James, for permission to use it.

12. Robert Breckinridge to John Breckinridge, 2 March 1792, Breckinridge Family Papers, Library of Congress, 8:1237, "Hon^d· by Mr. J. Madison."

13. Harrison, *John Breckinridge*, 36–37, 125. The effort was fruitless because Congress decided to open a land office for the area.

14. Archibald Stuart to John Breckinridge, 25 February 1792, Breckinridge Family Papers, Library of Congress, 8:1232–33.

15. J. Thompson to John Breckinridge, 2 March 1792, Breckinridge Family Papers, Library of Congress, 8:1239–40.

16. John Jordon to John Breckinridige, 2 March 1792, Breckinridge Family Papers, Library of Congress, 8:1238.

17. John Breckinridge to Lettice Breckinridge, 18 March 1792, Breckinridge Family Papers, Library of Congress, 8:1248–49, sent by James Preston. Regarding slavery, see Lowell H. Harrison, *The Antislavery Movement in Kentucky* (Lexington: The University Press of Kentucky, 1978), 1–2, 18–35; "An ACT concerning the IMPORTATION of SLAVES, into the District of Kentucky. Passed the 29th of December 1788," *The Kentucky Gazette*, 14 March 1789; Coleman, *Slavery Times in Kentucky*, 1–17; Clark, *A History of Kentucky*, 274–78.

18. J. Thompson to John Breckinridge, 22 March 1792, Breckinridge Family Papers, Library of Congress, 8:1254–55.

19. Robert Breckinridge to John Breckinridge, 6 May 1792, Breckinridge Family Papers, Library of Congress, 8:1265. A notation on the back of the letter, "Rich^d· Oct. 11[,], 1792[;] for^d" suggests that it was forwarded from Richmond on 11 October; hence, John did not receive it for more than five months.

20. James Monroe to John Breckinridge, 6 April 1792, Breckinridge Family Papers, Library of Congress, 8:1259.

21. Samuel Meredith [Jr.] to John Breckinridge, 17 May 1792, Breckinridge Family Papers, Library of Congress, 8:1270–71, sent by "Mr. P. Campbell" and answered on 30 August 1792.

22. William Russell to John Breckinridge, 19 May 1792, Breckinridge Family Papers, Library of Congress, 8:1272.

23. John Thompson to John Breckinridge, 14 June 1792, Breckinridge Family Papers, Library of Congress, 8:1230–31, sent "By Mr. P. Campbell, to the Care of Mrs. Breckinridge in Botetourt."

24. —— to John Breckinridge, 18 August 1792; John Davis to John Breckinridge, 10 March 1793, Breckinridge Family Papers, Library of Congress, 8:1296, 9:1403–4.

25. Mary Howard to John Breckinridge, 22 July 1792, Breckinridge Family Papers, Library of Congress, 8:1290–91.

26. Benjamin Howard to John Breckinridge, 22 July 1792, Breckinridge Family Papers, Library of Congress, 8:1288–89.

27. Documents dated 30 July 1792, Breckinridge Family Papers, Library of Congress, 8:1292.

28. John Breckinridge to Lettice Breckinridge, 19 August 1792, Breckinridge Family Papers, Library of Congress, 8:1298.

29. William Russell to John Breckinridge, 29 August 1792, Breckinridge Family Papers, Library of Congress, 8:1301–03.

30. William Breckinridge to John Breckinridge, 30 August 1792, Breckinridge Family Papers, Library of Congress, 8:1304.

31. Lettice Breckinridge to John Breckinridge, n.d., September 1792, Breckinridge Family Papers, Library of Congress, 8:1316–18; William Breckinridge to James Breckinridge, 17 September 1803, James Breckinridge Collection, Manuscripts Division, Special Collections Department, University of Virginia Library, shows William was planning to go to Kentucky; Breckinridge, "Cabell's Dale," 58, says both William and Betsy died in Fayette County, Kentucky, in 1838. See also, Harrison, *John Breckinridge*, 134 n. 41 and 174.

32. Samuel Meredith [Jr.] to John Breckinridge, 19 September 1792, Breckinridge Family Papers, Library of Congress, 8:1319.

33. Samuel Meredith [Jr.] to Lettice Breckinridge, 26 October 1792, Breckinridge Family Papers, Library of Congress, 8:1325.

34. James Hopkins to John Breckinridge, 21, 30 December 1792, Breckinridge Family Papers, Library of Congress, 8:1341, 1344.

35. W. Warfield to John Breckinridge, 11 February 1793, Breckinridge Family Papers, Library of Congress, 9:1381.

36. James Breckinridge to John Breckinridge, 19 March 1793, Breckinridge Family Papers, Library of Congress, 9:1408.

37. ——— to John Breckinridge, 23 March 1793, Breckinridge Family Papers, Library of Congress, 9:1414.

38. Dupre, "*The Kentucky Gazette* Reports the French Revolution," 164.

39. MS dated 9 April 1793, Breckinridge Family Papers, vol. 9 [unnumbered].

40. Harrison, *John Breckinridge*, 23.

Chapter 8. A Pleasant Journey and Arrival in Kentucky

1. Receipt for forty shillings paid to John Wharton for making an armchair, 15 March 1793, Breckinridge Family Papers, Library of Congress, 9:1406.

2. Joseph Cabell [Jr.] to Mary Cabell Breckinridge, n.d., May 1793, Breckinridge Family Papers, Library of Congress, 9:1461.

3. William Russell to John Breckinridge, 1 May 1793, Breckinridge Family Papers, Library of Congress, 9:1445.

4. Harrison, *John Breckinridge*, 39.

5. Joseph Cabell [Jr.] to Mary Cabell Breckinridge, n.d., May 1793, Breckinridge Family Papers, Library of Congress, 9:1461.

6. John Breckinridge to Joseph Cabell [Sr.], 10 May 1793, Breckinridge Family Papers, Library of Congress, 9:1455.

7. John Breckinridge to James Breckinridge, 10 March 1794, James Breckinridge Collection, Albemarle County Historical Society Collections, Manuscripts Division, Special Collections Department, University of Virginia Library; Harrison, *John Breckinridge*, 49.

8. Klotter, *The Breckinridges of Kentucky*, 32–33.

9. Note, n.d., Breckinridge Family Papers, Library of Congress, 3:431; Helen Congleton Breckinridge, "Descendants of John and Mary Cabell Breckinridge" (Lexington, Ky., unpublished paper, 1980); the cover page shows Joseph Cabell's years of birth and death as 1732 and 1798.

10. Lowell H. Harrison, "John Breckinridge: Western Statesman," *The Journal of Southern History* 18 (May 1952); 137–51; L. Harrison, *John Breckinridge*, 121; Klotter, *The Breckinridges of Kentucky*, 13–35.

11. L. Harrison, *John Breckinridge*, 198; Klotter, *The Breckinridges of Kentucky*, 34.

12. Breckinridge, "Cabell's Dale," 13–18.

13. Klotter, *The Breckinridges of Kentucky*, 39–41; Breckinridge, "Cabell's Dale," 18, 20, 26–28, 45, 62.

14. Klotter, *The Breckinridges of Kentucky*, 95–136; William C. Davis, "John C. Breckinridge," *The Register of the Kentucky Historical Society* 85 (Summer 1987): 197–212; Breckinridge, "Cabell's Dale," 73–81.

15. Klotter, *The Breckinridges of Kentucky*, 41.

16. C. W. Hackensmith, "John Fitch, a Pioneer in the Development of the Steamboat," *The Register of the Kentucky Historical Society* 65 (July 1967): 187–211.

17. See *The Salem Gazette*, printed by Samuel Hall in Salem, Mass., 26 July 1785, *The Essex Journal and New-Hampshire Packet*, printed by John Mycall in Newburyport, Mass., 24 August 1785, *The Independent Ledger, and the American Advertiser*, printed by John W. Folsom in Boston, Mass., 20 March 1786. Newspaper accounts too numerous to cite reported on Kentucky from the late 1770s, particularly Clark's campaigns and Indian wars; through the 1780s, they reported on migration also. The above citations are examples of a few that reprinted portions of Filson's history of Kentucky.

18. Emery and Emery, *The Press and America*, 93; Brigham, *History*, 1:146–81, 2:964–67, 1105–68. The first United States daily newspaper began in Philadelphia in 1783. No daily newspaper existed in Kentucky or Pittsburgh before 1820; the first successful daily newspaper in Virginia was the *Alexandria Advertiser and Commercial Intelligencer*, established 8 December 1800. A Richmond daily, *The Virginia Gazette: and Richmond Daily Advertiser*, established 1 October 1792, lasted only a few weeks. Another Alexandria daily, *The Times. [sic] Alexandria Advertiser*, established 10 April 1797, lasted five years.

19. Sprague, "Senator John Brown," 99–100.

20. L. Harrison, *John Breckinridge*, 109–10, 197–98; Klotter, *The Breckinridges of Kentucky*, 34.

21. L. Harrison, *John Breckinridge*, 188–89. Breckinridge seems to have relied fairly consistently on horseback travel. A trip that he began by carriage from Kentucky to Washington, reported by Harrison, was completed by horseback after the carriage overturned and was destroyed the fifth day of travel.

22. Daniel Czitrom, *Media and the American Mind: From Morse to McLuhan* (Chapel Hill: University of North Carolina Press, 1982), 3––29, discusses people's perceptions of the telegraph as it developed. See also Charles Briggs and Augustus Maverick, *The Story of the Telegraph and the History of the Great Atlantic Cable* (New York: Rudd and Carleton, 1858). The *New York Herald*, 5 Sept. 1858, gives extensive coverage to what was thought to be successful completion of the Atlantic cable.

23. Breckinridge, "Cabell's Dale," 31–36, 58. Mary Cabell Breckinridge went to Black Rock, N.Y., in 1825 and "made at least five trips to Virginia after . . . John died in 1806, the last one in 1838." No direct evidence was found of her riding on trains or steamboats, but she surely knew of them from newspapers and the travels of family members. Although sources refer to her becoming blind soon after her husband's death, Breckinridge includes a letter written by her in January 1826 in which she referred to seeing "a small paper published in Lexington"; at another point in the letter, she wrote, "I feared once I should never see to read again, not even with spectacles."

24. Emery and Emery, *The Press and America*, 65; Joseph C. G. Kennedy, Superintendent, United States Bureau of the Census, *Preliminary Report on the Eighth Census, 1860* (Washington, D.C.: Government Printing Office, 1862), 103.

25. Beaumont Newhall, *The History of Photography* (New York: Museum of Modern Art, 1982; distributed by New York Graphic Society Books and Little, Brown and Company of Boston), chaps. 1–5.

Bibliography

Primary Sources

NEWSPAPERS AND MAGAZINES

Boston. *The Continental Journal, and Weekly Advertiser.* Printed by John Gill, 30 May 1776–21 April 1785, and by James D. Griffith thereafter until 21 June 1787.

Boston. *The Independent Ledger, and the American Advertiser.* Printed by Edward Draper and John W. Folsom, 15 June 1778–3 November 1783, and by John W. Folsom thereafter until 16 October 1786.

Lexington, Ky. *The Kentucky Gazette.* Printed by John and Fielding Bradford, 11 August 1787–7 June 1788, and by John Bradford thereafter. Title was *The Kentucke Gazette,* 14 August 1787–7 March 1789.

Newburyport, Mass. *The Essex Journal and New-Hampshire Packet.* Printed by John Mycall, 9 July 1784–4 July 1787, when William Hoyt became printer and continued until 8 July 1789; John Mycall printed it thereafter until 1 April 1794.

New York. *New York Herald.* Published by James Gordon Bennett, Sr., 1835–ca. 1868.

Philadelphia, Pa. *Columbian Magazine.* Printed by William Spotswood, September 1786–December 1788, by John Trenchard, January 1789–February 1790, and by William Young, March 1790–December 1792. Title became *Universal Asylum and Columbian Magazine* in March 1790.

Pittsburgh, Pa. *The Pittsburgh Gazette.* Printed by John Scull and Joseph Hall, 29 July 1786–10 November 1786, John Scull, 18 November 1786–31 December 1786, John Scull and John Boyd, 6 January 1787–2 August 1788, and by John Scull thereafter.

Richmond, Va. *The Virginia Gazette.* Printed by John Dixon and Thomas Nicolson, 9 May 1780–21 April 1781.

Richmond, Va. *The Virginia Gazette, or Weekly Advertiser.* Printed by Thomas Nicolson and William Prentis, 29 Dec. 1781–7 May 1785, and by Thomas Nicolson thereafter. Title changed to *The Virginia Gazette, and Weekly Advertiser,* 16 February 1782; comma was omitted beginning 10 April 1784, and "The" was omitted beginning in January 1792.

Richmond, Va. *The Virginia Independent Chronicle.* Printed by Augustine Davis, 26 July 1786–6 May 1789. Title became *The Virginia Independent Chronicle, and General Advertiser,* 13 May 1789 and *The Virginia Gazette, and General Advertiser,* 25 August 1790.

Richmond, Va. *The Virginia Gazette, or, the American Advertiser.* Printed by James Hayes, 22 December 1781–23 August 1786, and James Hayes and Co. thereafter.

Richmond, Va. *The Virginia Gazette or Independent Chronicle.* Printed by John Dixon and

John H. Holt, August 1783–8 June 1787, John Dixon, 15 June 1787–27 April 1791, and John Dixon, Jr., 2 May 1791–16 February 1793. Title changed to *The Virginia Gazette and Independent Chronicle* in early 1784 and to *The Virginia Gazette, and Public Advertiser*, 3 October 1789.

Salem, Mass. *The Salem Gazette.* Printed by Samuel Hall, 18 October 1781–22 November 1785, and by Thomas C. Cushing thereafter until 12 January 1790.

Williamsburg, Va. *The Virginia Gazette.* Printed by William Rind, 16 May 1766–19 August 1773, Clementina Rind, 26 August 1773–25 September 1774, and John Pinkney, 29 September 1774–3 February 1776. Title changed from *Rind's Virginia Gazette* between 5 September and 27 November 1766.

Williamsburg, Va. *The Virginia Gazette.* Printed by Alexander Purdie, 3 February 1775–12 April 1779, and by John Clarkson and Augustine Davis thereafter until 9 December 1780.

Williamsburg, Va. *The Virginia Gazette.* Printed by William Parks, 6 August 1736–1 April 1750[?]. Ending date uncertain because last located issue is 25 September 1746, but Thomas, *The History of Printing*, 2:163, says the paper continued until Parks's death in 1750.

Williamsburg, Va. *The Virginia Gazette.* Printed by William Hunter, 3 January 1751–12 August 1761, Joseph Royle and Co., beginning 19 August 1761, Alexander Purdie and Co., beginning 7 March 1766, Alexander Purdie and John Dixon, 20 June 1766–31 December 1774, and John Dixon and William Hunter, Jr., 7 January 1775–4 December 1778.

Williamsburg, Va. *The Virginia Gazette.* Printed by John Dixon and Thomas Nicolson, 2 February 1779–8 April 1780.

UNPUBLISHED SOURCES

Department of Library Special Collections, Manuscripts, Western Kentucky University, Bowling Green, Ky.
Breckinridge, John. Letter to Brother, James, 18 March 1792.
Lipscomb, John. Journal, 11 June 1784–1 September 1784.
Shannon Family. Letters.
Division of Special Collections and Archives, University of Kentucky Libraries, Lexington, Ky.
Calk, William. Papers, 1753–1854.
Campbell, William, and William Christian. Letters to William Russell. Samuel Wilson Collection.
Crittenden Family. Papers. Samuel Wilson Collection.
Darbishire Family. Papers, 1780–89.
Hart, Thomas. Papers, 1767–90. Samuel Wilson Collection.
Hunt-Morgan Family. Papers, 1784–97.
Jouett Family. Papers. Samuel Wilson Collection.
Madison, James. Letter to John Brown, 21 January 1789. Samuel Wilson Collection.
Mason, George. Letter to George Washington, 9 March 1775.
Morgan, John. Letter to Hugh Mercer, 14 September 1773. Samuel Wilson Collection.
Preston, William. Papers, 1775. Samuel Wilson Collection.
Providence Church, Clark County, Ky. Transcript of the first record book.

Scott, Charles. Papers.

Shelby, Isaac. Letters.

Taylor, Hubbard. Papers, 1772–90.

Draper, Lyman C. Manuscript Collection. State Historical Society of Wisconsin Library, Madison, Wisconsin.

William Croghan Papers. Series N.

Draper's Life of Boone. Series B.

Draper, Lyman C. Notes. Series S.

Preston, William. Papers. Series QQ.

Kentucky Papers. Series CC.

Durrett, Reuben T. Collection. Department of Special Collections, University of Chicago Library, Chicago.

Beatty, Eskuries. "Diary of Major Eskuries Beatty, Paymaster of the Western Army, 1786–1787." Codex 11.

Clark, George Rogers. Diary, 25 December 1776–February 1778. Durrett, Miscellaneous Papers, Box 2.

Clarkson, Matthew. Journal, 1766–67. Codex 46.

Cowan, John. Journal, 1777. Codex 51.

Croghan, George. Journal, 15 May 1765–8 October 1765. Codex 53.

Croghan, William. Ledgers. Codex 54, 55, and 56.

Durrett, Reuben T. Miscellaneous Papers, Boxes 1–5.

———. Personal Papers, Boxes 1–2.

Gist, Christopher. Journal, 1750–51. Codex 76.

Gordan, Harry. Journal of 1766 Expedition Down the Ohio River. Codex 106.

"John Haggin, Early Settler in Kentucky." Codex 82.

Halley, John. Journal, 1789–91. Codex 83.

Hanson, Thomas. "Extracts of a Journal Kept on the River Ohio in the Year 1774." Codex 87.

Hart, Nathaniel. Letter from Spring Hill, 27 April 1839. Codex 89.

Henderson, Richard. Journal, 20 March–25 July 1775. Codex 93.

Hickman, William. "A Short account of My life and travels. For more than Fifty years; a Professed servant of Jesus Christ." Codex 94.

Hite, Isaac. Diary, 25 July 1773. Durrett, Miscellaneous Papers, Box 1.

Johnson, Cave. Autobiography, 1769–1850. Codex 104.

Linn, Colonel William. Papers. Codex 121.

Lynne, Edmund. Estate Papers. Durrett, Miscellaneous Papers, Box 1.

Maps, Sketches, Pictures. Forts and Stations. Durrett, Box 1.

McAfee, James. "Journal of a tour through Kentucky . . . 1773. . . ." Codex 129.

McAfee, Robert. "First Settlement on Salt River—New Providence Church." Codex 129.

———. "Historical Settlement of Kentucky." Codex 128.

———. Journal. Codex 130.

———. "Kentucky History." Codex 131.

———. "Life and Times. . . ." Codex 127.

McKee, Alexander. Letters from the Upper Shawnese Villages, 3 May, 4 June 1780, n.d., August 1780, 26 September 1781. Codex 132.

McKinney, John. "Encounter with a Wild Cat. . . ." Codex 133.

Nourse, James. "Diary of James Nourse, of Berkeley County, Va., 1775–1780." Codex 142.

Shelby, Isaac. Autobiography. Codex 165.

Smith, [no first name]. "Adventures with Indians at Boonesborough. . . ." Codex 169.

Smith, Daniel. Surveyor's Notes. Codex 170.

Smith, James. "Rev. James Smith, Three Journals to the Western Country from Powhatten County, Va.—1st Oct. 1785–Dec. 21st." Codex 171.

Smith, John, and James Sodosky. Depositions. Codex 172.

Sudduth, William. "Sketch of the life of W. Sudduth." Codex 179.

Todd, John. Diary. Codex 184.

Trabue, Daniel. Diary. Codex 186.

Walker, Felix. "Narrative of an Adventure in Kentucky in 1775." Codex 194.

Washington, George. Journal, 1753. Codex 196.

———. Journal, 1770 Trip to the Ohio. Codex 197.

Watkins, Joel. "Diary of Joel Watkins—1789." Codex 198.

Manuscripts Collections, Kentucky Historical Society, Frankfort, Ky.

Manuscript Department, The Filson Club, Louisville, Ky.

Boone, Daniel. Papers.

Boone, Squire. Papers.

Breckinridge-Marshall Papers. Breckinridge, Robert. Letter to James Breckinridge, 2 July 1788.

Campbell, Arthur. Papers, 1770–1811.

Johnston, William. Papers.

Logan, John. Account Book, 1790–92, regarding the wilderness road.

McDowell, Samuel. Letters to Andrew Reid, 1783–1814.

Meriwether, Nicholas. Nicholas Meriwether Papers, 1749–1828; copies from originals in the Manuscripts Collection, Kentucky Historical Society Library, Frankfort, Ky.

Meriwether, William. Correspondence, 1787–99.

Preston Family Papers-Davie Collection, 1658–1788. Correspondence, 1753–1896.

Shelby, Isaac. Papers. Correspondence, 1774–1824.

Taylor Family. Letters and Papers, 1744–1809.

Taylor, Francis. Diary, 1786–99.

Wallace, John. Journal, 1786–1802.

Trustees of the Town of Louisville. Minute Books, 7 February 1781–25 June 1793.

U.S. Congress. Act of 1791 for Admitting Kentucky into Statehood.

Wallace, Estill. Biographical Sketches of James and Samuel Estill.

Manuscript Division, Library of Congress, Washington, D.C.

Breckinridge Family. Papers, 9 Vols, 1752–93.

Innes, Harry. Papers.

Manuscripts Division, Special Collections Department, University of Virginia Library, Charlottesville, Va.

James Breckinridge Collection.

James Breckinridge Collection, Albemarle County Historical Society Collections.

Secondary Sources

ATLASES

Adams, James Turslow. *Atlas of American History.* New York: Charles Scribner's Sons, 1943.

American Heritage Pictorial Atlas of United States History. New York: American Heritage Publishing Co., 1966.

Brown, Lloyd A. *Early Maps of the Ohio Valley.* Pittsburgh, Pa.: University of Pittsburgh Press, 1959.

Clark, Thomas D. *Historic Maps of Kentucky.* Lexington: The University Press of Kentucky, 1979.

Colles, Christopher. *A Survey of the Roads of the United States of America, 1789.* Cambridge: Harvard University Press, 1961.

Cumings, Samuel. *The Western Pilot, Containing Charts of the Ohio River and of the Mississippi.* Cincinnati: N. and G. Guilford and Company, 1834.

Hutchins, Thomas. *The Courses of the Ohio River, 1766.* Cincinnati: Historical and Philosophical Society of Ohio, 1942.

Lord, Clifford L., and Elizabeth Lord. *Historical Atlas of the United States.* Rev. ed. New York: Henry Holt and Company, 1953. Reprint. New York: Johnson, 1972.

Paullin, Charles O. *Atlas of the Historical Geography of the United States.* Washington, D.C.: Carnegie Institution of Washington and the American Geographical Society of New York, 1932.

Sheafer, P. W. *Historical Map of Pennsylvania.* Philadelphia: Historical Society of Pennsylvania, 1875. Copy in the Library of Congress Map Division.

BIBLIOGRAPHIES

American Periodical Series. *List of Titles, 1741–1800.* Ann Arbor, Mich.: University Microfilms, 1952.

Brigham, Clarence S. *History and Bibliography of American Newspapers, 1690–1820.* 2 vols. Worcester, Mass.: American Antiquarian Society, 1947.

Bristol, Roger P. *Supplement to Evans' American Bibliography.* Charlottesville: University Press of Virginia, 1970.

Clark, Thomas D. *Travels in the Old South: A Bibliography.* Norman: University of Oklahoma Press, 1962.

Coleman, John W. *A Bibliography of Kentucky History.* Lexington: University Press of Kentucky, 1911.

Evans, Charles. *American Bibliography, 1639–1820.* Chicago: Blakely Press, 1903–14.

Jillson, Willard R. *A Bibliography of Early Western Travel in Kentucky, 1674–1824.* Louisville, Ky.: C. T. Dearing Printing Co., 1944.

————. *A Bibliography of the Lower Blue Licks: 1744–1944*. Frankfort, Ky.: The State Journal, 1945.

————. *An Historical Bibliography of Lexington, Ky., 1774–1946*. Frankfort, Ky.: Perry Publishing Company, 1947.

————. *Early Kentucky Literature, 1750–1840*. Frankfort: Kentucky Historical Society, 1931.

Lathem, Edward Connery. *Chronological Tables of American Newspapers, 1690–1820*. Worcester, Mass.: American Antiquarian Society and Barre, 1972.

McMurtie, Douglas C. *A Bibliography of Eighteenth-Century Kentucky Broadsides*. Louisville, Ky.: Extract from the *Filson Club History Quarterly* (January 1936).

Shipton, Clifford K., and James Mooney. *National Index of American Imprints through 1800*. Worcester, Mass.: American Antiquarian Society and Barre, 1969.

GENERAL WORKS

Abernethy, Thomas Perkins. *Three Virginia Frontiers*. Baton Rouge: Louisiana State University Press, 1940.

————. *Western Lands and the American Revolution*. New York: Russell and Russell, 1959.

Ambler, Charles. *Washington and the West*. Chapel Hill: University of North Carolina Press, 1936.

Arnow, Harriette Simpson. *Old Burnside*. Lexington: The University Press of Kentucky, 1977.

————. *Seedtime on the Cumberland*. New York: Macmillan, 1960. Reprint. Lexington: The University Press of Kentucky, 1983.

Bailey, Kenneth P. *Christopher Gist: Colonial Frontiersman, Explorer, and Indian Agent*. Hamden, Conn.: Archon Books, 1976.

Bailyn, Bernard. *The Ideological Origins of the American Revolution*. Cambridge: Harvard University Press, 1965.

Bakeless, John. *Daniel Boone*. New York: William Morrow, 1939.

Baldwin, Leland D. *Pittsburgh: The Story of a City*. Pittsburgh, Pa.: University of Pittsburgh Press, 1938.

————. *The Keelboat Age on Western Waters*. Pittsburgh, Pa.: University of Pittsburgh Press, 1941.

Billington, Ray Allen. *Westward Expansion*. New York: Macmillan, 1960.

————. *Westward to the Pacific: An Overview of America's Westward Expansion*. St. Louis, Mo.: Jefferson National Expansion Historical Association, 1979.

Bogart, W. H. *Daniel Boone and the Hunters of Kentucky*. Auburn, N.Y.: Miller, Orton, and Milligan, 1854.

Bond, Beverly W., Jr., *The Civilization of the Old Northwest: A Study of Political, Social, and Economic Development, 1788–1812*. New York: Macmillan, 1934.

Briggs, Charles, and Augustus Maverick. *The Story of the Telegraph and the History of the Great Atlantic Cable*. New York: Rudd and Carleton, 1858.

Brigham, Clarence S. *Journals and Journeymen: A Contribution to the History of Early American Newspapers*. Philadelphia: University of Pennsylvania Press, 1950.

Brown, Ralph H. *Historical Geography of the United States*. New York: Harcourt, Brace and Company, 1948.

Butler, Mann. *A History of the Commonwealth of Kentucky.* Louisville, Ky.: Wilcox, Deckerman and Company, 1834.

Campbell, Patrick. *Travels in the interior inhabited parts of North America in the Years 1791 and 1792.* Edinburgh: J. Guthrie, 1793.

Cannon, Jouett. *Kentucky's Active Militia [1786].* Anchorage, Ky.: Borderland Books, 1965.

Cartmell, Thomas Kemp. *Shenandoah Valley Pioneers and Their Descendants.* Winchester, Va.: The Eddy Press Corporation, 1909.

Caruso, John A. *The Appalachian Frontier.* Indianapolis, Ind.: Bobbs-Merrill Co., 1959.

Cassedy, Ben. *The History of Louisville From Its Earliest Settlement Till the Year 1852.* Louisville: Hull and Brother, 1852.

Chambers-Schiller, Virginia. *Liberty, A Better Husband: Single Women in America: The Generations of 1780–1840.* New Haven: Yale University Press, 1984.

Chastellaux, Francis Jean. *Travels in North America in the years 1780, 1781, 1782.* New York: The *New York Times*, 1968.

Clark, Thomas D. *A History of Kentucky.* New York: Prentice-Hall, 1937.

———. *Frontier America: The Story of the Westward Movement.* New York: Charles Scribner's Sons, 1959.

———. *Simon Kenton: Kentucky Scout.* New York: Farrar and Rinehart, 1943.

———. *Three American Frontiers.* Lexington: University Press of Kentucky, 1968.

Clark, Victor S. *History of Manufactures in the United States.* Vol. 1, 1607–1860. New York: McGraw-Hill, 1929.

Cleland, Hugh. *George Washington and the Ohio Valley.* Pittsburgh, Pa.: University of Pittsburgh Press, 1955.

Coleman, J. Winston. *John Bradford (1749–1830), Esquire, Pioneer Kentucky Printer and Historian.* Lexington, Ky.: Winburn Press, 1950.

———. *Slavery Times in Kentucky.* Chapel Hill: The University of North Carolina Press, 1940.

———. *Stagecoach Days in the Bluegrass.* Louisville, Ky.: The Standard Press, 1935.

———. *The British Invasion of Kentucky.* Lexington, Ky.: Winburn Press, 1951.

Collins, Lewis. *Historical Sketches of Kentucky.* Maysville, Ky.: L. Collins, 1847.

Collins, Richard H. *History of Kentucky.* 2 vols. 3d. ed. Covington, Ky.: Collins & Co., 1882.

Connelly, William Elsey. *Eastern Kentucky Papers.* New York: The Torch Press, 1910.

Corkran, David H. *The Cherokee Frontier.* Norman: University of Oklahoma Press, 1962.

Cotterill, Robert S. *History of Pioneer Kentucky.* Cincinnati, Ohio: Johnson and Hardin, 1917.

Coward, Joan Wells. *Kentucky in the New Republic: The Process of Constitution Making.* Lexington: The University Press of Kentucky, 1979.

Craven, Avery Odelle. *Soil Exhaustion as a Factor in the Agricultural History of Virginia and Maryland, 1606–1860.* Urbana: University of Illinois Press, 1926.

Cridlin, William Broaddus. *A History of Colonial Virginia.* Richmond, Va.: Williams Printing Company, 1923.

Cullinan, Gerald. *The Post Office Department.* New York: Frederick A. Praeger, 1968.

Czitrom, Daniel. *Media and the American Mind: From Morse to McLuhan*. Chapel Hill: The University of North Carolina Press, 1982.

Darter, Oscar H. *Colonial Fredericksburg and Neighborhood in Perspective*. New York: Twayne Publishers, 1957.

Davidson, Robert. *History of the Presbyterian Church in the State of Kentucky*. New York: R. Carter, 1847.

DeVorsey, Louis. *The Indian Boundary in the Southern Colonies, 1763–1775*. Chapel Hill: The University of North Carolina Press, 1966.

Drake, Daniel. *Pioneer Life in Kentucky, 1785–1800*. New York: Henry Schuman, 1948.

Dunbar, Seymour. *A History of Travel in America*. Indianapolis, Ind.: Bobbs-Merrill Co., 1915.

Durrett, Rueben T. *The Centenary of Kentucky*. Louisville, Ky.: J. P. Morton, 1892.

Earle, Alice Morse. *Stage-Coach and Tavern Days*. New York: Macmillan, 1912.

Eavenson, Howard N. *Map Maker & Indian Traders*. Pittsburgh: University of Pittsburgh Press, 1949.

Emery, Michael, and Edwin Emery. *The Press and America: An Interpretive History of the Mass Media*. 6th ed. Englewood Cliffs, N.J.: Prentice-Hall, 1988.

Ellis, David M., ed. *The Frontier in American Development*. Ithaca: Cornell University Press, 1969.

Filson, John. *The Discovery and Settlement of Kentucke*. Wilmington: James Adams, 1784. Reprint. Ann Arbor, Mich.: University Microfilms, Inc., 1966.

Fitzpatrick, John Clement. *The Writings of George Washington, 1745–1799*. Washington, D.C.: U.S. Government Printing Office, 1931.

Gordon, Mary McDougall. *Overland to California with the Pioneer Line: The Gold Rush Diary of Bernard J. Reid*. Stanford, Calif.: Stanford University Press, 1983. Reprint. Urbana: University of Illinois Press, 1987.

Green, Thomas Marshall. *Historic Families of Kentucky*. Baltimore: Regional Publishing Company, 1966.

———. *The Spanish Conspiracy*. Cincinnati, Ohio: R. Clarke and Co., 1891.

Gwathmey, John H. *Twelve Virginia Counties Where the Western Migration Began*. Richmond, Va.: The Dietz Press, 1937.

Hale, John P. *Trans-Allegheny Pioneers: Historical Sketches of the First White Settlements West of the Alleghenies, 1748 and After*. Cincinnati, Ohio: Samuel C. Cox, and Company, 1886.

Hanna, Charles A. *The Wilderness Trail*. Vol. 1. New York: G. P. Putnam's Sons, 1911.

Hardeman, Nicholas Perkins. *Wilderness Calling: The Hardeman Family in the American Westward Movement, 1750–1900*. Knoxville: University of Tennessee Press, 1977.

Harlow, Alvin F. *Old Post Bags*. New York: D. Appleton and Company, 1928.

Harper, Josephine L. *Guide to the Draper Manuscripts*. Madison: The State Historical Society of Wisconsin, 1983.

Harrison, Lowell H. *The Antislavery Movement in Kentucky*. Lexington: The University Press of Kentucky, 1978.

———. *John Breckinridge: Jeffersonian Republican*. Louisville, Ky.: The Filson Club, 1969.

Hartley, C. B. *Life and Times of Colonel Daniel Boone*. Philadelphia: G. G. Evans, 1869.

Hawke, David. *The Colonial Experience*. Indianapolis, Ind.: Bobbs-Merrill Co., 1966.

Heinemann, Charles B. *First Census of Kentucky, 1790*. Washington, D.C.: G. M. Brumbaugh, 1940.

Henderson, Archibald. *The Transylvania Colony and the Founding of Henderson, Ky.* Henderson, Ky.: N.p., 1929.

Hening, William Waller, ed. *The Statutes at Large: Being a Collection of All the Laws of Virginia*. . . . Richmond, Va.: By Directive of Virginia Assembly, 1819–23.

Henry, Ruby Addison. *The First West*. Nashville, Tenn.: Aurora Publishers, 1972.

Hepburn, Alonzo Barton. *A History of Currency in the United States*. New York: Macmillan, 1915.

Hess, Stephen. *America's Political Dynasties*. Garden City, N.Y.: Doubleday, 1966.

Hildreth, S. P. *Pioneer History*. Cincinnati, Ohio: H. W. Derby Co., 1848.

Hopkins, James F. *A History of the Hemp Industry in Kentucky*. Lexington: University Press of Kentucky, 1951.

Howard, Virginia W. *Bryan Station Heroes and Heroines*. Lexington, Ky.: Press of the Commercial Printing Company, 1932.

Hulbert, Archer Butler. *Historic Highways*. Vol. 4, *Braddock's Road*. Cleveland, Ohio: Arthur H. Clark Company, 1903.

———. *Historic Highways*. Vol. 2, *Indian Thoroughfares*. Cleveland, Ohio: Arthur H. Clark Company, 1902.

———. *Historic Highways*. Vol. 1, *Paths of the Moundbuilding Indians*. Cleveland, Ohio: Arthur H. Clark Company, 1902.

———. *Historic Highways*. Vol. 3, *Pioneer Roads*. Cleveland, Ohio: Arthur H. Clark Company, 1904.

James, James Alton. *The George Rogers Clark Papers, 1777–1781*. Springfield: Illinois State Historical Library, 1912.

Jennings, Walter W. *Transylvania: Pioneer University of the West*. New York: Pageant Press, 1955.

Jensen, Joan M. *Loosening the Bonds: Mid-Atlantic Farm Women, 1750–1850*. New Haven: Yale University Press, 1983.

Jillson, Willard R. *A Glimpse of Early Frankfort*. Louisville, Ky.: Standard Printing Company, 1936.

———. *Pioneer Kentucky*. Frankfort, Ky.: The *State Journal* Company, 1934.

———. *Tales of the Dark and Bloody Ground*. Louisville, Ky.: C. T. Dearing Printing Co., 1930.

———. *The First Printing in Kentucky*. Louisville, Ky.: C. T. Dearing Printing Co., 1936.

———. *The Kentucky Country*. Washington, D.C.: H. L. and J. B. McQueen, Inc., 1931.

———. *The Kentucky Land Grants*. Louisville, Ky.: The Standard Printing Co., 1925.

Johnson, J. Stoddard, ed. *First Explorations of Kentucky*. Louisville, Ky.: Filson Club Publication No. 13, 1898.

Johnson, Patricia Givens. *James Patton and the Appalachian Colonists*. Verona, Va.: McClure Press, 1973.

———. *William Preston and the Allegheny Patriots*. Pulaski, Va.: B. M. Smith, 1976.

Johnston, J. Stoddard, ed. *Colonel Christopher Gist's Journal of a Tour through Ohio and Kentucky.* Louisville, Ky.: J. P. Morton and Co., 1898.

Kegley, F. B. *Kegley's Virginia Frontier.* Roanoke, Va.: Southwest Virginia Historical Society, 1938.

Kenton, Edna. *The Jesuit Relations and Allied Documents: Travels and Explorations of the Jesuit Missionaries in North America, 1610–1791.* New York: Vanguard Press, 1954.

———. *Simon Kenton: His Life and Period, 1755–1836.* New York: Doubleday, 1930. Reprint. New York: Arno Press: 1971.

Kentucky Land Office. *Calendar of the Warrants for Land in Kentucky, granted for Service in the French and Indian War.* Abstracted by Philip Fall Taylor. Baltimore: Genealogical Publishing Company, 1967.

Kentucky Society of the Daughters of Colonial Wars. *Kentucky Pioneers and Their Descendants.* Franklin, Ky.: Roberts Printing Company, n.d.

Kerber, Linda. *Women of the Republic: Intellect and Ideology in Revolutionary America.* Chapel Hill: The University of North Carolina Press, 1980.

Kerr, Charles. *History of Kentucky.* New York: The American Historical Society, 1922.

Kincaid, Robert L. *The Wilderness Road.* Indianapolis: Bobbs-Merrill Co., 1947.

Klotter, James C. *The Breckinridges of Kentucky, 1760–1981.* Lexington: The University Press of Kentucky, 1986.

Kluger, Richard. *The Paper: The Life and Death of the New York Herald Tribune.* New York: Alfred A. Knopf, 1986.

Konwiser, Henry M. *Colonial and Revolutionary Posts.* New York: Jacques Minkus, 1947.

Kozee, William Carlos. *Pioneer Families of Eastern and Southeastern Kentucky.* Huntington, W. Va.: Standard Printing and Publishing Company, 1957.

Lederer, John. *The Discoveries of John Lederer.* Ann Arbor, Mich.: University Microfilms, Inc., 1966.

Lester, William Stewart. *The Transylvania Colony.* Spencer, Ind.: Samuel R. Guard and Co., 1935.

Lewis, Henry, comp. *The Valley of the Mississippi Illustrated.* Translated by A. Hermina Poatgieter and edited by Bertha L. Heilbron. St. Paul: Minnesota Historical Society, 1967.

Littell, William. *Political Transactions in and Concerning Kentucky, from the First Settlement Thereof, Until it Became an Independent State in June, 1792.* Louisville, Ky.: J. P. Morton and Co., 1926.

Lofaro, Micahel A. *The Life and Adventures of Daniel Boone.* Lexington: The University Press of Kentucky, 1978. Reprint. The University Press of Kentucky, 1986.

McAdam, Edna. *Kentucky Pioneer and Court Records.* Lexington, Ky.: The Keystone Printing Company, 1929.

Magill, John. *The Pioneer to the Kentucky Emigrant.* Lexington: University of Kentucky Publications Committee, Margaret Voorhies Haggin Trust, 1942.

Marshall, Humphrey. *The History of Kentucky, Including an Account of the Discovery, Settlement, Progressive Improvement, Political and Military Events, and Present State of the Country.* 2d ed. Frankfort, Ky.: Henry Gore, 1812.

Mason, Kathryn Harrod. *James Harrod of Kentucky.* Baton Rouge: Louisiana State University Press, 1951.

Meinig, D. W. *The Shaping of America: A Geographical Perspective of 500 Years of History.* Vol. 1, *Atlantic America, 1492–1800.* New Haven: Yale University Press, 1986.

Mereness, Newton D., ed. *Travels in the American Colonies.* New York: Macmillan, 1916.

Meyer, Henry Balthaser. *History of Transportation in the United States Before 1860.* Washington, D.C.: Carnegie Institution of Washington, 1917.

Moore, Arthur K. *The Frontier Mind: A Cultural Analysis of the Kentucky Frontiersman.* Lexington: University Press of Kentucky, 1957.

Morgan, Dale L., ed. *The Overland Diary of James A. Pritchard from Kentucky to California in 1849.* Denver: Old West Publishing Co., 1959.

Morrison, Alfred James. *Travels in Virginia in Revolutionary Times.* Lynchburg, Va.: J. P. Bell Company, 1922.

———. ed. *Travels in the Confederation (1783–84).* New York: Burt Franklin, 1968.

Morton, Richard L. *Colonial Virginia.* 2 vols. Chapel Hill: The University of North Carolina Press, 1960.

Mott, Frank Luther. *A History of American Magazines.* Vol. 1, 1741–1850. Cambridge: Harvard University Press, 1957.

———. *American Journalism: A History of Newspapers in the United States Through 250 Years, 1690 to 1840.* New York: Macmillan, 1941.

Nash, Roderick. *Wilderness and the American Mind.* New Haven: Yale University Press, 1967.

Newhall, Beaumont. *The History of Photography.* New York: Museum of Modern Art, 1982; distributed by New York Graphic Society Books and Little, Brown and Co. of Boston.

Nowlin, William Dudley. *Kentucky Baptist History, 1770–1922.* Louisville, Ky.: Baptist Book Concern, 1922.

Parker, William, and Julia Perkins Cutler. *Life, Journals and Correspondence of Rev. Manassah Cutler, L.L.D.* Cincinnati, Ohio: R. Clarke and Company, 1888.

Peckham, Howard H., ed. *George Croghan's Journal [1767].* Ann Arbor: The University of Michigan Press, 1939.

Perrin, W. H. *The Pioneer Press of Kentucky.* Louisville, Ky.: John P. Morton, 1888.

Perrin, W. H., J. H. Battle, and G. C. Kniffin. *Kentucky: A History of the State.* Louisville, Ky.: F. A. Battey and Company, 1887. Reprint. Easley, S.C.: Southern Historical Press, 1979.

Powell, Mary G. *The History of Old Alexandria.* Richmond, Va.: The William Byrd Press, 1928.

Pusey, William Allen. *The Wilderness Road to Kentucky.* New York: George H. Doran Co., 1921.

———. *Three Kentucky Pioneers: James, William and Patrick Brown.* Louisville, Ky.: J. P. Morton, 1930.

Ramsey, J. G. M. *The Annals of Tennessee to the End of the Eighteenth Century.* Charleston, S.C.: John Russell, 1853.

Ranck, George W. *Boonesborough.* Louisville, Ky.: J. P. Morton and Company, 1901.

———. *History of Lexington, Ky.: Its Early Annals and Recent Progress.* Cincinnati, Ohio: Robert Clarke, 1872.

Redford, Albert H. *The History of Methodism in Kentucky.* 2 vols. Nashville, Tenn.: Southern Methodist Publishing House, 1868.

Rice, Otis K. *The Allegheny Frontier: West Virginia Beginnings, 1730–1830.* Lexington: University of Kentucky Press, 1970.

Rich, Wesley E. *History of the United States Post Office to the Year 1820.* Cambridge: Harvard University Press, 1924.

Riley, Glenda. *Women and Indians on the Frontier, 1825–1915.* Alburquerque: University of New Mexico Press, 1984.

Robertson, James Rood. *Petitions of the Early Inhabitants of Kentucky to the General Assembly of Virginia.* Louisville, Ky.: J. P. Morton and Company, 1914. Reprint. New York: Arno Press and the *New York Times,* 1971.

Rohrback, Malcolm J. *The Land Office Business: The Settlement and Administration of American Public Lands, 1789–1837.* New York: Oxford University Press, 1968.

Rubin, Bernard, ed. *Small Voices & Great Trumpets: Minorities & the Media.* New York: Praeger Publishers, 1980.

Rutman, Darrett B. *The Old Dominion.* Charlottesville, The University Press of Virginia, 1964.

Sanders, Robert Stuart. *Presbyterianism in Versailles and Woodford County, Kentucky, 1784–1963.* Louisville, Ky.: The Dunne Press, 1963.

Scheele, Carl H. *A Short History of the Mail Service.* Washington, D.C.: Smithsonian Institution Press, 1970.

Schlesinger, Arthur M. *Prelude to Independence: The Newspaper War on Britain, 1764–1776.* Westport, Conn.: Greenwood Press, 1957.

Schlissel, Lillian. *Women's Diaires of the Westward Journey.* New York: Schocken Books, 1982.

Semple, Ellen Churchill. *American History and its Geographic Conditions.* New York: Houghton Mifflin, 1933.

Shank, William H. *Indian Trails to Super Highways.* Shepherdstown, W. Va.: American Canal and Transportation Center, 1974.

Smith, David G. *The Convention and the Constitution: The Political Ideas of the Founding Fathers.* New York: St. Martin's Press, 1965.

Smith, William. *The History of the Post Office in British North America, 1639–1870.* Cambridge: Cambridge University Press, 1920.

Sonne, Neils Henry. *Liberal Kentucky, 1780–1828.* New York: Columbia University Press, 1939.

Spalding, M. J. *Sketches of the Early Catholic Missions in Kentucky.* Louisville, Ky.: B. J. Webb and Brother, 1844.

Speed, Thomas. *The Political Club, Danville, Ky., 1786–1790.* Louisville, Ky.: J. P. Morton and Co., 1894.

———. *The Wilderness Road.* New York: Burt Franklin, 1886.

Spencer, John H. *A History of Kentucky Baptists from 1769–1885.* 2 vols. Cincinnati, Ohio: J. R. Baumes, 1886.

Staff, Frank. *The Transatlantic Mail.* London: Adlard Coles, in association with George C. Harrap and Company, 1956.

Staples, Charles R. *The History of Pioneer Lexington, 1779–1806.* Lexington, Ky.: Translyvania Press, 1939.

Stipp, George W., comp. *Western Miscellany*. Xenia, Ohio: N.p. 1827.

Stratton, Joanna L. *Pioneer Women: Voices from the Kansas Frontier.* New York: Simon & Schuster, 1981, first Touchstone Edition, 1982.

Summerfield, Arthur E. *United States Mail: The Story of the United States Postal Service.* New York: Holt, Rinehart and Winston, 1960.

Summers, Lewis Preston. *History of Southwestern Virginia, 1746–1786*. Richmond, Va.: J. L. Hill Printing Co., 1903.

Talbert, Charles G. *Benjamin Logan: Kentucky Frontiersman.* Lexington; University Press of Kentucky, 1962.

Talpalar, Morris. *The Sociology of Colonial Virginia.* 2d rev. ed. New York: Philosophical Library, 1968.

Thomas, Isaiah. *The History of Printing in America.* Edited by Marcus A. McCorison from the second edition. New York: Weathervane Books, 1970.

Thwaites, Reuben Gold, ed. *Early Western Travels, 1784–1846.* Cleveland, Ohio: Arthur H. Clark, 1901.

Thwaites, Reuben Gold, and Louise Phelps Kellogg. *Frontier Defense of the Upper Ohio, 1777–1778.* Madison: The State Historical Society of Wisconsin, 1912.

U.S. Bureau of the Census. *Historical Statistics of the United States, Colonial Times to 1957.* Washington, D.C.: U.S. Government Printing Office, 1960.

Van Every, Dale. *A Company of Heroes: The American Frontier, 1775–1783.* New York: William Morrow, 1962.

———. *Ark of Empire: The American Frontier, 1784–1802.* New York: William Morrow, 1963.

———. *Forth to the Wilderness: The First American Frontier, 1754–1774.* New York: William Morrow, 1961. Reprint. New York: First Quill Edition, n.d.

Varle, Charles. *A Complete View of Baltimore.* Baltimore: Samuel Young, 1833.

Verhoeff, Mary. *The Kentucky Mountains, Transportation and Commerce, 1750–1911.* Louisville, Ky.: J. P. Morton and Co., 1911.

Verhoeff, Mary. *The Kentucky River Navigation.* Filson Club Publication No. 28. Louisville, Ky.: J. P. Morton & Co., 1917.

Wainwright, Nicholas. *George Croghan: Wilderness Diplomat.* Chapel Hill: The University of North Carolina Press, 1959.

Walker, Thomas. *Journal of an Exploration in the Spring of the Year 1750.* Boston: Little, Brown and Co., 1988.

Wallace, Paul A. W. *Pennsylvania: Seed of a Nation.* New York: Harper & Row, 1962.

Walton, John. *John Filson of Kentucky.* Lexington: University Press of Kentucky, 1956.

Warfield, Ethelbert Dudley. *The Constitutional Aspect of Kentucky's Struggle for Autonomy, 1789–1792.* Vol. 4, Part 4, 347–65. New York: American Historical Association Papers, 1890.

Watlington, Patricia. *The Partisan Spirit: Kentucky Politics, 1779–1792.* New York: Atheneum, 1972.

Watts, William Courtney. *Chronicles of a Kentucky Settlement.* New York: G. P. Putnam's Sons, 1897.

Weibel, Kathryn. *Mirror Mirror: Images of Women Reflected in Popular Culture.* New York: Doubleday, 1977.

Whitsitt, William Heth. *Life and Times of Judge Caleb Wallace.* Louisville, Ky.: J. P. Morton, Co., 1888.

Woods, Neander M. *The Woods-McAfee Memorial.* Louisville, Ky. *Courier Journal* Job Printing Company, 1905.

Young, Chester Raymond. *Westward into Kentucky: The Narrative of Daniel Trabue.* Lexington: The University Press of Kentucky, 1981.

ARTICLES

Adams, Evelyn Crady. "Phillips' Fort [1780], Nolin Station." *The Register of the Kentucky Historical Society* 58 (October 1960): 308–21.

Altsheler, Brent. "The Long Hunters and John Knox, Their Leader," *Filson Club History Quarterly* 5 (October 1931): 167–85.

Ammon, Harry. "The Formation of the Republican Party in Virginia, 1789–1796." *The Journal of Southern History* 19 (August 1953): 283–310.

Barnhart, John D. "Frontiersmen and Planters in the Formation of Kentucky." *The Journal of Southern History* 7 (February 1941): 19–36.

Bayles, W. Harrison. "Postal Service in the Thirteen Colonies." *Journal of American History* 5, no. 3 (1911): 429–58.

Beckner, Lucien. "Captain James Harrod's Company." *The Register of the Kentucky Historical Society* 20 (September 1922): 280–82.

———. "Eskippakithiki: The Last Indian Town in Kentucky." *Filson Club History Quarterly* 6 (October 1932): 355–82.

———. "John Findley: The First Pathfinder to Kentucky." *Filson Club History Quarterly* 43 (July 1969): 206–15.

Bentley, James. "Letters of Thomas Perkins to Gen. Joseph Palmer, Lincoln County, Kentucky, 1785." *Filson Club History Quarterly* 49 (April 1975): 141–51.

Blair, John L. "Mrs. Dewees' Journal from Philadelphia to Kentucky." *Register of the Kentucky Historical Society* 63 (July 1965): 195–217.

Bliss, Willard F. "The Rise of Tenancy in Virginia." *Virginia Magazine of History and Biography* 58 (October 1950): 427–41.

Buckley, Leer. "Early Days of Kentucky's Government." *The Register of the Kentucky Historical Society* 40 (October 1942): 402–6.

Butler, Mann. "Details of Frontier Life." *The Register of the Kentucky Historical Society* 62 (July 1964): 206–29.

Cartlidge, Anna M. "Colonel John Floyd: Reluctant Adventurer. *The Register of the Kentucky Historical Society* 66 (October 1968): 317–66.

Clark, Thomas D. "Salt, A Factor in the Settlement of Kentucky." *Filson Club History Quarterly* 12 (January 1938): 42–52.

Clift, G. Glenn, comp. "John Bradford, 'the Caxton of Kentucky': A Bibliography." *American Notes and Queries* 8 (June 1948): 35–41.

Clough, Elizabeth T. "Bourbon County, Ky., Apprentice Bonds, 1788–1914." *National Geographical Society Quarterly* 60 (June 1972): 108–12.

Connelly, Thomas L. "Gateway to Kentucky: The Wilderness Road, 1748–1792." *The Register of the Kentucky Historical Society* 59 (April 1961): 109–32.

Coulter, E. Merton. "The Efforts of the Democratic Societies of the West to Open the Navigation of the Mississippi River." *Mississippi Valley Historical Review* 11 (December 1924): 376–89.

Dale, Edward E. "Medical Practices on the Frontier." *Indiana Magazine of History* 43 (December 1947): 307–28.

Davis, William C. "John C. Breckinridge." *The Register of the Kentucky Historical Society* 85 (Summer 1987): 197–212.

Doris, J. T. "Early Kentucky History in Madison County Circuit Court Records." *The Register of the Kentucky Historical Society* 43 (October 1945): 321–41.

Dupre, Huntley. "The *Kentucky Gazette* Reports the French Revolution." *Mississippi Valley Historical Review* 26 (September 1939): 163–80.

Everman, H. E. "Early Educational Channels of Bourbon County." *The Register of the Kentucky Historical Society* 73 (April 1975): 136–49.

Farnham, Thomas J. "Kentucky and Washington's Mississippi Policy of Patience and Persuasion." *The Register of the Kentucky Historical Society* 64 (January 1966): 14–28.

Fraas, Elizabeth. "An Unusual Map of the Early West." *The Register of the Kentucky Historical Society* 73 (January 1975): 61–69.

Garrison, George P. " 'A Memorandum of M. Austin's Journey from the Lead Mines in the County of Wythe in the State of Virginia to the Lead Mines in the Province of Louisiana West of the Mississippi,' 1796–1797." *American Historical Review* 5 (April 1900): 518–42.

Hackensmith, C. W. "John Fitch, a Pioneer in the Development of the Steamboat." *The Register of the Kentucky Historical Society* 65 (July 1967): 187–211.

Hadsell, Richard Miller. "John Bradford and His Contributions to the Culture and the Life of Early Lexington and Kentucky." *The Register of the Kentucky Historical Society* 62 (October 1964): 265–77.

Hagy, James W. "The Frontier at Castle's Woods, 1769–1786." *Virginia Magazine of History and Biography* 75 (October 1967): 410–28.

———. "The First Attempt to Settle Kentucky: Boone in Virginia." *Filson Club History Quarterly* 44 (July 1970): 227–34.

Hammon, Neal O. "Captain Harrod's Company, 1774: A Reappraisal." *The Register of the Kentucky Historical Society* 72 (July 1974): 224–42.

———. "Early Roads into Kentucky." *The Register of the Kentucky Historical Society* 68 (April 1970): 91–131.

———. "The Fincastle Surveyors in the Bluegrass, 1774." *The Register of the Kentucky Historical Society* 70 (October 1972): 277–94.

Harrison, Fairfax. "The Colonial Post Office in Virginia." *William and Mary Quarterly* 2nd ser., 4 (April 1924): 73–92.

Harrison, Lowell H. "John Breckinridge and the Kentucky Constitution of 1799." *The Register of the Kentucky Historical Society* 57 (July 1959): 209–33.

———. "John Breckinridge: Western Statesman." *The Journal of Southern History* 18 (May 1952): 137–151.

Henderson, Archibald. "Richard Henderson and the Occupation of Kentucky." *Mississippi Valley Historical Review* 1 (December 1914): 341–63.

———. "The Creative Forces in Westward Expansion: Henderson and Boone." *American Historical Review* 20 (October 1914): 86–107.

Henderson, H. James. "Constitutionalists and Republicans in the Continental Congress, 1778–1786." *Pennsylvania History* 36 (April 1969): 119–44.

Herold, Virginia Smith, ed. "Joel Watkins' Diary of 1789." *The Register of the Kentucky Historical Society* 34 (July 1936): 215–50.

Hiemstra, William L. "Early Frontier Revivalism in Kentucky." *The Register of the Kentucky Historical Society* 59 (April 1961): 133–49.

Jillson, Willard R. "The First Landowners of Frankfort, Kentucky, 1774–1790." *The Register of the Kentucky Historical Society* 43 (July 1945): 107–20.

———. "The Founding of Harrodsburg." *The Register of the Kentucky Historical Society* 27 (September 1929): 559–62.

———. "The Founding of Lexington." *Filson Club History Quarterly* 3 (October 1929): 237–46.

———. "George Washington's Western Kentucky Lands." *The Register of The Kentucky Historical Society* 29 (October 1931): 379–84.

———. "Harrod's Old Fort." *The Register of the Kentucky Historical Society* 28 (January 1930): 104–14.

———. "Narrative of a Caughnawaga Captive." *Filson Club History Quarterly* 37 (July 1963): 201–9.

———. "Old Fort Harrod," *The Register of the Kentucky Historical Society* 27 (September 1929): 563–68).

Jordan, Weymeuth T. "Some Problems of Colonial Tobacco Planters: A Critique." *Agricultural History* 43 (January 1969): 83–89.

"Journal of Col. John May, of Boston, Relative to a Journey to the Ohio Country, 1789." *The Pennsylvania Magazine of History and Biography* 45, no. 2 (1921): 101–79.

Keim, Ray C. "Primogeniture and Entail in Colonial Virginia." *William and Mary Quarterly* 3d. ser., 25 (October 1968): 545–86.

Kellogg, Louise Phelps. "A Kentucky Pioneer Tells Her Story of Early Boonesborough and Harrodsburg." *Filson Club History Quarterly* 3 (October 1929): 223–36.

Kilpatrick, Lewis H., ed. "The Journal of William Calk, Kentucky Pioneer." *Mississippi Valley Historical Review* 7 (March 1921): 363–77.

Lamb, Janie P. B. " 'Smithfield' Home of the Prestons, in Montgomery County, Virginia." *Virginia Magazine of History and Biography* 47 (January 1939): 109–25.

List, Karen. "Magazine Portrayals of Women's Role in the New Republic." *Journalism History* 13 (Summer 1987): 64–70.

McAfee, Robert B. "The Life and Times of Robert B. McAfee and His Family and Connections." *The Register of the Kentucky Historical Society* 25 (January 1927: 5–37.

Martin, Ged. "The British and Kentucky, 1786." *The Register of the Kentucky Historical Society* 73 (July 1975): 288–90.

Mason, Kathryn Harrod. "Harrod's Men—1774." *Filson Club History Quarterly* 24 (July 1950): 230–33.

Merkley, Florence. "The Cumberland Trace through Taylor County, Ky." *The Register of the Kentucky Historical Society* 70 (July 1972): 219–24.

Miles, Mrs. Harry Todd. "Old Churches in the Shenandoah—Their Descendants in Kentucky: Both People and Churches." *Filson Club History Quarterly* 34 (October 1960): 323–34.

Pusey, William Allen. "Three Kentucky Pioneers." *Filson Club History Quarterly* 4 (October 1930): 165–83.

Rainbolt, John C. "The Absence of Towns in Seventeenth-Century Virginia." *The Journal of Southern History* 35 (August 1969): 343–60.

Rice, Otis K. "Importations of Cattle into Kentucky, 1785–1860." *The Register of the Kentucky Historical Society* 49 (January 1951): 35–47.

Rives, George L. "Spain and the United States in 1795." *American Historical Review* 4 (October 1898): 62–64.

Robertson, John E. L. "Fort Jefferson." *The Register of the Kentucky Historical Society* 71 (April 1973): 127–38.

Rothert, Otto A. "John D. Shane's Interview with Mrs. John McKinney and Her Son Harvey, Bourbon County." *Filson Club History Quarterly* 13 (July 1939): 157–78.

———. "Shane, the Western Collector." *Filson Club History Quarterly* 4 (January 1930): 1–16.

Ryder, F. Van Loon. "The 'New Orleans'—the First Steamboat on Our Western Waters." *Filson Club History Quarterly* 37 (January 1963): 29–37.

Short, Howard Elmo. "Some Early Kentucky Church Experiences." *The Register of the Kentucky Historical Society* 49 (October 1951): 269–79.

Smith, James Morton. "The Grass Roots Origins of the Kentucky Resolutions." *William and Mary Quarterly* 3d ser., 27 (April 1970): 221–45.

Smith, William. "The Colonial Post Office." *American Historical Review* 21 (January 1916): 258–75.

"Some Letters of John Preston." *William and Mary Quarterly* n.s., 1 (January 1921): 42–51.

Staples, Charles R. "The Bryan Family Papers." *The Register of the Kentucky Historical Society* 34 (April 1936): 196–200.

Still, Bayrd. "The Westward Migration of a Planter Pioneer in 1796." *William and Mary Quarterly* 2d ser., 21 (October 1941): 318–43.

Talbert, Charles G. "John Logan, 1747–1807." *Filson Club History Quarterly* 36 (April 1962): 128–50.

———. "Kentuckians in the Virginia Convention of 1788." *The Register of the Kentucky Historical Society* 58 (July 1960): 187–93.

Talbert, Charles G., and Clifford C. Gregg. "George Michael Bedinger, 1756–1843." *The Register of the Kentucky Historical Society* 65 (January 1967): 28–46.

Talley, William M. "The Cabin Creek War Road." *The Register of the Kentucky Historical Society* 63 (January 1965): 17–23.

———. "Salt Lick Creek and Its Salt Works." *The Register of the Kentucky Historical Society* 64 (April 1966): 85–109.

Tapp, Hambleton. "Colonel John Floyd, Kentucky Pioneer." *Filson Club History Quarterly* 15 (January 1941): 1–24.

Thompson, Dorothy Brown. "John Taylor as a Biographer of Pioneer Baptist Preachers." *Filson Club History Quarterly* 37 (July 1963): 258–80.

Tuchman, Gaye. "Women's Depiction by the Mass Media." *Signs: Journal of Women in Culture and Society* 4 (Spring 1979): 528–42.

Turner, Frederick Jackson. "The Significance of the Frontier in American History." American Historical Association *Annual Report for the Year 1893* (Washington, D.C., 1894).

Von Nardoff, Ellen. "The American Frontier as Safety Valve—The Life, Death, Reincarnation, and Justification of a Theory." *Agricultural History* 36 (July 1962): 123–42.

Warren, Elizabeth. "Senator John Brown's Role in the Kentucky Spanish Conspiracy." *Filson Club History Quarterly* 36 (April 1962): 158–76.

Watlington, Patricia. "Discontent in Frontier Kentucky." *The Register of the Kentucky Historical Society* 65 (April 1967): 77–93.

———. "John Brown and the Spanish Conspiracy." *Virginia Magazine of History and Biography* 75 (January 1967): 52–68.

Welch, Sylvia Pettit. "Six Letters by Pioneer John McKinney." *Filson Club History Quarterly* 14 (April 1940): 103–28.

Williams, D. Alan. "The Small Farmer in 18th-Century Virginia Politics." *Agricultural History* 43 (January 1969): 91–101.

Williamson, Hugh P. "An Overland Journey in 1849." *The Register of the Kentucky Historical Society* 66 (April 1968): 147–58.

Wilson, Samuel W. "West Fincastle—Now Kentucky." *Filson Club History Quarterly* 9 (April 1935): 64–94.

Wood, Eleanor Duncan. "Limestone, a Gateway of Pioneer Kentucky." *The Register of the Kentucky Historical Society* 28 (April 1930): 151–54.

Yanchisin, Daniel A. "John Bradford, a Public Servant." *The Register of the Kentucky Historical Society* 68 (January 1970): 60–69.

DISSERTATIONS, THESES, AND PAPERS

Breckinridge, Helen Congleton. "Cabell's Dale: The Story of a Family, 1760–1876." Lexington, Ky.: unpublished paper, copyright, 1983.

———. "Descendants of John and Mary Cabell Breckinridge." Lexington, Ky.: unpublished paper, 1980.

Cantrell, Timothy A. "A History of Baptists in Clinton County, [Ky.]." Master's thesis, Western Kentucky University, 1969.

Golladay, Victor Dennis. "The Nicholas Family of Virginia, 1722–1820." Ph.D. diss., University of Virginia, 1973.

Holmes, Oliver W. "Stagecoach and Mail from Colonial Days to 1820." Ph.D. diss., Columbia University, 1956.

Klotter, James Christopher. "The Breckinridges of Kentucky: Two Centuries of Leadership." Ph.D. diss., University of Kentucky, 1975.

Lockhart, Quinn Hartwell. "Colonel Arthur Campbell, 1743–1811: A Biography." Ph.D. diss., University of Georgia, 1972.

Maraman, Wenonah E. "Some Phases of Pioneer Education on the Kentucky Frontier with Emphasis on Nelson County, 1785–1860." Master's thesis, University of Louisville, 1943.

Mikkelson, Dwight. *"Kentucky Gazette:* 'The Herald of a Noisy World.' " Ph.D. diss., University of Kentucky, 1963.

Nyland, Keith Ryan. "Doctor Thomas Walker (1715–1794 Explorer, Physician, Statesman, Surveyor, and Planter of Virginia and Kentucky." Ph.D. diss., Ohio State University, 1971.

Sprague, Stuart Seely. "Senator John Brown of Kentucky, 1757–1837: A Political Biography." Ph.D. diss., New York University, 1973.

Washington, Wanda. "Press Agentry and the Emergence of Daniel Boone as an American Folklore Hero." Master's thesis, University of Wisconsin, 1973.

Index